Social Studies That Sticks

Social Studies That Sticks

How to Bring Content and Concepts to Life

Laurel Schmidt

HEINEMANN
Portsmouth, NH

Heinemann
A division of Reed Elsevier Inc.
361 Hanover Street
Portsmouth, NH 03801–3912
www.heinemann.com

Offices and agents throughout the world

Library of Congress Cataloging-in-Publication Data
Schmidt, Laurel J.
    Social studies that sticks : how to bring content and concepts to life / Laurel Schmidt.
        p. cm.
    Includes bibliographical references and index.
    ISBN-13: 978-0-325-01059-5
    ISBN-10: 0-325-01059-5
    1. Social sciences—Study and teaching—United States. 2. History—
Study and teaching—United States.   I. Title.
LB1584.S366 2007
300.71—dc22   2007019224

Editor: Danny Miller
Production: Vicki Kasabian
Cover design: Jenny Jensen Greenleaf
Typesetter: SPi Publishing
Manufacturing: Steve Bernier

Printed in the United States of America on acid-free paper
11 10 09 08 07   VP   1 2 3 4 5

To my students at SMASH,

and always

Durnford King

Contents

1

Putting the Social Back in Social Studies

Teaching So Kids Learn

Education is not preparation for life; education is life itself.
—John Dewey, "My Pedagogic Creed"

What's the Big Idea About Social Studies?

So you're going to teach social studies? Welcome to a four-billion dollar-a-year industry. And that's just the textbook publishing segment. Add in the sales of edible maps, talking globes, atlapedias, inflatable volcanoes, make-a-mountain kits, blackline masters, CD-ROMs and videos, plus product-choked conferences and those dazzling four-color professional publications that few teachers have time to read, and you can see that big dollars—public dollars—are changing hands. That could come as quite a surprise to teachers who are starting the school year with a world map featuring the Holy Roman Empire, pre-dot.com reference books, and a set of supplementary materials printed midway through the Carter administration. They feel lucky indeed if they just get their hands on a full set of relatively new social studies texts, since many teachers must beg, borrow, or violate copyright laws to provide for their students.

So what does four billion dollars buy in the way of student achievement?

Not much. Despite state standards issued in volumes the size of the Manhattan phone book, and testing programs with security procedures that would make a nuclear reactor site proud, here's what we know about our kids' proficiency in social studies.

In 2005, the scores on standardized tests were bad—57 percent of high school students *scored Below Basic* on social studies assessments. Lower than math, reading, and science. The only lower scores went to the varsity surfing squad in Iowa. And social studies scores actually head south the longer kids stay in school. As test questions become more complex, the proportion of low-performing students increases.

Now, that wouldn't necessarily be cause for alarm in itself, since it's widely known that standardized tests measure only a fraction of what students know.

And they do it in such perverse ways that some students actually do better using the *Quick-Pick* lottery method—circling their favorite letters or numbers—than they would if they stopped to think about the convoluted questions and deliberately confusing array of answers offered up for their cranial torment.

But setting standardized tests aside, there's other news that is truly disturbing. It appears that our current approach to social studies instruction is producing wholesale, widespread ignorance. In July 2005, the *Boston Globe* reported that most fourth graders couldn't identify the opening passage of the Declaration of Independence. When presented with the challenge to name two reasons why pioneers moved west, only 5 percent gave the right answer. Forty-eight percent gave responses that were deemed totally inappropriate, presumably something like "to be able to play tennis outdoors all year round." One in four eighth graders didn't know why the Civil War was fought, and one in five high school seniors thought Germany was a U.S. ally during World War II.

Even with strong visual prompts, students are stymied. Given photographs of two segregation signs—*We Wash for White People Only* in front of a laundry, and *For Whites Only* next to a picnic area at a beach—59 percent of the students gave an incorrect response when asked what the signs indicated, even when supplied with the multiple-choice answers: prejudice, poverty, political protest, and environmental conservation.

A survey conducted in 2006 by the National Geographic Education Foundation found that more than half of the young Americans queried couldn't find Saudi Arabia or Iraq on a map, despite daily news reports emanating from the region. Three-quarters could not locate Indonesia, the sight of a massive tsunami, and closer to home, fewer than half could pinpoint New York or Ohio on a map of the United States.

Our education system seems to be producing a generation of citizens suffering from a serious strain of amnesia when the topic is ourselves—who we are and how and why we came to be. So what's going on—or not—in social studies?

The Battle Between Priorities and Best Practices

State and federal mandates focusing on language arts and math have created a fierce battle for time and space in the classroom. And sadly, subjects that used to be considered pillars of a well-rounded education haven't been on the winning side of the struggle. Music and art were early casualties, followed by almost anything else that didn't directly promote decoding, comprehension, and computation. Social studies is certainly among the walking wounded. So what remains? Precision reading exercises reminiscent of drill team practice, formulaic writing prompts that urge students to communicate with a pantomime audience for a pantomime purpose, and rote computation—all presented by teachers who move through their lessons at a clip that makes you think someone is chasing them.

As a result, many teachers feel lucky if they actually get to *teach* social studies. That's right. It's simply not a priority. The No Child Left Behind Act of 2001 dealt a severe blow to social studies instruction by omitting it from the new nationwide accountability system. Which is why some states and local districts subtly discourage or explicitly dismiss social studies instruction in favor of reading and math—the publicly accountable subjects, for which performance is announced in the newspapers, with schools ranked by scores. In many classrooms, social studies has been reduced to a brisk trot through the highpoints of history and geography, with a dash of civics thrown in during election years. In some cases, the shiny, full-color textbooks never escape their shrink-wrap, remaining pristine from year to year because teachers feel there's simply no time.

No doubt, there's a handful of teachers who are thrilled with the eclipse of social studies. These closet history-haters are more than content to teach extra math and skip the dates-faces-and-battles curriculum that makes them wince. Their nod to social studies is to assign chapters for homework, as punishment assignments when the class gets rowdy, or as padding for days when a substitute teacher is filling in.

But even if teachers are determined to squeeze social studies into the schedule, the challenge can be daunting. According to John Goodlad (2004), social studies has been voted off the island—its students least favorite subject, which is puzzling, because it has the potential to be endlessly fascinating. The problem is that over time, social studies instruction has been sucked dry of the humanity and audacity that made possible the very events that it's supposed to explore. How could the westward movement be boring with the Donner Party out there, eyeing each other with knives and forks? Who wouldn't be moved by the twenty-seven-year imprisonment and ultimate triumph of Nelson Mandela? Or fascinated by the upheaval in fourteenth-century Europe when savvy peasants who'd survived the plague, discovered that they—simple, unskilled, grunt laborers—were the most valuable commodity in the market, and opted for revolution over continued servitude? Wouldn't you just love to get your teeth into stories like that? So would most kids. So what's up with hating social studies?

For the most part, social studies has been reduced to memory exercises—lists of dates, battles, and political events—that are quickly forgotten. Lessons are long on forced-fed factoids and short on human interest, stripped of the heartbreak, adventure, conflict, invention, competition, disappointment, treachery, heroism, strategic brilliance, and spectacular foibles that allow kids to discover what they have in common with people who lived in other places, times, and cultures. In short, we've taken the *social* out of social studies. As a result, many students graduate from high school without ever realizing what history buffs have always known—that history is first and foremost an engrossing story about people, full of daredevils, dunderheads, and scoundrels. Far too many students leave school ignorant of the bliss to be found wandering through the Middle Ages in the company of a knight, or viewing the imperial court of China through the eyes of Marco Polo. If asked, these unfortunates swear that "they *hate* history."

In fact, they may not hate history at all. They just hate the way it's taught, which is odd since the educational frameworks insist that history is supposed to be "a story well told." Unfortunately, when it's history time in many classrooms across America, students may feel like they've wandered into a game show and chosen the wrong category. The teacher peppers them with one-liners, all of which require numeric responses—1812, 1776, 1929, 1849. Where's the story? Or she reviews the list of Top Ten Treaties. No one's pulse races. Battles seem like a more promising topic—action, carnage, winners, and losers—but instead the textbook reads like the diary of a real estate broker—who got what property and where the losers decamped to sulk.

Sulking is probably too strong a word. Instruction—and some instructors— seem to be lavishly unemotional. Entire cultures are annihilated through contact with disease-bearing traders; amazing libraries burned to the ground taking with them the history of the ancient world; utopian communities crushed, totalitarian leaders elevated. No outcry. Not even a sigh. "It's a good day to die" comes as close to an emotional revelation as you're likely to get, then it's "turn to the last page of the chapter and answer the questions." Not a story well told.

The results are disheartening but predictable. Our national drive to standardize and quantify learning has failed to do the very thing it set out to accomplish—help kids learn. Test scores and student disinterest confirm that stripping instruction of its humanity has reduced it to a hollow, boredom-inducing obligation that most students and teachers simply endure. Our mistake was taking the *social* out of social studies—and it's time to put it back.

Putting the Social Back in Social Studies

When I talk about putting the social back in social studies, I'm looking at three aspects of instruction—content, learning, and outcomes—that need to be reconnected with the fundamental humanity of this discipline.

1. *Putting the social back in content* means re-establishing human beings as the central subject of social studies—their lives and stories, their triumphs and abysmal failures, the enduring dilemmas embedded in the study of family and society over time.

2. *Putting the social back in learning* means creating learning environments and using instructional practices that are compatible with the natural recurring cycle of learning in human beings.
3. *Putting the social back in outcomes* means incorporating into your curriculum challenging problems, authentic experiences, and real-life tasks that have consequences in the community or world, and teaching your students to accomplish them.

Let's look at each of these in greater depth.

Putting the Social Back in Content

Social studies is the original big tent of elementary and middle school curriculum, embracing a huge array of discrete subjects, from archaeology to psychology. Taken together they paint a vivid picture of what we human beings have been up to for a very long time. Social studies touches on everything from why people invented communication systems and the size and shape of their houses, to how much they're willing to fork over for a head of cattle or a gallon of gas, and who can wear stiletto heels in public without inviting scorn. The subject is ourselves.

In its fullest, most glorious incarnation, social studies is all about people: what we've done, where, why, and what were the consequences. And what are we doing now? How does our own current behavior mirror history? What impact can we have on our community? How can we influence the future? It encompasses everything people do to survive, thrive, and evolve as social beings. With such a broad sweep, it's not surprising that social studies programs typically include elements of a long list of disciplines, including the following:

Archaeology: How people investigate life in the past.
Anthropology: How people developed physically, socially, and culturally.
Economics: How people use, value, amass, and exchange resources.
Geography: How people and the earth's physical systems affect each other.
History: The things that people did with such brilliance or brutality that they stand out over time. They are documented, memorable, and historic.
Law: How people create rules to regulate behavior in society.
Philosophy: How people think about truth and values.
Politics: How people use power in society.
Psychology: How people understand the mind and human behavior.
Religion: How people express beliefs about God or the supernatural.
Sociology: How humans form groups and behave in society.

Unfortunately, contemporary curriculums and textbooks have stripped away much of that social fabric, leaving content that is so antiseptic and dehumanized, we may as well be studying another species. But what does putting the social back in content mean? Simply that instruction needs to refocus on faces, problems, context, and continuity.

- **Faces of individuals, not just a list of celebrities.** Students need to hear the stories of actual people, powerbrokers and commoners, women and children who lived in, participated in, and shaped the past and present.
- **Problems, not simply events.** Students need to learn to analyze events as manifestations of larger problems that people are facing. Events may be solutions to problems or evidence of our collective failure.
- **Context, not just locations and dates.** Students need to recognize that human activities are shaped by the natural surroundings and social environments in which people are trying to survive and thrive.
- **Continuity from the past to the present.** Students need to understand that we are grappling with some of the same problems that vexed the Mesopotamians, Romans, Chinese, Mayans, Tuaregs, the Dogon, and the Bushmen of the Kalahari.

Many students slouch reluctantly into their social studies classes, drop into their seats as if they've been shot, and whine rhetorically, "What does this have to do with me?" An entire year may pass without a single ray of light falling upon that question. But if you revive the social element in content by emphasizing faces, problems, context, and continuity, students soon discover that there are stunning parallels between their existence and the lives of people in other states, countries, or centuries. They're intrigued. Presented with decontextualized, fact-driven oratories, they quickly lose heart and revert to more rewarding activities, such as text-messaging cryptograms, having a rich fantasy life, or napping.

Putting the Social Back in Learning

Historically, schools in the United States have been organized around recitation teaching. The teacher broadcasts knowledge to be memorized by the students, and reproduced on demand. This was uniformly the case up to the 1900s, when most education was delivered in rural one-room schoolhouses, sheltering local students of all ages and abilities. The sole teacher was usually an unmarried, often untrained, woman. Using only the most basic resources—slate, chalk, a few books, a fistful of threats, and a paddle—teaching and learning consisted mainly of literacy, penmanship, arithmetic, and good manners. Recitation, drilling, and oral quizzes at the end of the day were the norm. Urban teachers, faced with waves of immigrant children, relied on recitation and memorization as the most efficient way to deal with the diversity in their classrooms. Little thought was to given to the nature of learning itself, or the best way for individual students to learn.

Due to the less-than-spectacular success of this approach, researchers began to investigate how humans learn, and lots of informative theories emerged, including the following:

- **Lev Vygotsky** believed that children's learning is affected in large and small ways by the culture—including the culture of their family environments.
- **Paulo Friere** advocated for the empowerment of learners through dialogue, critical thinking, and using knowledge to take action in the real world.
- **Howard Gardner** identified at least nine distinct ways that people learn about and understand the world. Each of these "intelligences" is a distinct set of skills that can be used to find and solve problems.
- **Renate Caine** explored the idea of brain-based learning, which suggests that every person is born with a brain that functions as an immensely powerful processor. Traditional schooling, however, often inhibits learning by discouraging, ignoring, or punishing the brain's natural learning processes.
- **Jean Piaget's** theory was based on the idea that children build cognitive structures—in other words, mental "maps" or networked concepts for understanding and responding to physical experiences in their environment.
- **Benjamin Bloom** identified three domains of educational activities including cognitive, affective, and psychomotor skills. He is well known for his taxonomy of cognitive skills that includes: knowledge, comprehension, application, analysis, synthesis, and evaluation.
- **John Dewey** felt it was vitally important that education not be the teaching of mere dead facts, but that the skills and knowledge that students learn be integrated fully into their lives as human beings and citizens.
- **Daniel Goleman** explored the idea of *emotional intelligence*, which describes the ability to perceive, assess, and manage the emotions of one's self, others, and groups. Emotional intelligence has proven to be a better predictor of future success than GPA, IQ, and standardized tests.
- **Albert Bandura's** social learning theory emphasizes the importance of learning by observing and modeling the behaviors, attitudes, and emotional reactions of others.

Each of these individuals uncovered evidence about how people learn—through talking, observing, modeling, collaborating, sensing, responding emotionally, and having physical experiences in their environment.

The Learning Cycle

If I'm not mistaken, you didn't need someone named Vygotsky to tell you how people learn. First of all, you're in the learning profession. And secondly, you've been a learner all your life. So you have only to review your own behavior as a learner to come up with some pretty accurate ideas about how learning happens. I'm not talking about compulsory learning like graduate courses in *Theories and Application of Critical Pedagogy*. I mean human learning—the way you behave when you really want or need to learn something, and you're left to your own devices.

Here's an example. You dine with an old friend who proudly announces that she just got back from Paris, and it was "fab-u-lous." *Paris. Why didn't I think of that?* You realize that the fantasy of Parisian anything has lingered in the lymbic region of your brain since the fifth-grade talent show when you belted out *I Love Paris* by Cole Porter, to the exquisite embarrassment of your siblings. Beyond that? Speak French? *Non*. Eat snails? Double *non*. The truth is you couldn't find France on an unmarked map, even at gunpoint. The closest you've come to franglicizing your life is ordering a chocolate croissant with your latte, and mumbling *merci* to the startled barrista. But suddenly you can't stop thinking that a junket to the City of Light will be the trip of a lifetime, or even life itself if Mr. or Ms. Right crosses your cobblestoned path.

So what do you do? Hit the Internet. Obeying a single impulse, you type in the keyword *Paris* and within a nanosecond, you have four hundred million choices to explore. For the next two hours, you cyberprowl *la Ville Lumière*—click, read, click, read, as if your mouse has a bad case of OCD. Hotels, museums, sewer tours—you're indiscriminate in your pursuit. You even bookmark a live webcam of the Eiffel Tour so you can eavesdrop 24-7. Next, you pester well-traveled friends, join a conversational French dinner group, gain five pounds, call the French Embassy after hours just to listen to the accent on their answering machine, and monitor transatlantic airline fares with the intensity of a day-trader. Finally you clear your calendar, lay down the credit card, throw your chic-est togs in a bag, and depart for your brilliant adventure.

You would go through this same sequence if you were intent on learning to play golf, speak Japanese, prepare gourmet meals, mix killer martinis, alter digital photographs, or rewire a lamp. You get a notion, explore it, develop some expertise, and then use your new knowledge.

All human learning follows this distinct and predictable cycle. It begins with awareness, proceeds to exploration, which leads to inquiry, and culminates in action or use. Then the cycle frequently begins again, with another round of learning stimulated by deeper understanding and more questions. It can take five minutes or eat up your entire summer vacation.

$$AWARENESS \rightarrow EXPLORATION \rightarrow INQUIRY \rightarrow ACTION$$

Here are some descriptors to help flesh out this picture of the learning cycle.

AWARENESS	EXPLORATION	INQUIRY	ACTION
Idea shows up on mental radar and captures interest	*Broad spectrum curiosity*	*Direct intense focused investigation*	*Use of new knowledge*
glimpse	browse	ask	teach
sniff	poke	gather data	present
glance	prod	analyze	write and publish
stumble upon	snoop	challenge	demonstrate
catch your eye	rummage	question	invent
eye-opener	survey	compare and	advocate change
encounter	sample	contrast	create visual art
bump into	probe	research	compose and
confronted by	sift	test	perform
sense possibilities	seek out sources	pick brains	present
wonder	wander	obsess	dramatization
puzzled	dead ends	refine sources	debate
intrigued		dig	organize social
first impressions		contact experts	action
		become experts	launch campaign

Now let's think about the learning cycle in students and in your classroom.

Awareness engages kids' minds and sets that stage for learning in two ways. First, when children become aware of something, their brains ask: *How is this like other things I've already seen or experienced?* This triggers the hunt for prior knowledge. Neural pathways locate memories, to which the new information is attached and stored for use. Second, during the awareness stage, the brain also asks: *How is this thing unique? I wonder what this is all about?* That curiosity provides the energy to move forward into exploration. *Awareness gets students ready to expand their cognitive real estate by locating prior knowledge from their cultures, families, and experiences in the world, and stimulating their curiosity. Engaging the brain is the first, absolutely essential step toward learning.*

Exploration is the stage for finding out. You can clearly observe exploration in babies who seem to live in a perpetual state of exploration. Picture the fussing six-month-old who is given a set of keys for distraction. In rapid succession the baby touches the keys, smacks them on any available surface, shakes them to discover their full range of noises, gives them a thorough, slobbering examination with lips and tongue, and finally offers them to anyone who might be interested. In a similar spirit, young kids coming across a pile of discards in the garage can fill an entire afternoon examining, combining, and rearranging a few pieces of lumber, an inner tube, several yards of canvas, and a folding chair. First it's a boat, then a space capsule, then a wilderness shelter with an inflatable fire pit. *Exploration lets students use all their senses, multiple intelligences, and different learning styles to get a first look at new ideas, formulate more questions, pursue hunches, make discoveries, and compare their impressions with other students.*

Inquiry is the stage for digging in. You've probably seen the inquiry stage of learning in young kids who become dinosaur fanatics, mastering the names, weights, and dietary habit of the top twenty-five dinosaurs, along with a raft of esoteric facts that they share with anyone who will stand still long enough to listen. If you've ever been accosted by a five-year-old asking, "Did you know that stegosaurus had a brain the size of a walnut?" you've had a close encounter with a child in the thrall of inquiry. Inquiry involves collections, research, frequent trips to the library, passionate conversations, and staying up late. It is a question-driven activity, but the work becomes very focused, complex, and challenging. Students doing inquiry work in social studies discover that there are very few right answers but enormous opportunities to pose their own questions, ponder human motivation, imagine alternative scenarios, evaluate human behavior, propose solutions for the present, and puzzle about the future. *Inquiry lets students focus, probe deeply, devise and test theories of their own, obsess and become an expert.*

Action is the product and the reward for all the investigation, research, and experiments. For all the blind alleys and half-baked ideas that finally produce a solid body of knowledge that can be used to change what is, or invent something new. If students collect lots and lots of data, but are never challenged to process what they've learned into a product, their knowledge is like an appendix, a vestigial organ. It's there, but it serves no purpose. But the goal of social studies is to help students acquire the habits of good citizens, globally aware individuals and productive adults. And habits come from action. In-the-world, in-the-moment, strategic, bold, creative action. *Action lets students use their knowledge to address problems, work on solutions, create new knowledge that can be shared, and see the impact of their learning in the world.*

That's about as social as learning can hope to be.

> *The native and unspoiled attitude of childhood, marked by ardent curiosity, fertile imagination, and love of experimental inquiry, is near, very near, the attitude of the scientific mind.*
>
> —John Dewey,
> *How We Think*

Why This Approach Makes Sense

Picture this scenario. The teacher directs his students to "Take out your social studies books, turn to page 1,153, read the chapter and answer the questions at the end." No connections, no relevance, no curiosity, no choices, no diversity of learning styles, no conversation, no interaction, no opportunity for debate or invention. It's the equivalent of solitary confinement for the brain—and the brain's response is generally to shut down or incite a riot. Either way, very little learning occurs.

But research studies now show that teaching strategies based on social development theories are far more effective than other approaches. Scaffolding, reciprocal teaching, cooperative learning, classroom dialogues, problem solving, culturally relevant materials, place-based learning, and guided instruction are strategies that have been effective across the curriculum with diverse groups of students.

What does this mean for you? Simply this. You can work your kids like rented mules, but if you're working against the brain, using strategies that ignore the natural cycle of learning in children, how will you reach your goal? With struggle and resistance? Marginally and only with the very bright students who learn no matter what methods are used?

It can only be to your advantage to harness the natural mechanisms of the brain to achieve your goals. If we want kids to learn social studies effectively, meaning they understand the concepts and retain relevant information to use for writing, social action, *and* passing standardized tests, we need to tailor our instruction to capitalize on the natural learning cycle—awareness, exploration, inquiry, and action.

Putting the Social Back in Outcomes

Without action, social studies is just voyeurism. So is it any wonder that many students stare glumly at their five-pound textbooks and lament, "We can't change history, so why do we have to study this stuff? What's the point?" The answer is that we study history/social science to gain knowledge from people in the past so that we can act in the present and influence the future. That's the point. But that requires action.

> *When Cicero had finished speaking, the people said, "How well he spoke." When Demosthenes finished speaking, the people said, "Let us march."*
> —Adlai Stevenson

The challenge is moving students from passivity to activity by helping them understand that the stuff of history is simply what human beings do, in any society, at any time. Which means that there's a world of need and possibility—exploitation, poverty, discrimination, and social injustice—right outside their classroom door. When you put the social back in outcomes, you teach your students that they *can* and *should* get involved. In the process of acting or acting up, they exercise the skills required for dynamic citizenship in a democracy. They experience the challenge and reward of raising their voices for the good of their neighborhood, the environment, or the global community.

How does that look? Kids who have been involved in outcome-based social studies have initiated changes that range from small neighborhood improvements to feats bordering on the miraculous. Here's a short list. Students:

- Created the largest abolitionist movement of the twentieth century to fight slavery in Sudan.
- Forced the federal government to clean up toxic dumps in their neighborhood.
- Created a campaign to end child slavery and raised funds to provide education for children who had been indentured laborers.
- Lobbied city officials to create a park to provide a safe haven for children who had no place to play ball but the streets.
- Saved thousands of square miles of rain forest from destruction.
- Boycotted corporations to exert their economic power in support of fair-trade chocolate.
- Raised funds to restore historic murals in their community.
- Fought developers at city meetings and in the press to save historic buildings.

One of the awe-inspiring possibilities of including outcomes in your social studies program is that your students actually have the opportunity to become better human beings. They can use their understanding of the past to act in the present in order to pass on a better world to their descendants. They can have a say in the future, rather than waiting passively for it to unfold. With your guidance, they'll view their education as a tool for change and say, "Let us march."

What About Standards?

You may be thinking that this all sounds fascinating, but there are standardized tests lurking out there, and you're not eager to be the poster-person for the latest failed educational experiment. Authentic learning sounds tempting, but what about all those federal, state, and local standards?

Well, there are plenty of them, that's for sure. For a start, you have the National Council on Social Studies (NCSS) that guides K–12 social studies instruction across the country. The NCSS has mercifully described its standards in humanistic terms, choosing ten thematic strands that run throughout social studies instruction. They are:

- culture
- time, continuity, and change
- people, places, and environments
- individual development and identity

- individuals, groups, and institutions
- power, authority, and governance
- production, distribution, and consumption
- science, technology, and society
- global connections
- civic ideals and practices

These themes allow teachers to address the breadth of social studies content and, at the same time, focus on skill development that will allow students to do authentic work in the areas of history, geography, economics, politics, and social justice.

But the NCSS has been quite explicit about the kinds of skills students should acquire in order to make sense of the ten social studies themes. Thinking skills. Research skills. Decision-making and getting along skills. They are:

Data-Gathering Skills

Acquire information by observation.
Locate information from a variety of sources.
Compile, organize, and evaluate information.
Extract and interpret information.
Communicate effectively orally and in writing.

Intellectual Skills

Compare and contrast things, ideas, events, and situations.
Classify items or ideas in categories.
Ask appropriate and probing questions.
Draw conclusions or inferences from evidence.
Arrive at generalizations.
Make defensible predictions from information.

Decision-Making Skills

Consider alternative solutions.
Consider the consequences of each solution.
Make decisions and justify them in relation to democratic principles.
Take action based on those decisions.

Interpersonal Skills

See issues from others' points of view.
Understand your own beliefs, feelings, and abilities, and how they affect relationships with others.
Avoid stereotyping and classifying people through generalizations.

Work as an effective member of a group.

Give and receive constructive criticism.

Accept responsibility and respect the rights and property of others.

Call me crazy, but when I scan that list, the first thing that occurs to me is that the majority of these skills can only be achieved in the context of social learning. Look again at that list and ask yourself how many can be effectively addressed via the open-your-book-answer-the-questions method. They can't. In fact, these standards fairly beg for a more dynamic and diversified approach to instruction.

To ensure that students actually learn these skills, it's simply not enough to document what's been presented, or check off what's been "covered" as if we are all in the upholstery business. Because here's that thing. Teaching hasn't happened until students learn. What do I mean by that? Suppose I offer to teach you to ride a bicycle. I talk and wave my arms and pummel you with suggestions. Three months later, you're bruised, bandaged, and scared—a loser against the forces of gravity. You take the bus or walk everywhere. So I ask, *Did I teach you to ride a bike?*

Kids *have* to learn or we haven't done our job. Great teachers know that. They keep their eyes on state and national standards, but their overarching guidance comes from an internal gyroscope that prompts them to consistently construct rigorous, challenging yet engaging lessons, units, and projects that lure students into authentic, active learning. As they plan, replan, and assess their work with students, they make a habit of asking themselves:

- What do I want my students to understand?
- What do they need to learn about how to learn?
- What do I want them to do with what they understand?
- How will their learning affect the way they relate to other people?

Answering these questions can help you integrate subject areas and skills naturally, identify the critical material that needs to be addressed, and provide ample opportunities for students to apply it to real-world situations so that what they learn gets hard-wired into their brains and hearts.

And that's what this book is all about. Teaching social studies so kids learn.

A Map of This Book

I think of this book as a conversation between two really smart colleagues who are passionate about teaching social studies. I'm sitting at my computer. You're in your classroom or tucked in bed, reading before sleep overcomes you. That could be in three or four paragraphs if you've had a hectic day. Think of this as a recipe book or a brain booster to help catapult your instructional program to higher levels of authentic achievement for your students. You can open to any page and read it on the run, because that's what busy teachers need. I know. I taught for twenty-three years, every grade from kindergarten through eighth. Social studies was always my favorite subject and the best part of the day according to my students. So I've organized the book with your needs in mind. Here's how it works.

Section One: Getting the Big Picture

Chapters 1 and 2 examine the *what* and *how* of social studies instruction. They identify the essential questions at the heart of social studies—the big problems that people were trying to solve over time, and the efforts that caused the human race to change, develop, evolve, and occasionally devolve.

Section Two: Tools of the Trade

Chapters 3 through 5 provide activities, strategies, and resources for using primary source documents, biographies and first-person narratives, objects and art, place-based explorations and other nontraditional materials to investigate social studies topics. Students have the opportunity to explore the tools and processes used by real historians and social scientists in the course of their work.

Section Three: Real-World Connections

Chapters 6 through 9 encourage teachers and students to embrace real-world learning using the skills presented in the first two sections of the book. Students learn through investigating their community as classroom, examining cultural perspectives, comparing current and historic events, and pursuing social justice projects.

Chapter Format

As I have indicated, the opening chapters of the book constitute a collegial conversation about teaching and learning in the social studies classroom. The narrative is designed to help you think through some of the big issues and clarify your unique approach.

The remaining chapters have a common structure intended to be as clear, efficient, and user-friendly as possible. They are well stocked with ideas you can use or modify to enrich your program. The components in each chapter begin with the fundamentals for planning, move through the stages of the learning cycle, and end with ideas for assessment. In each chapter you will find these sections:

- Thematic Strands
- Learning Layers
- What's the Big Idea?
- What About Standards?
- Awareness
- Exploration
- Inquiry
- Action
- The Learning Ledger

Let's spend a little more time looking at these elements.

Thematic Strands

This section helps you keep your eye on the ten themes described by the National Council on Social Studies (NCSS) by indicating which themes are addressed in the chapter. For example, in Chapter 3 on primary source documents, the thematic strands are: People, Places, and Environments; Global Connections; and Individuals, Groups, and Institutions.

Learning Layers

Time is the most precious commodity in a twenty-first-century classroom, ranking even higher on most teachers' wish lists than copy paper, sticky notes, and unoccupied restrooms. Harried teachers, caught between compulsory programs and standardized tests, might find themselves echoing the words Queen Elizabeth whispered on her deathbed in 1603, "All my possessions for but a moment of time."

The number of minutes in the teaching day has been aggressively poached by federal, state, and local mandates that require teachers to present vast swaths of curriculum, often at a breakneck pace. Given the persistent time crunch, you can make the most of the minutes at your disposal by consistently crossing disciplinary boundaries to layer your lessons with three, four, or five different disciplines. That's the concept of learning layers—that many subjects can be integrated into one unit of instruction. Even the simplest social studies lesson can strengthen analytic thinking, reading for comprehension, persuasive writing, Internet research, drawing, explicating literature, debate, and public speaking. On top of that, you can blend in concepts from geography, history, anthropology, sociology, ethics, politics, mathematics, and on and on, all of which will increase exponentially the amount of learning students can do in a single lesson, without consuming any extra time.

For example, suppose you give your students a copy of an etching entitled *The Town of Pomeiooc* by Theodore De Bry (available online). It shows a bird's-eye view of a Native American village in the region of North America that would later become Virginia. Studying the print, students can make observations and speculate about architecture, village planning, defense, agriculture, diet, natural vegetation, tool making, topography, social hierarchies, climate, weather, and religious and cultural rituals. After discussing the print, you can ask your students why it might be interesting to live in a place like this village and how it would be different from life as they know it.

All that content is layered with skill development, including the ability to analyze visual images, describe what is seen using adjectives and similes; pose questions; and higher-level thinking including speculating, hypothesizing, extrapolating, comparing and contrasting; historic empathy; and an imaginative leap. There are layers and layers of learning possible for all students, including second-language learners and students with reading challenges.

It takes only five to ten minutes to accomplish all of that. And asking your students to examine a picture rather than read a section of text is surprising, so your students' attention and retention are greater, motivation to stick with the topic is stronger, and you could actually have some fun!

What About Standards?

In each chapter I identify the skills that will be strengthened through the suggested strategies and activities. The skills are not tied to specific content areas, such as *Students will be able to name three causes of the Civil War*, because content varies by grade, region, and subject. Rather, the skills cited are fundamental to learning social science content at many grade levels.

The Learning Cycle

Each chapter has one section for each stage of the learning cycle (Awareness, Exploration, Inquire, Action). The activities, strategies, and resources will help you build lessons and plan experiences to create intense awareness of a topic, provide opportunities for exploration, followed by deeper inquiry, and finally, action using new knowledge. Now let's take a closer look at social studies instruction through the learning cycle.

 Awareness

The good news about creating awareness about social studies is that it's a subject that's loaded with intriguing topics that students love. Plus, it has elements of television, tabloids, and gossip columns—who did what to whom and why. What's not to love? When you introduce social studies in a way that emphasizes the social element, your students will be all ears.

The Trick of It: Destination Brand Promise

The first time I encountered the term *destination brand promise* was in my local newspaper where I read that my fair city was spending fifty thousand dollars and having dozens of citizens' meetings to create a slogan that will capture the imagination of potential tourists. The end result was "Santa Monica . . . the best way to discover LA." It goes on to mention unforgettable beaches, eye-catching people, cutting edge culture, and bold innovations. That's destination brand promise, and if it works, tourists in droves will be headed for the broad white beaches of Santa Monica, with high expectations, eager hearts, and credit cards at the ready.

That's what you're doing with Awareness activities. You advertise your social studies topic and convince your kids that it will be a great destination. You present a whiff, a glimpse so intriguing that kids can't help thinking, "I want to go there." The next thing you know they're diving into books on Mesopotamia, puzzling over cuneiform writing, and reading, reading, reading.

You will find two kinds of activities in the Awareness section of each chapter. You Are Here activities help you assess your students' prior knowledge of the new subject. Waking Magoun's Brain is designed to capture their interest and motivate them to engage in active learning.

You Are Here: *Assessing Prior Knowledge*

All students approach new learning tasks with rich funds of intellectual, social, emotional, and practical knowledge. You Are Here activities encourage them to reveal what they know, so they can feel smart before they ever crack a book. As you flush out that information, you get an accurate idea of who knows what and where to start teaching. In effect, you're putting an arrow on a learning map that says *You Are Here.* If you encourage students to do these activities in pairs or groups, you send a message that you are a community of learners in which dialogue, exchange, collaboration, and mutual support are the norm.

In each chapter you will find a variety of approaches to assessing prior knowledge, including activities, verbal prompts, and suggestions for using concrete objects and images to start a discussion about what your students already know.

Waking Magoun's Brain

It's possible that some students will know little or nothing about a new topic when you first mention it. You Are Here activities can create an initial level of awareness, but they may not be enough to capture the attention of Magoun's brain—a small and largely unknown part of the brain that is only stimulated by novelty. Its job is to notice anything new, alert the learner, and begin to make sense of the new material. The activities in this section ratchet awareness up to curiosity and perhaps excitement by waking Magoun's brain.

You can get Magoun's attention in a heartbeat and keep it, simply by sharing tantalizing tidbits such as these with your students.

- Magellan's men were so crazed by starvation on their marathon voyage that when they'd finished off all the rats, they stripped the leather off the ships railings, boiled and ate it. In the medieval Islamic world, hospitals were built in all the major cities. The Qalawun Hospital in Cairo could care for eight thousand patients, and had a staff that included physicians, pharmacists, nurses, a dispensary, and research facility. Muslim doctors were removing cataracts with hollow needles over one thousand years before Westerners attempted such an operation.

- Students fascinated with the bubonic plague will perk up when you share details of the horrible but swift death, also known at the Black Death. The Italian writer Boccaccio said victims often "ate lunch with their friends, and ate dinner with their ancestors in paradise." The first signs were generally aching limbs and vomiting of blood. Then the lymph nodes in the neck, armpits, and groin would swell for three or four days until they burst. The plague killed twenty-five million people—one-third of Europe's people.

- It may surprise students living in the twenty-first century, where social status is determined by fame and wealth, to learn that in Tokugawa, Japan (1600–1867) the samurai were at the top of the social ladder, followed by rice farmers, craftsmen, artisans, fishermen, and finally, merchants, who were despised as parasites. But the bottom of the barrel was occupied by entertainers. Social mobility was out of the question—no American Idol syndrome for the Japanese. Each person occupied his or her allotted place and was expected to stay in it.

- Give them a glimpse of royal vanity by sharing that when Queen Elizabeth I contracted smallpox in 1562, she took to wearing a thick layer of white lead makeup to cover the scars on her face. In later life, when she lost her hair and teeth as well, she banished mirrors from every room in her palace.

Why Is Awareness So Important?

If we never capture students' attention, we can't activate the natural learning cycle. If they hear the word *history* and react as if offered a phlegm cocktail, they'll never get to the level of exploring ideas, or even be able to retain rudimentary facts long enough to pass a standardized test. So while awareness would seem to be a gigantic "No-duh" in planning instruction, it is often skipped in the headlong rush to accountability.

 ## Exploration

Once you succeed in stimulating your students' curiosity about the Renaissance, historic preservation, local politics, or the civil rights movement, you don't want to dash that budding enthusiasm by presenting them with a single textbook that is less than fascinating, beyond their reading level, below their thinking level, or culturally irrelevant. What you do want to do is give your students multiple entry points into the subject and license to rummage. The exploration stage is akin to Googling a keyword and then following the trail from one website to another, clicking, browsing, cutting, and pasting, getting totally lost in the subject and its tangents. Exploration activities are a buffet from which students can pick and choose according to their learning styles, prior experiences, and intelligences.

Why Is Exploration So Important?

The desire to learn grows when students have the opportunity to get their hands, eyes, and brains on new material and just muck about with it, satisfying their curiosity *before* they're hit with prescribed tasks and assignments. Without exploration, the initial impulse to learn may be frustrated, particularly for students who are strong in visual, spatial, kinesthetic, and interpersonal intelligence. Without various avenues for exploration, students may never reach the inquiry stage where they can probe deeply into content and carve out areas for personal mastery.

 ## Inquiry

Inquiry is the stage in the learning cycle where students and teachers take the plunge. They submerge themselves in a topic, getting to know as much as possible until they begin to feel like experts. Students can even choose their own research targets within an area determined by the teacher. For example, while the whole class is studying the age of exploration, one student may focus on types of ships, while others study cartography, mythology, gunpowder, individual explorers, the emerging opportunities created by technologies such as the sextant, astrolabe, and chronometer, and life and death at sea. Once students decide what they want to find out, they have to discover how to do it. They may develop a list of questions or hypotheses, then launch their search for information, using a wide range of strategies and technologies, including: interviewing, surveys, Googling, reading books, consulting primary and secondary sources, collating data, making firsthand observations, and taking notes.

This is when kids who have been voluntary illiterates may finally reach for a book. Some will read widely and above grade level. Typically they all work harder and longer in sustained sessions that go beyond the bell without any prompting from you. Barbara Lewis, author of *A Kid's Guide to Social Action* (1991), reported that while her fifth-grade students were working to eliminate a toxic dump in their neighborhood, they routinely consulted medical journals to learn about the hazards of heavy metal pollutants in ground water.

This level of mastery is incredibly satisfying to students who are accustomed to being hitched to a fast-moving curriculum vehicle that whisks them across the surface of a subject, then comes to an abrupt halt and demands that they recapitulate the journey via a written test. Inquisitive students who object to this style of high-speed learning by asking probing questions are often rewarded with the retort, "We're not talking about that now," whereupon thinking and learning end.

Why Is Inquiry So Important?

Inquiry is time consuming—no doubt about it. Teachers who incorporate this level of thinking and research into their classroom program are very busy people. This stage requires teachers to: consult learning goals, locate primary source documents, find links in literature, identify compelling questions to guide thinking, help students choose topics for deep inquiry, teach research skills, orchestrate authentic assessments, and organize social justice efforts.

So why do good teachers do it? Because inquiry is the template for how we become an expert on any subject, at any point in our lives. Students who engage in inquiry learn how to do their own learning. They know that to truly understand something they must use questions to pierce superficial explanations, get the facts, synthesize various sources of information, think about the implications, and draw their own conclusions.

Action

If we're going to teach social studies in a way that sticks—that grabs students' attention and doesn't let go until they've discovered an active role in society—then we need to create opportunities for them to use their knowledge to address real-world problems and create products, presentations, or events to share what they've learned. This type of learning is a dynamic process that frequently links the school and community. Students tackle problems that are important—often urgent—to them. Their work has consequences beyond the classroom door and beyond the end of the school year.

The easiest way to describe this approach to learning is to give you a few examples. Students at a Kentucky elementary school conducted surveys, did research, built models, and took field trips with the goal of determining the best kind of new bridge to build over the Ohio River. Second graders in Newport News, Virginia, curious about the number of medicines a classmate took and her frequent trips to the doctor, investigated—with the classmate's permission—the causes of cystic fibrosis. They invited experts to tell them about the disease, wrote up their research, used graphs and a PowerPoint presentation to tell the story, sold pledges to a cystic fibrosis walkathon, and participated in the walkathon. Students in classrooms across the nation lobbied chocolate manufacturers to purchase Fair Trade cocoa in order to eradicate slave labor among children on cocoa plantations in Central and South America.

Why Is Action So Important?

Students who are excited about learning tend to dig in and expand their interest to a wide array of subjects. They retain what they learn rather that forget it as soon as they scribble the last answer on a test. They make connections and apply their learning to other problems. They learn how to collaborate, and their social skills improve. They're more confident talking to other people, including adults. When students are involved in compelling activities and projects, test scores improve along with attendance and discipline. Compared with lessons derived exclusively from textbooks, active learning typically produces a deeper knowledge of subject matter, increased self-direction and motivation, improved research, and sharpened problem-solving skills.

But there are even greater implications. We are the faces in history for the generations that will follow us. The problems we face and our success or failure to solve them will influence the way the next generations live. Your students have the power, by their actions, to help humans evolve.

The Learning Ledger

Developing the Self-Assessment Habit

The Learning Ledger is a tool for regular, focused self-assessment. It's definitely a form of accountability, but without the sting. *Accountable* suggests "to someone else," with the added attraction of that someone being the judge of what's good enough and what's not. It has a negative tone.

In contrast, Learning Ledgers put kids in the judge's seat. Ledgers help them account for their day, like a diary or journal with the expressed purpose of capturing concrete descriptions of their work and its effects on them by answering three questions:

1. *What did I do?* focuses on one type of work they did that day—how they spent their time—or a product. For example, a student might write, *I interviewed two kindergarteners about what kind of animals makes the best pets* or *I worked on an invention for opening the cafeteria door without using your hands.* It's brief and paints a picture of a learning activity.

2. *How did I do it?* asks students to identify their abilities and how they used them to accomplish the task, including comments about preparation, sequence, knowledge, or inventions required to execute the work. The student telling about the pet interviews might write, *First I wrote out all my questions and collected pictures of ten kinds of animals. Then I went to the kindergarten and chose two kids. I sat with them in the library center and asked them to point to pictures of animals they would like for a pet. Then I asked why and wrote down their answers.*

3. *What did I learn?* is where students tally their growth as learners by deliberately highlighting the new knowledge that resulted from their labor. The student working on the cafeteria door invention might explain, "*I learned that when you're making an invention, you should do some real tests to see if it works while you're building it, not wait until the end because you can waste a lot of time that way if you get the first part wrong.*"

In each chapter you will find sample Learning Ledger questions that address specific areas of academic content and skills. You can amend the Learning Ledger to suit yourself and your kids, but keep it short. It's serious brain-work, but it shouldn't become a gauntlet kids have to run at the end of the day. You don't want to unwittingly introduce a dread factor by making the activity too long, too writing-intensive, too repetitive, or too boring. And keep the tone positive. Avoid questions about what was hard or what could they do better next time. Hang on to the *what I did, how I did it,* and *what I learned* elements because the purpose of this is to train students to habitually notice *what* and *how* they learn.

Among your students you may have some reluctant writers, visual-spatial learners, or second-language students who need extra support with any writing task. Encourage them to fill their ledgers with pictures, symbols, or annotated drawings—simple sketches combined with words that explain or augment the images. Don't worry about writing mechanics. Keep your eyes on the prize. You're looking for thinking, introspection, insight into learning—dare I say it, metacognition!

At the end of one hundred and eighty school days, students have dozens of indicators, like mile markers, that help them explain how they got from there to here, and what they've learned that will help them in future learning situations. Ledgers reinforce the critically important idea that learning is a personal possession—an asset like an investment or savings account—to be used and developed over time. Ultimately it is only meaningful to the learner, the user of the skills and ideas.

Do-It-Yourself Ledgers

What does a ledger look like? It's a lot like a journal, but before you run out to buy dozens of those black and white composition books, ponder this. Ledgers, like journals, are very personal creations. The thoughts they contain are totally unique to the writer. So I suggest that you have your kids make their own ledgers. This is a lot easier than it sounds because the ledger I'm thinking of is just a front and back cover made from recycled paper, a few pages inside and a clip. That's it.

A few more details. The cover can be cut from magazine advertisements, colored paper, a poster, cardboard, a cereal box, heavy wrapping paper. It could even be a couple of baseball cards clipped together. Forget about eight-inch-by-eleven-inch rectangles. Ledgers can be palm-sized since many kids love tiny anythings. How about a circle or triangle? The more unusual and personal, the better.

Reflecting

One of the surest ways to help students embrace the benefits of the Learning Ledger is to model evaluating your own performance. Talk out loud every day about what puzzles you, what you want to master, how you conduct your own research, what stumps you, what intrigues you, how you can find out more, and what *you* are doing well as a learner.

Periodically let your students review and reflect on their Learning Ledgers. Every few weeks, let your students get comfortable and just read through their entries to track what's happening to them as learners. Encourage them to look for recurring challenges or breakthroughs. They can use marking pens to highlight epiphanies or put stars all over their best days. Give them time to share their findings with a partner in a pair-share format. This is the educational equivalent of putting marks on the doorjamb to see how much they've grown. It's serious work, but you can create a festive atmosphere by letting kids sit on the floor, play music that is conducive to introspection, even have special snacks. While they're looking at how much they've learned, take note and take credit. You're the reason this is happening.

To Text or Not to Text: The Up- and Downsides

You can embrace the mandated social studies text in your school with slavish devotion, consult the pacing chart like a dieter counting calories, lecture from dawn to dusk, pepper your students with hundreds of facts, assign questions, and administer tests of encyclopedic proportions. But in the end, there's just one question on the achievement test for teachers: Have your students learned? So when deciding what materials to use, including textbooks, the bottom line is always—will they help you ensure that your students will learn?

What's Right with Textbooks?

Textbooks provide a de facto curriculum when schools don't have their own guidelines. If it's a choice between *tabula rasa* and a textbook, a book may jumpstart the process, particularly if teachers are new to the subject, or if their own education in history and social science was inadequate or a big turnoff. Sadly, that might be the majority. I was asked to teach the Social Studies methods course at my local university and was scandalized when I learned that I would have nine hours and ten minutes to get the job done. In just under the amount of time it takes to wash and dry five jumbo loads of laundry, I was expected to take my graduate education students from apathy to "I can't wait to teach this!" So a text may be a godsend. Contemporary texts have excellent graphics and rich visual material, including maps, paintings, etchings, portraits, and photographs of objects and artifacts. Some critics observe, and rightly so, that the pages in many texts mimic Web pages, with icons, sidebars, colorful graphics and boxes filled with snippets of information—everything but the keyboard, mouse, and electrical cord. But the visual material can be helpful in teaching content, critical thinking, and visual literacy by engaging visual learners and providing content for second-language learners who would get little or nothing from staring at a page of solid text.

Social studies texts can be a great help to parents who may be rusty on the fine points of NATO or the struggle between agribusiness and migrant laborers. They can scout ahead in the text, then help their kids with homework without being embarrassed. This could even lead to some interesting dinner table conversations.

The Downside of Textbooks

As I told you in the beginning of this chapter, textbooks are big business and very competitive. A publisher can lose tens of millions of dollars in sales if a textbook adoption committee doesn't find the keywords it's looking for in a computerized search. With their eye on the marketplace rather than learning, publishers are churning out textbooks that mention many, many terms—often in bold type—without any attempt at an explanation. Coverage is king, and as a consequence the actual content can be devoid of the details, personalities, tragedies, epiphanies, heroic feats, disasters, human turmoil, and triumph that grab students' attention and challenge them to think.

Textbook authors must also work while fashionably attired in a political straightjacket. Content is diluted and deformed by bias-and-sensitivity reviewers, hired by the publishers to avoid trouble. This phenomenon was explored by Diane Ravitch in her groundbreaking and influential book, *The Language Police: How Pressure Groups Restrict What Students Learn* (2003). Dozens and dozens of words, images, and foods are routinely banned from school texts to avoid the possibility of giving offense to anyone. For example, the word *hut* was deemed ethnocentric and replaced with *small houses*.

Despite this hyperscrutiny, textbooks manage to be culturally skewed and loaded with inaccuracies. Plus, they're very expensive. Publishers have been supersizing their products, with the cost of textbooks doubling or tripling in an era when teachers' salaries increase in increments that will buy them a fast-food meal—hold the onion rings.

So let's see. We took away the really juicy, engrossing, fascinating, intriguing stuff about this business of being humans, and forced teachers and kids to plow through what remains in a way that is almost guaranteed to blunt their interest. And we assiduously avoid activities that bear any resemblance to the actual work performed by historians, economists, political and social scientists, relying on a didactic presentation of factoids to pass muster when it's accountability time.

Students go through the motions of learning but since the product is unpalatable, they partake reluctantly; what they manage to ingest, they misunderstand or forget. When test time rolls around, they regurgitate the little they can recall, sit back, and wait for their miserable scores.

The Reality for Now

As dire as the textbook situation sounds, the reality is that the majority of teachers are going to use a social studies text at some time, for some lessons. Researchers say that even the best teachers rely on them more than they think. Shadow studies that track teacher activities have shown that between 80 and 90 percent of classroom and homework assignments are textbook driven.

Some teachers may even be required to make textbooks the mainstay of instruction, although most school systems and districts have confined their stringent implementation practices to reading and math, leaving teachers free to teach any social studies lessons they can squeeze in the time remaining in their crowded day.

So here's the reality about social studies textbooks in the instructional program. You may be directed to use them. You may need to use them sometimes. You may want to use them as a framework for establishing basic material. But make no mistake. That teacher's guide simply describes a system that, when conscientiously executed, only provides documentation of what has been *presented*.

If you want to be truly accountable, you must remember—teaching hasn't happened until kids learn.

Goal of This Book

The goal of this book is to help kids *learn* social studies by modeling how you can restructure your teaching to capitalize on the four stages of the learning cycle, and reinject critical social elements into the content, process, and outcomes, whether you are following the structure of a textbook or creating lessons of your own.

You can use this book side-by-side with the social studies text, choosing activities that feed your students' curiosity, encourage exploration, promote inquiry, and guide them to take action—in effect, putting your textbook on steroids. For example, Chapter 3 shows you how to select primary source documents that inject detailed content into classroom discussions. Give your students time to examine the ledger of George Washington during the Revolutionary War, and they'll discover that his expenses included a vet bill for his sick horse and payments to spies for vital information about the enemy. Chapter 4 demonstrates how selections from autobiographies, diaries, and journals can bring unique voices and faces into your classroom. For example, through Gold Rush diaries your students can discover the harsh reality of pregnancy, birth, injury, sickness, and starvation on a slow-moving wagon train headed west. Chapter 5 gives you dozens of ways to use visual objects and images as powerful learning tools, including examining photographs of four-year-olds toiling twelve hours per days as newsboys, coal sorters, and mill workers to feed their siblings and parents.

Maybe you're already a social studies superstar, or heading in that direction with fiery determination. Your approach to social studies resembles an intricate collage, combining the standard curriculum with rich resources that raise complex questions and provide diverse points of view on a given topic. The ideas in this book can help you galvanize your students into action by giving them opportunities to identify their own questions for research, piece together their understanding from a variety of sources, and demonstrate their mastery through authentic assessments.

If you're fortunate enough to have complete autonomy over the style and content of your social studies program and you have boundless energy, this book offers dozens of ideas that you can modify to meet your needs. You'll also learn how to shift the burden of work to your students, where it belongs. As they select areas for personal research, they learn to delve deeply into a single aspect of a topic, and then meet the challenge of formatting their expert knowledge into presentations that teach others. At its most breathtaking, social studies instruction produces students who challenge and change conditions in their community or globally.

This book is meant to be a user-friendly handbook for social studies instruction, and a powerful tool for learning—yours and your students. So I encourage you to experiment, apply some trial-and-error, and please, have some fun. For novice or master teacher, this is a guidebook for teaching social studies so that kids learn.

Back to the Future

While I was working on this book, I decided to contact some of my former students, to see if their recollections about this approach to learning bore any resemblance to what I'm telling you. I was heartened by many of their comments, the spirit of which is captured in this letter from Ryan Malanaphy, an aspiring filmmaker who graced my classroom fifteen years ago.

> Dear Laurel,
>
> Simply put, I feel that your curriculum taught us how to teach ourselves. Generally, classes do not extend beyond the textbook or the chalkboard. In your class, we went outside the classroom and discovered that learning was also drawing and discussing architecture, visiting landmarks, attending local government meetings, and even participating in those meetings. As a result, we began to view the world around us as an extension of school where knowledge was waiting to be discovered. When we studied a historical period, we explored it in great depth and that period became our world. During the Renaissance Fair in fifth grade, we transformed the classroom into the sixteenth century using murals, costumes, and props. In the Santa Monica History Fair, we brought our reports to the rest of the school, becoming a teacher to our peers. Textbooks were thrown out and we were set loose to research as many different sources as we could get a hold of. Finally, and I don't want to underemphasize this point because it is no easy feat for a teacher, learning in your class was fun. The day-to-day variation in activities and assignments, as instructive as they were, kept us engaged and on our toes. I think that all that I have mentioned here, ultimately cultivated a passion in us for our studies. That passion proved to be, and remains so today, more valuable than any fact we could have memorized.
>
> First cool learning memory that comes to mind: the way you brought the library into the classroom. Lining the chalkboard with books made learning into a kind of treasure hunt. And yes, it was our first experience with original source material.

Architecture field trips. The class once took a trip to my old house on seventh to study its Spanish style. At the time it felt good knowing that my one bedroom triplex was worth class time.

The Renaissance fair and Santa Monica Fair. For the Renaissance Fair, Andrew and I dressed up as Leonardo Da Vinci's apprentices and delivered a report on Da Vinci while our parents watched on—oh my god, I think my dad has a video of that somewhere. The Santa Monica Fair: first video project I ever did.

City Council Meetings! How can I forget the late nights at City Hall with Tommy. And the day we spoke to the council urging them to reject an ordinance that would ban rollerblading on the promenade. We won because we were able to prove that there were no skating alternatives in the city.

It certainly influenced the way I think. For example, I have a genuine interest in Santa Monica's historical heritage and future development, which first developed in your class. If someone intends to build an obnoxious twenty-story tower over the Santa Monica Place, I'm watching those city council meetings and reading our local paper for updates. I know from experience that if need be, my involvement will count for something. After all, I once saved rollerblading on the promenade. I can't walk past an architecturally significant building without giving it a good going over. That definitely is your doing. It seems there are more subtle influences too, such as a curiosity and appreciation for human culture, that started in your class and matured over the years with high school and college.

Best wishes and good luck with the book.

Ryan

2

What's Your Problem?

Human Dilemmas at the Heart of Social Studies

History must be presented, not as a mere statement of what happened, but a forceful acting thing. The motives—that is, the motors—must stand out. To study history is not to amass information, but to use information to construct a vivid picture of how and why men did thus and so, achieved their successes and came to their failures.

—John Dewey, *The School and Society*

What's the Big Idea About Problems?

How do we . . . ? is an all-purpose question that humans have been asking since the beginning of time whenever they encountered a problem. Let's take the problem of *How do we survive when food is scarce?* Faced with famine, death, and possible extinction in any location or era, humans resort to a fairly consistent pattern of problem-solving behavior—self-sacrifice, sharing, stealing, looting, usury, piracy, shifts in power, need for protection, migration, innovation, and invention. An early example of this occurred in 6000 BC, when hunting nomads experienced a drought that wiped out the animal herds upon which they depended. After they'd skipped one too many meals, someone asked, *How do we survive?* The answer was to move down from the plateaus in search of food and water. Arriving in a fertile valley, they harvested naturally occurring plants, got comfortable, and then asked, *How can we guarantee the recurrence of these plants in sufficient amounts so that we can stay put and give up our nomadic life?* The answer was tilling the land and the invention of the plough. With the plow came surplus crops that needed to be stored. Hence, the invention of pottery. Next question, *How can we label the storage jars to indicate ownership?* The answer was writing. This cascade of new conditions, questions, innovations, and inventions brought the world scribes, administrators, math, canal building, more tools, metallurgy, weapons, barter, stone buildings, and eventually, the pyramids. From an isolated plateau to the Pyramids of Giza, thanks to problems and questions.

Once humans got rolling with this questions game, they found that the sky was the limit. Each new question triggered a new arena for exploration, develop-

30

ment, and more questions, until it became an addiction. *Why do birds migrate?* led to zoology. *What makes a healthy person die?* gave us medicine. *What if we cut open a dead body?* begot anatomy. *What causes rain?* spawned meteorology. *How do we honor the dead?* gave rise to elaborate funerary rites. *Why is it easier to carve some stones into building blocks, while others shatter or resist?* Geology. *How can we use the snout, tail, and stomach of a pig?* Behold the culinary arts. *How do we indicate status among the people in the community?* Enter jewelry making, face painting, tattoos, and ritual scarification. *What do we do with people who take a life?* Criminal justice. *And what is the meaning of life, anyway?* Philosophy is born. Even in the so-called Dark Ages, there were more inventions developed and applied usefully in less than a century than in the previous thousand years of human history all over the globe.

So human life is a question-based enterprise, moving from problem to solution, and then repeating the cycle to refine ideas and evolve. Therefore, it would be logical to expect social studies to be a question-based discipline, in which students identify the big questions that have been the levers of human development, and examine the problems and solutions that have occupied residents of this planet for eons. Sounds fascinating, doesn't it?

However, when teachers first tackle the task of planning a week's or a year's worth of social studies instruction, they're hit with a description of social studies that's enough to cause brain freeze. Observe.

What Is Social Studies?

Social studies seeks to examine and understand communities, from the local to the global, their various heritages, and the nature of citizenship within them. Students acquire knowledge of key social science concepts, including change, culture, environment, power, and the dynamics of the marketplace. They learn about the United States and the role of citizens in a democratic society within a culturally diverse and interdependent world. They also acquire skills of inquiry and communication through field studies and other research projects; the use of maps, globes, and models; and the consideration of various forms of historical evidence. Students apply these skills to develop an understanding of American identity and democratic values, to evaluate different points of view, and to examine information critically in order to solve problems and make decisions on issues that are relevant to their lives.

How do you even get your mind around devising activities that force words like "culture, environment, power, and the dynamics of the marketplace" to get up off the page and explain themselves to your students? This could be particularly challenging if your students have had little or no previous social studies instruction—a real possibility these days. What if they're new arrivals to the country and the culture, speak little or no English, or are so politically and economically disenfranchised that they doubt that anyone is interested in helping them *solve problems and make decisions on issues that are relevant to their lives?* How about students who are stymied by a text that is too difficult, or so culturally lopsided that the whole learning enterprise is thwarted?

Perhaps your dilemma lies on the other end of the spectrum. Your kids are fluent readers and speakers, but have made it pretty clear that their only interest in the "dynamics of the marketplace" is cruising the local mall or shopping on line. Social studies? No thanks!

What's a teacher to do? You could look to the National Council for Social Studies (NCSS) for guidance, but most teachers are lucky if they have time to glance at the state and local standards, which typically run to five or six pages of microprint, exhaustive in their breadth and encyclopediac in their attention to detail. For example, the California State Standards for fourth graders—nine-year-olds—lay out the following challenge:

> Students learn the story of their home state, unique in American history in terms of its vast and varied geography, its many waves of immigration beginning with pre-Columbian societies, its continuous diversity, economic energy, and rapid growth. In addition to the specific treatment of milestones in California history, students examine the state in the context of the rest of the nation, with an emphasis on the U.S. Constitution and the relationship between state and federal government.

For a start, it looks like the author was intent on hoarding punctuation marks, particularly periods, as if they were primetime cell phone minutes. The friendliest word in the whole statement is *story*, yet this mouthful is followed by thirty-two objectives, most of which sound more like SAT material than storytelling. For example:

- Describe the effects of the Mexican War for Independence on Alta California, including its effects on the territorial boundaries of North America.
- Understand the purpose of the California Constitution, its key principles, and its relationship to the U.S. Constitution.
- Describe the similarities (e.g., written documents, rule of law, consent of the governed, three separate branches) and differences (e.g., scope of jurisdiction, limits on government powers, use of the military) among federal, state, and local governments.
- Describe the mapping of, geographic basis of, and economic factors in the placement and function of the Spanish missions; and understand how the mission system expanded the influence of Spain and Catholicism throughout New Spain and Latin America.

These are but a few of the expectations handed down from on high. Add in the local guidelines for implementation and you have a whole lot of "what needs to be taught." Considering the sheer volume of material in the average social studies syllabus, an obvious question arises. How can you teach so many discrete topics in a way that kids gradually, steadily understand events in the past and apply that insight to their role in the present? Forget about it. You can't do it, and people who try get very cranky.

So it's no wonder some teachers simply force-march their students through a textbook that they may or may not understand, assigning the questions at the end of each chapter and congratulating themselves if they manage to keep up with the other teachers in their grade level. It looks more like a military maneuver than learning. Conscientious students spend most of their time memorizing meaningless facts, like reluctant College Bowl contestants. The others are AWOL.

What seems to have been lost in the great effort to list, categorize, and number to the third decimal place all the skills that should be taught, is the *reason* for teaching social studies So let's think about it. Why should we set aside precious classroom time to ruminate over our past? Or prod at the sharp edges of other cultures? What do ten-year-olds need with the separation of powers or the process for amending the state constitution, when their biggest concerns are getting to the cafeteria before the sausage pizza runs out, and not being the last person picked for dodgeball? Why do we do this social studies stuff, anyway?

Social Studies—What's It Really All About?

Interestingly, the NCSS has a simple, relevant, and highly compelling answer. The primary purpose of K–12 social studies is *citizenship education*. Why? Because the thinkers in the Council believe that in order to maintain our democratic system, citizens must care about the common good and participate in public life. To achieve that, social studies programs must prepare students to identify, understand, and work to solve the problems facing them in their communities, as well as in our increasingly diverse nation and interdependent world. Specifically, social studies instruction should:

* Foster individual and cultural identity.
* Examine the forces that hold society together or pull it apart.
* Provide opportunities for participation in the school and community.
* Address critical issues in the world.
* Prepare students to make decisions based on democratic principles.
* Teach the skills needed for citizen participation in public affairs.

Here it is at last—the *social* element that has been stripped from so many social studies programs—society, cohesion, interdependence, citizenship, decisions, participation, the common good. This is the small bright kernel that tells us why we simply must include social studies in our classrooms on a daily basis. Yet the message is buried in a mass of federal, state, and local mandates so arcane and densely packaged that even veteran teachers feel like they need an interpreter.

And teachers aren't the only ones who are puzzled. Many students are at a dead loss to explain why they're required to take social studies at all. It simply doesn't make sense. Unwieldy chunks of history, often studied wildly out of order. This year the thirteen colonies. Next year Mesopotamia. After four or five years of disjointed instruction, it would take an honor student with lots of time on his hands to find any connection between Captain John Smith and King Nebuchadnezzar. And yet those two leaders were up to the very same tasks, four thousand years apart. Organizing workers, fending off enemies, expanding their real estate, consolidating power. Or consider Marco Polo, Lewis and Clark, and John Glenn. The parallels in their adventures are fascinating and illustrate that every age produces people with born-to-roam DNA. Strikingly similar situations keep recurring throughout history—in politics, international relations, social standards, religion, law, and personal behavior. But unfortunately, all that most students seem to extract from their close encounters with the past is an intense and abiding dislike for the subject. They don't get it, and as a result, they hate it.

And who can blame them when social studies is presented as a list of battles with matching dates? But alternatively, if you were to ask students *What drives people to butcher each other for a cause?* you'll have a hell of a conversation on your hands, fueled by lots of fresh details about the Sudan, the Middle East, and the inner cities of the United States, lifted right from the front page of your local newspaper or from your students' own experiences. Ask kids to memorize the highlights of the Magna Carta and you're in for a snooze festival. Ask them to debate the appropriate limits of free speech on their campus and you'll hear their synapses positively crackling.

Rather than approaching social studies as a bunch of unrelated events lashed to a time line, the goal is to help your students discover that social studies is a multimillennial chronicle of human beings trying to solve a handful of basic problems through experimentation and invention. And guess who's writing the latest chapter in the story? They are, along with their parents, friends, enemies, and strangers across the globe. Driven by curiosity and necessity, we the people, persist in our quest to find solutions to the four basic problems that mankind has faced, tackled, solved, or botched over time:

* How do we survive?
* How do we thrive?

- How do we evolve?
- What causes us to devolve?

Every topic in your social studies book is tied to one of these four questions. The trick of teaching social studies is to help kids identify the basic problems behind the events, so they begin to see social studies as a *human problem-solving activity*. The goal is to teach them that our actions in the present are connected to actions in the past; that we struggle to solve the same problems as our ancestors; and that our choices and actions will influence the lives of the people who inherit the planet from us in generations to come.

Basic Problems and the Brain

Now let's go back for a moment to the problem of information overload—that mountain of names, dates, and concepts that you must present to your kids or else. Let's be clear about this. It's impossible to transfer all that information into your kids, unless you liquefy it and inject it directly into a main vein. And even if you could hook every student up to a social studies intravenous drip, mainlining data is a doomed strategy because the human brain simply will not retain isolated, unrelated facts for more than a nanosecond.

But the brain *will* seize upon big ideas that can be examined and applied over and over. So that's your goal. To teach your kids about these four basic concepts—survive, thrive, evolve, devolve—that they can use to make sense of the whole of human history, including the present. And you want them to recognize that we all continue to work on those same problems, with varying degrees of success.

Focus on the Four Basic Problems

So let's take a look at the four basic problems and see how they connect to the topics you're likely to address in any social studies unit or year. The goal here is to illustrate how you can continuously link ideas, events, and inventions back to the four basic problems to help your students begin to construct the big pictures in social studies, rather than trying to master a curriculum that is served up in a thousand tiny pieces, like a plate that's been dropped on a hard floor.

Problem 1: *How do people survive?*

Survival may not be a daily topic of conversation for most of your students, but it is a persistent theme in social studies, beginning with the Paleolithic era, the hunter-gatherer societies, the rise of the cities, the great plagues, the dangers and disasters in the age of exploration, invasions, and world wars. You are tapping into the problem of survival whenever you examine or discuss exploring unknown regions, forced or voluntary migration, radical shifts in climate and environmental disasters, natural or man-made calamities, persecution, economic distress, and homelessness. You're examining evidence of the attempt to survive when you handle artifacts such as tools, weapons, clothing, animal traps, implements for cooking or discuss fire, heating, shelter, and fortifications.

Problem 2: *How do people thrive?*

Thriving is a far more familiar topic for your students, although they may view our obsession with upgrading computers, having the latest clothing or shoes, home furnishings, or micromusic systems as simply the status quo. The notion of thriving is a persistent theme in social studies, beginning with the early civilizations of Mesopotamia, Egypt, and Kush, and the development of agricultural technology, the rise of cities, commerce, and trade. You're tapping into the problem of *how* we thrive when you examine or discuss the origins of architecture, medicine, formal codes or laws, water supply systems, lighting, plumbing, or the domestication of animals. You're examining evidence of thriving when you study artifacts such as textiles, weaving, furniture, baskets, pottery, simple machines, boats, plows, carts, and the tools required to make these things.

Problem 3: *How do people evolve?*

With the notion of evolving, you begin to see people extending their thinking, looking beyond the dinner table, to devise ways to improve their lives and make sense of human existence on a larger scale. The notion of evolving is a persistent theme in social studies, beginning with the early civilizations of Mesopotamia, China, and India, the development of architecture for distinct purposes (temples, courts, schools, stables), the invention of writing, paper, and books, math, calendars, art, and music. You're tapping into the problem of how we evolve when you examine or discuss the origins of religions, moral codes, literature, mythology, philosophy, philanthropy, science, drama, forms of government, politics, division of labor, citizenship, overland and maritime expeditions. You're examining evidence of evolution when you study artifacts such as maps, musical instruments, pumps, bridges, coins, armor, stirrups, astronomical instruments, statuary, etchings, and paintings.

Problem 4: *What causes us to devolve?*

With the notion of devolving, you begin to see the dark side of human thinking and invention, as people devise ways to wield power over others, often with devastating effects. Sometimes devolution is the result of natural disasters that reduce people to stone-age conditions, and challenge them to start all over again. The notion of devolving is a persistent theme in social studies, beginning when early civilizations organized themselves around hierarchies or caste systems. You're tapping into the problem of how we evolved when you examine or discuss behaviors such as discrimination, slavery, bondage, genocide, invasions and warfare, torture, germ warfare, dropping atomic bombs, anarchy, wholesale looting, and rioting. People also endure a form of devolution when subjected to widespread and prolonged natural disasters such as famine, pestilence, plague, tsunamis, volcanic eruptions, toxic pollution, and the destruction of their environment. You're examining evidence of devolution when you study about the Holocaust, the African Slave Trade, imprisoning the innocent, child-bonded labor, genocidal wars, institutionalized racism, systematic discrimination, and economic oppression.

Retooling Your Thinking

What does this basic-problem approach to social studies require of you, the teacher? You'll need to make a fundamental shift in your head, quite possibly swimming against a rather strong current, from looking at *social studies as events* to *social studies as problem-solving behavior*. Instead of talking about an event such as the Battle of Hastings in the abstract, as if it spontaneously occurred in 1066, you talk about specific people doing something observable in order to solve a problem—Normans and Anglo Saxons trying to survive and prevail in hand-to-hand combat in order to control the government of England. Here's another example. Instead of referring to a *demonstration*, you would say that *protesters demonstrated* in order to force their local government to pass a living wage law that would allow poorly paid workers and their families to survive. In a way, it's as simple as turning nouns into verbs, then putting a human subject in place. Let's see a few more examples of thinking about social studies as human behavior.

Social Studies as Events	vs.	Social Studies as Problem-Solving Behavior
The French Revolution	→	Peasants, wage-earners, and bourgeoisie revolted against Louis XVI to achieve economic changes that would allow them to thrive.
Nuclear Treaty	→	Faced with the problem of mutually assured destruction, two leaders agreed to stop

		developing nuclear weapons that could cause widespread slaughter and destruction.
Secession	→	Faced with the abolition of slavery, the voters in North Carolina decided that the only way they could continue to thrive was to sever their ties with the U.S. government in order to prevent the emancipation of their slaves.

Thinking About Utopian Communities

Now let's apply this *social-studies-as-problem-solving-behavior* approach to the topic of utopian communities. That may sound a little esoteric, until you think about the fact that the colonization of North America was in many ways a utopian venture. Granted, most of the people fleeing England were intent on solving the problems of *how do we survive?* and *where can we thrive?* Puritans needed a safe haven where they could practice religion without persecution. Ditto the Baptists. Second sons, cheated of any inheritance by the *primo genitur* rule of birth order, voyaged to the colonies to thrive, intent on acquiring the land, power, and status they'd never enjoy if they stayed home. Their dreams were fueled by Thomas More's *Utopia*, which was plagiarized to create advertisements to lure people to the colonies. It was wildly successful with the impoverished and unemployed who had a choice between three seasick months on the Atlantic or debtor's prison. They were all intent on surviving and thriving, but they also harbored the dream of a fresh start, the good life, their particular version of Utopia. How much more Utopian can you get than Philadelphia—the city of brotherly love.

And it didn't stop there. In the eighteenth and nineteenth centuries several hundred groups launched model communities in the United States, including settlements in Oneida, New York; New Harmony, Pennsylvania; and Zoar, Ohio. The approaches were as diverse as they were imaginative; the people had to overcome problems that were immense.

If we consider these utopian communities using the *social-studies-as-events* approach, they might just seem like the failed experiments of charismatic eccentrics and their idealistic or delusional followers. But suppose we view these utopianists as people trying to solve the problem, *How do we evolve?* They wanted to achieve paradise on earth, to establish perfect societies in which their followers enjoyed equality, freedom from want, peace, and harmony. Now we're in very fertile territory for thinking about all the challenges involved in forming a functional community, from the first cities in Mesopotamia to the present day in our hometowns.

Starting with the utopian community as the *solution*, we probe for the *problem* they were trying to solve by asking questions, such as:

- What were these people concerned about?
- What was their problem before they started the community?
- What were they trying to accomplish by inventing a new form of community?
- What do you think they were trying to fix, change, or avoid?
- How did they do it?
- What was the effect?
- Did it achieve their goals?
- What else happened as a result?
- What do you wonder about them?
- What would you have done?
- What are your thoughts about organizing a utopian community?
- What are your thoughts about living in a utopian community?
- Do any of these communities still exist?
- How could we find out more?

Now you can connect utopian movements of the past to present-day efforts to build successful communities by guiding your students to ask themselves the same questions that drove utopian projects:

- How do we live together?
- What makes for a successful community?
- What rules do we need?
- What values must be shared?
- What are worthy goals?
- How can we achieve economic stability?
- How are material goods distributed?
- What type of leadership is necessary?
- How is power shared?

Ask your students if they think people still struggle with these questions. In our classroom or school? In the community? In our country?

- What part of our society seems to be getting closer to a utopian ideal?
- What part is moving farther away?
- What is one change we would need to make if we wanted to live in utopia?
- What else?
- Do you think people want to live in a utopian society? Why?
- How would our laws change if we were utopianists?

Baby Steps: Effect → Cause Thinking

Tracking down problems and studying their solutions can take you to some pretty interesting places. Cognitively speaking, it's a huge improvement over "read the chapter and answer the questions at the end." But how do you get started, especially if you're teaching students who are used to text-driven lessons that require little more than basic reading skills and the patience of a hunger striker? Baby steps. You have to take this a little at a time, just like you'd start an exercise regime after years of being a couch potato. John Dewey gave us a valuable clue about how to construct learning experiences that emphasize the problems at the heart of human activity. He said, "History must be presented, not as a mere statement of what happened, but as a forceful acting thing. The motives—that is, the motors—must stand out" (1899, 136). Dewey said we must "use the information to construct a vivid picture of how and why men did thus and so, achieved their successes and came to their failures" (1899, 136). He's talking about the big problems that motivate people—survive, thrive, evolve, devolve.

You can teach your students to unearth the motives behind historic events, meaning the problems people were trying to solve, by introducing them to **Effect → Cause** thinking. It's pretty simple, but it can train students' minds to look for problems and solutions throughout the social studies curriculum. Here's what you do. Ask your students to focus on an object, custom, event, or institution in the present, and treat it as the end-product of a problem that people were trying to solve. Ask them, "What problem were people trying to solve when they came up with this?" and then let them attempt to think their way back to its origin, creation, invention, discovery, or purpose. That's what Dewey meant by making the motives stand out. Here are a few simple examples.

Show students a brick.
Ask: *What problem were people trying to solve when they invented bricks?*
Possible answers:

> How to build if you have no trees
> How to build a fire-proof building
> How to build a higher, stronger building
> How to use the natural resource of clay
> How to have windproof and waterproof walls

Show a picture of a judge.
Ask: *What problem were people trying to solve when they decided to have judges?*
Possible answers:

> How to settle arguments
> How to ensure that people are treated fairly
> How to make sure people follow rules

How to make new rules
How to deal with dangerous people

Show a picture of a shelter, house, or building.
Ask: *What problem were people trying to solve when they invented architecture?*
Possible answers:

How to keep dry in the rainy season
How to keep safe from wild animals
Where to sleep when it's cold
Where to keep food and belongings

Other examples:

Show a classroom.
Ask: *What problem were people trying to solve when they invented schools for children?*

Show a voting booth.
Ask: *What problem were people trying to solve when they invented voting?*

Show a dam.
Ask: *What problem were people trying to solve when they invented dams?*

Thinking backward to find the link between solutions and problems isn't just an intellectual exercise. In the process, students get ideas for solving problems in the present, and they're constructing a working model for improving the future. This is a big shift for students (and adults) who see contemporary problems such as poverty, violence, pollution, or the crisis in health care as simply facts of life. Effect → Cause thinking suggests—none too subtly—that problems are opportunities for people to create solutions by thinking. That's what humans have been doing for eons, and it's time that your students get to work, too.

In Closing

Students frequently complain that social studies, particularly history, is irrelevant to their world and their lives, giving them license to ignore it and you. Using the four basic questions you can help your students see that the study of the past is not about guts, governments, and glory. It's about the recurring questions that humans must face in any era and how they arrive at their answers. You can also give them a new perspective on their own times. As they realize that some of the dilemmas they face in the twenty-first century have been puzzling humans since the time when the world was lit by fire, they can use models from the past to become problem solvers and change agents in their own lives, in their community, and in the global village.

3

Investigations

Discovering the World Through Primary Sources

There is nothing like first-hand evidence.
—Sherlock Holmes

Thematic Strands:
People, Places, and Environments
Global Connections
Individuals, Groups, and
Institutions

Learning Layers: Geography, history, deciphering historic texts, Internet research skills, language arts, sociology, cultural anthropology, economics, analytic and inferential thinking, contextual analysis

What's the Big Idea About Primary Sources?

Using primary sources may be the hardest fun you can have in your classroom. It's a bit like playing charades—lots of clues, but what's the message? This is particularly true with primary source texts. Some read haltingly, like emergency, grammar-free English. Others are written in a Baroque fashion, the sentences so clogged with *wherefores* and *whereases*, dependent and independent clauses, that you may feel compelled to send out a search party to locate the final punctuation mark. A simple shop announcement can read like a church sermon.

So what can your kids learn from wrestling with primary source documents? For a start, what Ferdinand and Isabella promised Columbus:

> For as much of you, Christopher Columbus, are going by our command, with some of our vessels and men, to discover and subdue some Islands and Continent in the ocean, and it is hoped that by God's assistance, some of the said Islands and Continent in the ocean will be discovered and conquered by your means and conduct, therefore it is but just and reasonable, that since you expose yourself to such danger to serve us, you should be rewarded for it. And we being willing to honour and favour You for the reasons aforesaid: Our will is, That you, Christopher

Columbus, after discovering and conquering the said Islands and Continent in the said ocean, or any of them, shall be our Admiral of the said Islands and Continent you shall so discover and conquer; and that you be our Admiral, Vice-Roy, and Governour in them.

—*Privileges and Prerogatives Granted by Their Catholic Majesties Ferdinand and Elizabeth to Christopher Columbus, 1492*

And what happened to disloyal colonists who violated the boycott on British tea in 1773:

Resolved, that whoever shall be aiding, or assisting, in the landing, or carting of tea, from any ship, or vessel, or shall hire any house, storehouse, or cellar or any place whatsoever, to deposit the tea, while it is subject, by a British Act of Parliament, to the payment of a duty, for the purpose of raising revenue in America, he shall be deemed an enemy to the liberties of America, and we will not deal with, or employ, or have any connection with him.

—*Association of the Sons of Liberty, December 1773*

And how to behave toward native people encountered on voyages of exploration:

To exercise the utmost patience and forbearance with respect to the Natives of the several Lands where the Ship may touch.

To check the petulance of the Sailors, and restrain the wanton use of Fire Arms.

To have it still in view that sheding the blood of those people is a crime of the highest nature: They are human creatures, the work of the same omnipotent Author, equally under His care with the most polished European; perhaps being less offensive, more entitled to His favor . . .

—*Hints from the Royal Society offered the consideration of Captain Cooke, 1768*

And how to treat small pox when you've run out of vaccine:

As we had no vaccine, we decided to inoculate with the smallpox itself. The smallpox matter should have been taken from a very healthy person, but unfortunately Mr. Halsey was not sound, and the operation proved fatal to most of our patients.

—*Charles Larpenteur,* Forty Years a Fur Trader on the Upper Missouri, 1833–1872

And rules for Native American visitors to Plymouth Colony:

When their men came to them, they should leave their bows and arrows behind them.

—*Of Plymouth Plantation by William Bradford, 1620–1647*

In the land of primary sources, your students can even learn how to dress a "Beef-Stake, sufficient for two Gentlemen, with a fire made of two newspapers":

Let the beef be cut in slices, and laid in a pewter platter, pour on water just sufficient to cover them, salt and pepper well cover with another platter inverted; then place your dish upon a stool bottom upwards, the legs of such length as to raise the platter three inches from the board; cut your newspapers into small strips, light with a candle and apply them gradually, so as to keep a live fire under the whole dish, till the whole are expended when the stake will be done; butter may then be applied, so as to render it grateful.

—*Amelia Simmons*, American Cookery *(2d ed.), 1796*

In short, primary sources help you and your students get as close as possible to what actually happened. They're artifacts of a certain time, created at the time being studied, by the people being studied. The word *artifact* can have a slightly inner tone, bringing to mind something decayed and likely to disintegrate at the slightest exploratory poke. But as you can see, that's the very opposite of how primary source documents behave. In the right hands, they're chatty, gossiping insiders—flesh-and-blood eyewitnesses to history in the distant past and in the making. The Last Will and Testament of Thomas Jefferson is a primary source. So is a scarab ring from Queen Hatshepsut and the diary of a Vermont farm child. How would we know that Leonardo da Vinci designed an armored vehicle, a scythed chariot, a pile driver, a revolving crane, a lagoon dredge, and a flying ship if not for primary sources—his drawings and notebooks preserved over the centuries for our delight and edification? The past would be a large black hole without primary sources.

But primary sources aren't just tools for investigating the past. Your daily newspaper and last night's city council agenda are also primary sources that help us understand issues in the present. Julia Roberts got an Academy Award for playing Erin Brockovich—a woman with a knack for unearthing primary sources. Brockovich—the real-life heroine—used friendly persuasion, a plunging neckline, and a truckload of these documents to defeat the Pacific Gas and Electric Company, accused of bringing a toxic plague down upon the southern California town of Hinkley, by contaminating the drinking water with hexavalent chromium. The twenty-eight-billion-dollar settlement was a testament to the power of primary sources and unrelenting research.

Primary sources can be divided into three broad categories.

1. Written documents that provide textual evidence about the times being studied, including: arrest records, eviction notices, advertisements, speeches, recipes, laws, ledgers, newspapers, guidebooks, obituaries, and wills.
2. First-person, eyewitness accounts about the times being studied, including: journals, diaries, letters, autobiographies, and memoirs.

3. Physical objects and images created at the time being studied, including: photographs, newsreels, tools, clothing, simple machines, paintings, vehicles, and buildings.

Teachers typically use all three types in combination to construct rich learning environments, but we're going to study each category separately. This chapter concentrates on strategies to help students decipher primary source documents including: public records, birth and death records, census reports, church records, newspapers, treaties, legal documents, deeds, government documents, accounting books or ledgers, ships' logs, travel guides, city directories and business papers, pamphlets, newspapers, audio and videotapes. (Chapter 5 highlights first-person accounts and Chapter 6 examines images and objects.)

Where's the Beef?

No doubt your textbook includes snippets of primary source texts set out in sidebars or colored boxes. Sometimes these excerpts are couched in explanatory text, almost like subtitles translating the content, but they can't begin to capture the complexity and vivid detail of the intact documents. It's like scanning a menu in the window of a restaurant versus sitting down to a full meal. A slipping glimpse compared to a visceral experience. No, if you're intent on doing rigorous, full-blooded social studies, you need to give your kids the whole-hog version.

In a sense, reading primary source texts is like snooping through someone else's mail. And snooping is inherently fascinating, so poring over undigested, unadulterated, unabridged primary source documents typically generates intense interest. None of the brainwork is done for your students, and yet they seem to enjoy it immensely, exactly because of the mystery factor. They're playing detective, piecing together raw material from what at first glance seems like a really cold case.

Using primary source texts stimulates cranial activity—and that's a departure in itself for students raised on nothing but textbooks and worksheets. Even a rudimentary glance raises questions—evidence that the brain is on the job. You might hear outbursts like, "What's with this handwriting? I can't *read* this," particularly if your students are trying to decipher a text like Thomas Paine's *Common Sense* (1791). Here's a sample sentence that will have them scratching their heads: *The fentiments are not yet fufficiently fashionable to procure general favor.* Eventually kids crack the code—that *f* is a long *s*, so their decoding becomes more fluid, but what do the words mean? They may need a few trips to the dictionary for the more archaic ones. With persistence, they'll have a rough translation, and then they're ready to get to the heart of the matter. What was Paine's purpose? Who was his audience? What does this tell us about the times and the people?

Reading primary source texts can be puzzling, as when students encounter the Blue Laws in Texas that prohibited selling pots, pans, and washing machines on Sunday until 1985. There are surprises—the discovery that in 1813 Thomas Jefferson wrote a letter to Alexander von Humboldt in which he concluded that Indian support for Great Britain "would oblige us now to pursue them to extermination, or drive them to new seats beyond our reach." Kids learn valuable information in unexpected ways. Plundering the obituary archives of the *New York Times* they can glean facts not included in textbooks—that Ralph Abernathy accompanied Martin Luther King Jr. to jail seventeen times for leading civil rights demonstrations in the South; Eleanor Roosevelt quit the DAR because they refused to rent their concert hall to Marion Anderson, an African American singer; Nikola Tesla is credited with seven hundred inventions; James Baldwin was denounced by blacks and whites for his writings on race relations in the United States; on her deathbed Susan B. Anthony, pioneer leader of the cause of woman suffrage, uttered this regret: "To think I have had more than sixty years of hard struggle for a little liberty, and then to die without it seems so cruel."

Primary source texts are the original reality show, so it's absolutely worthwhile to spend some of your planning time locating a sampling of unique documents that bear witness to the period, event, or theme you're studying. Then your job is to stoke the inquisition in your classroom, because witnesses are only useful if you can make them talk. So the focus of this chapter is teaching your kids how to get the story out of primary source texts by looking, thinking, and asking questions, especially *how do we know?*

What About Standards?

When you decide to use primary source documents to provide textual evidence about the times you are studying, you're asking your students to use authentic historical-investigation strategies to learn more about social studies. In the process, they will develop and demonstrate skills that are fundamental to a rigorous standards-based approach to social studies. The following list suggests the range of challenges students will face as they undertake a thorough examination of documents from the past and present created by a wide variety of individuals for many different purposes.

Students will:

* Read a wide range of primary sources to acquire new information.
* Apply a wide range of strategies to comprehend and interpret primary source texts.
* Compile, organize, and evaluate information.

- Ask appropriate and probing questions.
- Draw conclusions or inferences from evidence.
- Compare and contrast things, ideas, events, and situations.
- See issues from various points of view.
- Develop historical research capabilities, including the ability to formulate historical questions, interrogate historical documents, and obtain historical data.
- Synthesize knowledge of an historic time and place from primary source documents to construct a story, explanation, or historical narrative.

 ## Awareness

Assessing Prior Knowledge About History and Documents

It's hard to overestimate the value of asking kids what they already know *before* we haul out the textbooks and write assignments on the board. And most teachers truly understand that. But in our rush to get to the content and cover the required material, we sometimes forget that all students come to school with rich funds of intellectual, social, emotional, and practical knowledge garnered from conversations with their families, experiences in the neighborhood, personal reading or even watching television.

Your students probably know a lot about history, but they may not know they know it. That's your first challenge: to get them to toy with this idea of history, and reveal what they know. Asking, instead of telling, lets your students display how smart they are. In the process, they often surprise themselves.

Assessing what your students already know about history and primary source documents also gives you an authentic starting place from which to launch the explorations and inquiry stages of the learning cycle, instead of reteaching familiar material or making assumptions that leave gaps in their learning.

The activities in this Awareness section ask students to examine the question, *How do we know what we know?* about events outside of our own experience, particularly those that happened in the past, even thousands of years ago. Posing the *How do we know?* question leads naturally to the topic of primary source texts and how they're used as research tools. The following activities begin with open-ended questions that let your students dabble in the role of historian as a warm-up to tackling something like *The Great Binding Law* of the Iroquois Nation or the *Code of Hammurabi*. These activities can be done in pairs, small groups, or as a whole class. Working collaboratively is a boon to all students because it provides modeling, scaffolding, and creates opportunities for dialogue and debate.

You Are Here: What Is History?

So let's get started. The goal of this activity is to develop a working definition of *history*. You begin by asking a very straightforward, open-ended question to find out what history means to your students, then charting their responses. After each student response, ask "What else?" to encourage multiple responses. Ask: *What do you think of when you hear the word* history? or *What does the word* history *mean to you?*

You can do this as a whole-group activity, listing all their comments on the board. When you have many responses, help them summarize and agree on a definition of history. Or you can divide students into groups and ask them to brainstorm the question and agree on a list of ideas that begin to build a class definition.

Once you've established a draft definition, ask students to find the word *history* in various dictionaries, online, and in a thesaurus. Have them read the definitions and synonyms out loud and compare the information with your draft. Encourage students to fine-tune their definition, then write it on a chart and post it for frequent reference.

The History of . . .

Although initially your students may not seem to know a lot about the history found in their textbooks, they do know a lot about the history of themselves, their families, and their belongings. Asking students to re-create a single aspect of their personal history can tell you a lot about their sense of time, chronology, notable events, and what's important to them. This activity asks students to write a brief history of a personal possession.

Begin by asking your students, *Does everything have a history?* Elicit many responses and encourage students to ask clarifying questions and provide examples if they disagree. Then model the process you want students to follow. Show them a common object such as a tennis racket, a wooden spoon, a doll, a metal tool, an old book, a hiking boot, a watch. Ask: *What might the history of this (object) be?*

Invite students to speculate, and ask them to explain their comments if their logic isn't apparent. List their responses. If they make comments about chronology—what came first and next—help them place the events in order by numbering them, listing them chronologically, or constructing a simple time line. Then tell them that they'll have an opportunity to construct a brief history of an object that's important to them. It could be their favorite shoes, baseball mitt, pet, skateboard, a tree in their backyard, a favorite hat or book, or a cherished baby toy. If possible, give them time to decide on an item and bring it to class.

Ask them to represent the history of the item using any of the following techniques, or a combination of them:

- Draw a series of pictures to show the major events in the history of your _____.
- Write a story describing the history of your _____.
- Make a story map showing the history of your _____.
- Make a list of words or phrases that tell the history of your _____.
- Write a short play or monologue to present the history of your _____.
- Construct a time line showing major events in the history of _____.
- Write a first person narrative in which your _____ tells its life story.

Have students share their histories in pairs or small groups, and ask clarifying questions. After the small-group discussions, ask:

- How long is the history of your _____? (months, years, generations)
- When did the history of your _____ start?
- What is the most interesting part of your history?
- How do you know all these things? Who did you talk to for information?
- What do you think will happen to your _____ in the future?
- What types of events in history do we usually remember? (*dangerous, frightening, joyful*) Why?

What Did We Learn About Being an Historian?

After working on their personal history projects, students should have some notions about what it takes to work like an historian. The goal of this conversation is to be explicit about the skills, activities, and resources historians—novices or veterans—use in their work. Record all students' ideas on a chart with a title such as *How Historians Work*. Ask:

- What did you have to think about to write your history?
- What did you need to do to discover the history of your _____?
- What kinds of information did you include?
- How did you get that information?
- How did you think about organizing your history?
- What was the most useful thing you did?
- What problems did you have to solve?
- If you decided to create another history, what would you choose as your subject?
- What might you do differently?

Waking Magoun's Brain

Now that your students have experienced a bit of what it feels like to poke around in the past, it's time to generate some curiosity about primary source documents—historians' tools. This exercise can help your students see the potential and limitations of primary sources as material for investigating history, both in the distant past and in-the-making.

Our Town: The Recycling Bin as Resource

Most of us live in cities or towns that are generating primary source documents by the ton on a daily basis, most of which end up in the dumpster, recycling bin, or lining the gutters. But this ephemeral material is not trash when viewed with an inquisitive eye, because it holds clues about your community and the people who live there. *Our Town* is an activity that helps students recognize the primary source material in their daily environment, and begin to read it to construct a picture of the place they call home.

To prepare for this activity, you'll need to collect a broad range of text items generated in your community, such as:

- junk mail
- discount coupons for fast food or auto repair shops
- a map of the town (get from chamber of commerce or telephone book)
- pages from the telephone or business directory
- flyers from a health food store
- calendar section of the local newspaper showing events of the week
- announcement for a yard sale
- obituary page from newspaper
- application for a library card
- real estate brochures
- bus schedules
- brochures for political campaigns
- ticket to an amusement park

Divide students into small groups. Give them a selection of six to eight documents and ask them to discuss what each document is, and what it tells about their town. It may help them to imagine that they're detectives, anthropologists, or historians, investigating the town. Ask, *What could an outsider guess about your town based on these text documents? Is there any connection between the documents? Is there any contradiction or irony? Is anything in these documents news to you?*

When the groups complete their observations, have them share their materials with the class and tell what they think is revealed about the community. Ask the other students, *What's another interpretation? What else could this document indicate? How could we be sure?* Post their ideas along with the documents on a bulletin board with a caption such as *What does this say about our town? What's missing?* Encourage students to bring in additional documents to round out the picture.

The Paper Trail: The Story of You

This activity helps older students understand that they personally generate primary source documents containing information about who they are, where they went, and what they did every day. This paper trail could be used to document a piece of their existence by retracing their movements, actions, and interactions. Here is how the activity works.

1. Ask students to mentally review the past twenty-four hours of their lives, as if they're rewinding a videotape. They should try to remember where they went and what they did. Were they alone or with others? Ask them to make a list of each thing they did in chronological order (for example, breakfast, carpool, gym class, text messaging, band practice, soccer, the library, homework club, dinner with family, computer research).

2. Next, ask students to circle any activity that was recorded in some way—on paper, electronically, or audiovisually. They might have created the record themselves, as in sending emails. Or it might have been created externally, by a teacher taking attendance or a video surveillance camera filming them at a convenience store.

3. Now have students focus on the records created about them in that twenty-four-hour period. Ask, *Do the records tell a full and accurate story about who they are and how they spent their time? What's missing? What important things did they do that left no trace?*

4. Ask them, *If someone who didn't know you looked at the records only, what conclusions might they reach about you? What wouldn't they understand?*

From this activity students should conclude that primary source documents provide valuable clues but may paint an incomplete or misleading picture of what really happened.

 ## Exploration

Discovering More About Primary Source Texts

Once you succeed in stimulating your students' curiosity about how we know about history, including their own experiences with primary source documents, give them some hands-on time with authentic material related to your social studies theme. One approach is to present a buffet of documents and let them sample, graze, and return for second helpings.

It used to be that you had to break into the local archives after hours, or bribe an historian to get your hands on certain primary source documents. Now they're as accessible as fast food. Full texts are available all over the Internet. For one-stop convenience, go to www.uidaho.edu/special-collections/Other.Repositories.html for a listing of more than five thousand websites describing holdings of manuscripts, archives, rare books, historical photographs, and other primary sources for the research scholar.

You can spend hours looking at primary sources online, but the most practical approach for classroom use is to print out copies that your kids can examine, compare and contrast, and annotate as part of their exploration. Try to find an assortment that will appeal to different student interests—ledgers for the future accountants, historic advertisements for consumers, antique guidebooks for the restless, campaign literature for the budding politicians, and municipal codes for students interested in the law or its enforcement. Here's a sampler of documents you can locate with the click of a mouse.

Primary Source Text Documents: A Sampler

Arrest Records: Arrest records contain important information about the types of laws people make and how they are applied. They tell about community values and social upheaval. Arrest records aren't just about villains. Many environmental activists, antiwar protesters, suffragettes, and labor organizers have been arrested and view their jail time as evidence of their efforts to reform a failed justice system. Rosa Parks' arrest record for not moving to the back of the bus is available online.

Advertisements: Photographs of billboards, print advertisements, trade cards, calendars, almanacs, and product leaflets provide evidence about daily life—fashion, food habits, home furnishings, sports, and personal hygiene that are often absent in more traditional historical sources.

Catalogues: Browsing through a catalogue is like going through the drawers and closets of an era. The material culture is laid out with enticing descriptions and price tags. Catalogues show the accoutrements of class and wealth.

Census: The United States Census Bureau conducted its first survey in 1790, and maintains a website with vast amounts of information about people and businesses in our country. For example, the section on People and Households addresses population numbers and distribution, housing, income, poverty, health insurance, and genealogy. There is a large section to help teachers use census data in the classroom.

City Directories: City directories are the precursors to the Yellow Pages or telephone book. Typically they contained listings of the people residing in a city, giving name, address, and occupation. Directories also included listings of businesses by name and by type (e.g., saloons, hotels, tanners, etc.) with advertisements.

Guidebooks: The oldest surviving guidebook, *Descriptions of Greece*, was written in about 160 AD for wealthy Romans, and they have flourished ever since. Guidebooks provide vital information for travelers, including weather, geographic hazards, dangers, lodging, transportation routes, and must-see natural or cultural features.

Laws: Documents enumerating laws range from the Mesopotamian *Code of Hammurabi* to the test prep manual for people applying for a driver's license. There are striking similarities in common law and municipal codes over the ages that testify to our persistent attempt to create an orderly society.

Ledgers: A ledger is a book for recording commercial transactions. Some contain all of the financial accounts of a business, including debits and credits. Household and personal ledgers generally list transactions recorded as they occurred, like a diary of expenses.

Newspapers: Julius Caesar published an early version of the newspaper called *Acta Diurna*—news of the day—a series of daily reports from Rome posted throughout the Empire. Most newspapers inform readers of current events, but some are published by special interest groups primarily to promote causes such as abolition, civil rights, and secession and strengthen ties among cultural, business, academic, and ethnic groups.

Obituaries: Obituaries reveal information about individuals and their culture. They offer hints about who and what people value, social status, virtues, gender roles, and the way people view death.

Patents for Inventions: The idea of patents may have originated in ancient Greece, but in 1474 Venetians officially decreed that new and inventive devices must be registered with the Republic in order to obtain legal protection against potential infringers. England followed with the Statute of Monopolies in 1623 under King James I. Patents document attempts to invent solutions to problems.

Receipts of Purchase: Receipts are documents that serve as legal evidence of an exchange or purchase. They provide information about goods and services, the economy, the participants in the transactions, and relative values of items purchased.

Recipes: Recipes give clues to regions, agriculture, resources, and traditions. In colonial times, a recipe book was kept by the mistress of the household as a guide for cooking as well as her treasury of family recipes. Printed cookbooks were expensive and scarce, so a young woman leaving home copied her mother's book.

Sheet Music: The lyrics in sheet music hold clues to current events, social change, and customs of a period. Students can compare and contrast songs from the Civil War and the Vietnam War eras, or the lyrics from songs in the prosperous 1920s and the Depression. This is an intriguing way for students with musical intelligence to process content.

Ships' Logs: Logs record important events in the management, operation, and navigation of a ship, with notations written at regular intervals. Taken as a whole, they show the activities required for running the ship as well as incidental observations and weather changes.

Transcripts of Trials: Transcripts give a play-by-play account of the judicial system at work. Students can learn about laws, logic, crimes and punishment, and use transcripts as text for Readers Theatre, skits, or simulations.

Wills: A will is a legal declaration of how a person's possessions should be distributed after death. Wills provide a survey of the material culture of a time and give readers an idea of what people of different classes possessed, valued, and passed on.

Exploring Primary Source Documents

Once you've gathered a tantalizing selection of documents, you'll need to give your students plenty of browsing time. If the document is antique or technical or from another culture, their first encounter can be akin to listening to someone with an unfamiliar accent, so they may need time to tune their ears and eyes before they can concentrate on the content. The following activities provide examples of strategies that allow students to practice decoding a broad array of documents.

Newspaper Articles

The newspaper is a rich source of details about life in many places and periods, starting with this morning's news and working your way back in time. Many websites publish newspapers from around the globe, so you can monitor daily events such as tsunamis, revolutions, elections, or medical advances with the click of a mouse. There are also tremendous newspaper archives online, organized by date, theme, location, or event. The following is from the *New York Times: On This Day* website (New York Times 1964).

Martin Luther King Wins the Nobel Prize for Peace

Dr. King Is Winner Of Nobel Award

Special to The New York Times

Oslo, Norway, Oct. 14, 1964—The Nobel Peace prize for 1964 was awarded today to the Rev. Dr. Martin Luther King Jr. The 35-year-old civil rights leader is the youngest winner of the prize that Dr. Alfred Nobel instituted since the first was awarded in 1901.

The prize honors acts "for the furtherance of brotherhood among men and to the abolishment or reduction of standing armies and for the extension of these purposes."

The Norwegian state radio changed its program schedule tonight to broadcast a 30-minute program in honor of Dr. King. In a broadcast from Atlanta, Ga., Dr. King said that he was deeply moved by the honor.

Dr. King said that "every penny" of the prize money, which amounts to about $54,000, would be given to the civil rights movement.

"I am glad people of other nations are concerned with our problems here," he said. He added that he regarded the prize as a sign that world public opinion was on the side of those struggling for freedom and dignity.

He also said he saw no political implications in the award. "I am a minister of the gospel, not a political leader," he said.

After reading, ask:

- Why do you think Martin Luther King was given the Nobel Prize for peace?
- What words tell how Dr. King felt about getting this award from a group in Norway?
- How do you think people in the United States felt in 1964 about Dr. King receiving the award?
- What surprised you in this newspaper article?
- Who else has received the Peace Prize?
- Do you think Martin Luther King was a leader? Why?

Let students go on the Internet to find pictures of the civil rights movement. Ask them to observe:

- What is happening in the pictures?
- What are the protesters doing?
- What are the law enforcement people doing?
- What are segregationists doing?
- What kind of techniques did Dr. King teach people to prepare them for a demonstration?
- What happened to many demonstrators?
- Did Dr. King's life end peacefully? Do you think he felt like he had succeeded?

Recipes

You can find historic recipes on the Internet or in your library, and used bookstores are excellent sources for regional cookbooks. Here's a section of a traditional recipe from the Louisiana area (Junior League of Baton Rouge 1959).

Squirrel Pie
6 squirrels
2 cups chopped celery
2 cups chopped onion

1 cup salt meat
1 quart water
Red and black pepper
2 hard cooked eggs
Salt
Cut squirrels in pieces. Put in heavy pot and add celery, onions, salt meat and seasoning. Cover with water. Simmer for about an hour until squirrels are tender.

Read and discuss the recipe, then ask:

- How is this recipe different from food you eat? How is it similar?
- What ingredients might we use instead of squirrel?
- What might this tell you about the region? What else?
- Who do you think ate squirrel pie? Why?

Select a cookbook from another era, or find the menu for meals consumed by famous people such as Henry VIII, Marie Antoinette, or Leonardo da Vinci. Look at the items served. What do they tell you about the lifestyle and types of foods available at the time? For example, if they decide to research the culinary habits of the Emperors of China, they might consult the *Rites of the Zhou Dynasty*, which states, "When the emperor gives a banquet, there must be six cereals and six animals for food, the six clears for drink, 120 delicacies, eight dainties, and 120 urns of sauce." The six cereals included rice, millet, broomcorn, sorghum, wheat, and wild rice stem. The six animals were the horse, cow, sheep, pig, dog, and chicken. The six clears were water, thick liquid, li wine, chun wine, yi wine, and ye wine. Ask your students, *What can you guess about life in the Imperial Court in China from this description?* Compare and contrast the Chinese banquet with this menu from a Civil War regiment, found in the journal of Thomas Wentworth Higginson, the leader of the first black regiment in the war:

For drink we aim at the simple luxury of molasses & water, a barrel per company. Liberal housekeepers may like to know that for a barrel of water is allowed three gallons of molasses, half a pound of ginger & a quart of vinegar, this last being a new ingredient for my untutored palate though the rest are amazed at my ignorance. Hard bread with more molasses, with subsequent tobacco, complete the repast destined to cheer but not inebriate.

Students with strong kinesthetic intelligence may learn best by researching and preparing a common recipe such as bread, soup, or pie from different eras. Have them consider, *What are the differences in the vocabulary? How have terms for measurement, ingredients, portion size, and accompaniments changed?* Encourage them to hold a taste test to let students compare and contrast the results.

Catalogues

Find or photocopy pages from catalogues of different periods to research fashion trends, household articles, the cost of living, and lifestyles. Ask your students,

- What can you tell from the advertising text?
- Who do you think did the household purchasing? How can you tell?
- What were considered necessities of the time?
- What were the latest inventions or innovations?
- What were considered luxuries?
- How do the catalogue pages reflect attitudes of that time about gender, work, family, and dress?

Compare and contrast the items advertised in an historic catalogue with similar advertisements in your local newspaper.

Laws

Reading laws can give students instant insight into the civil expectations of an era or region, and raise questions about what is a just law. The Blue Laws are a great place to start as they provide endless fodder for discussion. They're still in effect in many states and easily located on the Internet. The following is an excerpt from *Blue Laws of the Colony of Connecticut* written in 1655:

> No one shall be a freeman or have a vote unless he is converted and a member of one of the churches allowed in the dominion.
> No food or lodging shall be offered to a Quaker, Adamite or other heretic.
> No one shall cross a river on the Sabbath but authorized clergymen.
> No one shall travel, cook victuals, make beds, sweep houses, cut hair, or shave on the Sabbath.
> No one shall kiss his or her children on the Sabbath or feasting days.
> Whoever wears clothes trimmed with gold, silver, or bone lace above one shilling per yard shall be presented to the grand jurors and the selectmen shall tax the estate 300 pounds.
> Whoever brings cards or dice into the dominion shall pay a fine of 5 pounds.
> No one shall eat mince pies, dance, play cards, or play any instrument of music except the drum, trumpet, or jewsharp.

Ask your students,

- What do these laws tell you about living in Connecticut in 1655?
- What do they tell about the practice of religion?
- Which law seems the most unusual? Why?
- Do any of the laws seem unfair? Why?

- Which law is the most like our times?
- Who do you think wrote these laws?
- What do you think was the reason for making these laws?
- Who do these laws favor?
- What kind of community did they want?
- Would you have liked to live in Connecticut in 1655?

Find a copy of the municipal codes for your town. Are there any similarities? What are the main differences? If you know a lawyer or law student, ask him or her to review the Blue Laws and comment on how individual rights have changed since 1655. Then reach way back in history to the Code of Hammurabi, the earliest known written legal code, composed about 1780 BCE by Hammurabi, the ruler of Babylon. The Code lays out the basis of both criminal and civil law, and defines procedures for commerce and trade. Here are a few samples that have a contemporary ring, despite being nearly four thousand years old:

> If fire break out in a house, and some one who comes to put it out cast his eye upon the property of the owner of the house, and take the property of the master of the house, he shall be thrown into that self-same fire.

> If a judge try a case, reach a decision, and present his judgment in writing; if later error shall appear in his decision, and it be through his own fault, then he shall pay twelve times the fine set by him in the case, and he shall be publicly removed from the judge's bench, and never again shall he sit there to render judgment.

Have students compare and contrast all three sets of laws, then speculate on new laws that may need to be written in the next decade or century to address emerging technology, spyware, undersea and space exploration, real estate ownership out in the cosmos, responsibility for global environmental pollution, and other emerging areas of regulation or conflict.

Receipts of Purchase

Receipts of purchase tell what people bought, in what quantities, and how much they paid for it. They provide a view of daily life through the pocket book. The following document reveals the contents of a ship arriving in England from New York, referred to as New Netherland, and the purchase of the island that is now Manhattan.

> Rcvd. 7 November 1626
>
> High and Mighty Lords,
>
> Yesterday the ship the Arms of Amsterdam arrived here. It sailed from New Netherland out of the River Mauritius on the 23d of September. They report that our people are in good spirit and live in peace. The women also have borne some children there.

They have purchased the Island Manhattes from the Indians for the value of 60 guilders. It is 11,000 morgens in size [about 22,000 acres]. They had all their grain sowed by the middle of May, and reaped by the middle of August They sent samples of these summer grains: wheat, rye, barley, oats, buckwheat, canary seed, beans and flax. The cargo of the aforesaid ship is:

7246 Beaver skins
178 Otter skins
675 Otter skins
48 Mink skins
36 Lynx skins
33 Minks
34 Muskrat skins

Many oak timbers and nut wood. Herewith, High and Mighty Lords, be commended to the mercy of the Almighty,

Your High and Mightinesses' obedient, P. Schaghen

(Letter To The Directors of the Dutch West India Company, 1626)

Read and discuss the letter, then ask:

* What does it tell you about natural resources in New Netherland?
* What does it tell about the diet of the people?
* Why do you think they were shipping lumber to England?
* Why did people in England want animal pelts?
* Who do you think benefited from this trade? Who else?
* How might the colonizing of New Netherland have affected the Native Americans living in the area?
* How do you think they reacted?
* How could you find out more?
* Who were the High and Mighty Lords?

Obituaries

Reading obituaries is a fascinating and efficient way to get to know the dead. The articles are packed with the highpoints of a life, but are also spiced with unusual details that bring out the personality of the departed. Obits may not be your first stop in the daily newspaper, but they definitely belong in your social studies program. Google *obituaries* and the underworld is yours—including these tributes to George and Martha Washington.

Mount Vernon, December 16, 1799

It is with inexpressible grief that I have to announce to you the death of the great and good General Washington. He died last evening between 10 and 11 o'clock, after a short illness of about twenty-four hours. His disorder was inflammatory sore throat, which proceeded from a cold of which he made but little complaint on Friday. On Saturday morning about 8 o'clock he became ill. Every medical assistance was offered but without the desired effect. His last scene corresponded with the tenor of his life. Not a groan or complaint escaped him, in extreme distress. With perfect resignation and a full possession of his reason he closed his well spent life.

The Spectator, New York

Read and discuss the obituary. Ask:

- How is this similar to obituaries in our newspaper? How is it different?
- What type of person did the writer think Washington was?
- What did he admire about him?
- What words tell you how he felt about Washington?
- How was his death like his life?
- How has illness and medicine changed since then?

Now look at Martha Washington's obituary in *The American Mercury* newspaper, June 3, 1802.

Died, at Mount Vernon, on Saturday evening, Mrs. Martha Washington, widow of the late illustrious Gen. George Washington. To those amiable and Christian virtues which adorn the female character, the added dignity of manners, superiority of understanding, a mind intelligent and elevated. The silence of respectful grief is our best eulogy.

Read and discuss this one. Ask:

- How is this different from George's obituary?
- What might that tell us about the times?

Read several obituaries from your local paper. Compare and contrast them with the Washingtons'.

Inquiry

Digging Deeper into Primary Source Documents

Now that your kids have a working knowledge of many kinds of primary source texts, they're poised to discover the wealth of information hidden in a single document. Inquiry is the stage in the learning cycle where students move from surveying the field to drilling down deep to expose the meaning and messages in primary source texts. But it's all up to you. Researchers have found that elementary-level students are capable of deep historical understanding, but only if carefully guided by a teacher. Without you, they simply can't get below the surface. The studies showed that when faced with multiple sources of information, students tended to view all of them as equally useful, reliable, and valid, and mistakenly concluded that the information in long texts was better than in short ones, simply based on length. So you will need to actively model the process of making documents talk. It takes a bit of time at first, but it's worth it.

How to Make Primary Source Documents Talk

The most important skill in the inquiry process is just that—inquiring. Students can catch the spirit of inquiry if they imagine that they are colleagues of the master detective, Sherlock Holmes, who was famous for using astute observation and logic. In other words, looking and thinking. That's what you're going to teach your kids to do—to look and to think. They can wring a huge amount of crisp, detailed information out of primary source documents simply by observing and asking thoughtful questions. Here's a four-step questioning process that can help them make any primary source talk.

Step 1: What Is the Document?

Here is my lens. You know my methods.

—Sherlock Holmes

- What type of document is this?
- Is it from a newspaper or magazine?
- Is the author writing as an individual or for an organization?
- When and where was it written?
- Is it handwritten or machine printed? What does that suggest?
- What do you notice about the typeface or design?
- Can you identify the author?
- What do you know or can you guess about the author?
- How could you find out more?

Step 2: What Does It Say?

It is a capital mistake to theorize before one has data.

—Sherlock Holmes

- Who or what is the story or information about?
- What do the words say?
- What do they mean?
- What's unusual about the language?
- What information does this source add to your research?
- What are the important facts you learned from the document?
- Does the author have first- or secondhand knowledge about what he or she has written?

Step 3: What's the Point?

> *It has long been an axiom of mine that the little things*
> *are infinitely the most important.*
>
> —Sherlock Holmes

* Why was this document written?
* Was it written for a public audience or a specific group?
* Is it personal, or for a few people?
* How do you know who it is for?
* What does the author hope to do with this document (inform? argue? persuade?)?
* What phrases or words indicate the author's intent?
* What biases might the writer have?
* Why might the author have that bias?
* What ideas, words, or phrases suggest bias?

Step 4: What Else Do I Want to Know?

> *One true inference invariably suggests others.*
>
> —Sherlock Holmes

* What do I wonder about this document?
* What else do I want to know?
* What guesses (inferences) can I make from this?
* What other primary or secondary sources might help answer my questions?
* How can I find information on the Internet?
* Who still knows about this event?
* Who else could give me more information?

The first time you model this Holmesian process of interrogating a document, it's a good idea to start with something short, captivating, and easily accessible to all students. I've chosen a very brief but intriguing advertisement that appeared in a California newspaper in 1860. With a mere twenty-one words, you can show your students how to make a Pony Express advertisement sing like a bird.

Saddle Up: Analyzing a Pony Express Advertisement

First, a bit of background. The idea behind the Pony Express—a horseback relay mail service—is an old one. In thirteenth-century China, Marco Polo saw post stations twenty-five miles apart, and the Chinese had been using the system for at least a thousand years before that. In 1849, the Gold Rush made California a mecca for fortune hunters, adventurers, and people bored with life in the east. But the transplants were hungry for news from their families and business connections. In addition, political tensions between the North and South were increasing, and the government was determined to keep the far west, with its treasures of gold, in the Union. Mail service was urgently needed. The Pony Express was born.

One hundred and eighty-three men rode for the Pony Express during its eighteen-month existence, each receiving $100 per month in pay. Most of them were lightweight young men, often teenagers, but there was one by the name of Bronco Charlie Miller who was only eleven years old. In 1860, the Pony Express published this advertisement in California.

PONY EXPRESS!

**WANTED: YOUNG, SKINNY, WIRY FELLOWS
NOT OVER 18, MUST BE EXPERT RIDERS,
WILLING TO RISK DEATH DAILY.
ORPHANS PREFERRED.**

In preparation for this inquiry activity, you may want to download some pictures of Pony Express riders. Share the pictures and background information with your students. Check your textbook for additional information, then give them copies of the Pony Express advertisement and have them read and discuss it in pairs or small groups. Finally, work through these questions as a whole-group activity.

What Is It?

What type of document is this?
A want ad similar to the classified section of contemporary newspapers. May have been in the newspaper or printed on paper and posted around the city.

When and where was it written?
In California in 1860.

Who do you think wrote this?
The owner of the company, his business manager or advertising man, a person who worked for the newspaper, an employment recruiter.

What Does It Say?

Who or what is the story or information about?
It's about a company that needs a certain type of rider to deliver the mail. About delivering mail on horseback. About getting the mail across the western half of the country fast. About the difficulties of traveling west on horseback.

What do the words tell about the job?
That the riders might not live through the journey because of the dangers of overland travel at the time. That lighter people seem to be more successful in the job.

Why do you think they only want skinny young men?
Horses can run faster, longer with a light man in the saddle and this business is about being the fastest mail service to the west coast and back. Young men are strong and willing to take risks.

What's unusual about the advertisement? How is it different from job descriptions in your paper?
That they tell riders/applicants that they might be killed on the job. They don't try to make the job sound fun or glamorous.

What are the important facts you learned from the document?
That they risked death. That they used such young riders. That young people then were expert riders.

What does it tell about conditions between Missouri and San Francisco? What were the dangers?
The territory is dangerous, perhaps because of no real roads, hostile Native Americans, poisonous snakes, wild animals, heat, snowstorms, floods, and robbers.

What's the Point?

Why do you think this document was written?
To recruit appropriate riders for the Pony Express.

Why do you think they were advertising in California?
There were lots of young men there who didn't get rich in the gold fields and were looking for jobs.

Why do you think they prefer orphans?
They don't have to tell anyone if the rider dies. They don't have to ship the body or personal belongings home. They don't have to give his pay to anyone.

What does that make you feel about the Pony Express Company?
That they cared more about their business than about their employees.

What does the author hope to do with this document (inform? argue? persuade?)?
To persuade men to apply for the job. To appeal to their egos. To attract daredevils who will ride fast and keep up the reputation of the company.

What biases might the writer have?
He doesn't want fat men of any age, nor old men and not women of any shape or age. He prefers to hire people with no family.

Why might the author have that bias?
He has in mind a specific type of rider that he thinks will be the fastest, most successful and/or the least trouble. Women were not employed in this type of job, except in disguise.

What Else Do I Want to Know?

What do I wonder about this document?
Did many people respond to an ad like this?

What else do I want to know?
What type of person rode for the Pony Express?
How long did they stay in the job?
What did they like about the job?
What type of mail were they carrying?
Were the riders paid well?
Did many riders die? How?
Did any women ride in disguise?

What guesses (inferences) can I make from this?
It was not unusual for a young person to be employed in a potentially deadly job that involved riding hundreds of miles alone through dangerous territory. This was hard work but it paid well because of the risks. California had a supply of young men who might want to work for the Pony Express.

What other primary or secondary sources might help answer my questions?
California newspapers form 1860, history of the Pony Express, history of the Post Office

How can I find information about Pony Express Riders?
On the Internet, encyclopedia, museums.

That's how you make a primary source document talk, talk, talk. Fun, isn't it?

On Their Own

You'll need to model this process numerous times with a variety of documents, until students have acquired an appetite for inquiry. Gradually, they'll gain the skills and confidence to interrogate documents on their own. Each time you lead students through this comprehensive thinking exercise, you're reinforcing strategies they can use across the curriculum—in literature, economics, ethics, for substantive essays and standardized tests. Paramount among these are the abilities to extract information and interpret its meaning, draw conclusions or inferences from evidence, and compile, organize, and evaluate information.

One way to encourage investigative independence in your students is to introduce the element of choice into your curriculum. As you teach your way through a body of general knowledge with the whole class, tell your students that they may select a topic to investigate on their own. For example, if you're studying the Middle Ages, discussing daily life, feudal systems, art, architecture, and commerce, let students stake out their special territory—warfare, medieval healing techniques, simple machines, witchcraft, science, the plague, cartography, or the monastic system. As they scour text documents for information, they may also find images, objects, and first-person narratives that contribute to their research. Eventually they can present their expert findings to the class and everyone gets smarter.

How to Make Literature Talk About Social Studies

Most great teachers are experts at using literature to teach social studies themes. They choose class sets such as *My Brother Sam Is Dead* (Collier and Collier 1974) to transport their kids to colonial America during the Revolutionary War, or *The Power of One: Daisy Bates and the Little Rock Nine* (Fradin 2004), to let them glimpse growing up in segregated Arkansas. Efficiency is the obvious reason, since reading thematic literature doubles your social studies time while giving your kids the pleasure of devouring a really good book.

But what does reading literature have to do with primary source texts? Plenty. Research shows that kids learn information more readily and retain it longer if it is embedded in a narrative format that connects factual information to particular people in a specific place. So reading literature is a companion activity that multiplies the effect of your work with primary sources. Here's why. Your students have been scouring documents for facts, which are like pieces of a puzzle. But facts are useless unless they're assembled into a coherent picture. Enter literature—the glue that holds all the pieces together. A great novel transforms facts into vivid pictures that the brain can retain. Fiction readers or listeners can almost smell the meat smoking over an open fire, feel the coarse embrace of a single blanket on a freezing battlefield, experience lessons in a prairie classroom, feel the excitement of explorers sighting land and the apprehension of those watching from on shore—all the while learning volumes of explicit information covered in your social studies standards.

Now cast your mind back to Chapter 1 and the grim statistics about how U.S. students perform on standardized social studies tests that specialize in the recollection of isolated facts—a dismal 57 percent failure rate for high school students. So it's not unreasonable to think that one way to attack that deficiency would be to reintroduce narratives—good solid stories—into our instructional plans.

More encouragement about this literature-social studies connection came from four researchers, Levstik (1986), VanSledright (1995), and VanSledright

66

and Kelly (1996), who conducted naturalistic studies of elementary school students who were learning social studies using multiple texts, including children's trade books (Nelson and Nelson 1999). They concluded that students' interest in the subject matter as well as their ability to learn and retain information increased significantly when their instruction included literature. Moreover, they observed that, given a choice, students were more likely to read works of fiction or nonfiction than standard textbooks.

Another reason great teachers use literature to delve into social studies is that some periods, cultures, or groups of people will not be well represented using the visual arts, artifacts, or primary source texts as investigative tools. During the period of slavery in the United States, African Americans did not appear often in paintings or photographs; their material culture was sparse; because it was illegal to teach them to read or write, they produced few texts that have survived. But they did pass down songs, folktales, stories, and a collection of narratives recorded after the Civil War, all of which have been folded into literature about slavery in America.

Well-chosen literature—either class sets or read-aloud selections—reinforces what students uncover in their own research and introduces additional content. And speaking of read-alouds, there is a vast store of social studies knowledge hidden in fiction books written for adults. You don't have to read the whole book, or even whole chapters, just unique passages selected for their descriptive power. For example, *The Durable Fire* by Virginia Bernhard (1990), is an amazing evocation of life in Jamestown, as the colony struggled with incompetent leadership, uncertain financial backing, Native Americans bent on annihilation, and an untamed wilderness. As you read sections aloud, your students will glean so many details of the daily struggle for life during this near-catastrophic time that they'll feel as if you dumped them in a snowdrift outside the stockade.

Through read-alouds, you're developing their ears for good literature *and* increasing the prospect that they will become proficient readers. That's right. In 1985, *Becoming a Nation of Readers*, the groundbreaking study on literacy, stated "the single most important activity for building the knowledge required for eventual success in reading is reading aloud to children" (Anderson 1985). So when you're reading aloud to students of any age, you're building a foundation for literacy.

 ## Action

Using Knowledge About Primary Source Texts

Action is the stage of the learning cycle where you create a more dynamic relationship between students and the material they are studying. In this case, the goal is to use primary source texts as a basis for role playing, public speaking, individual research, and a bit of their own history making.

You Were There: *Historic Simulations*

When I was studying the Renaissance with my students, they were in love with Marco Polo and his million stories about the Silk Route. They could practically feel the grit in their teeth as they read about the highwaymen attacking Marco's caravan under the cover of a sandstorm. They were mesmerized by the notion of a human kite, and were frankly impressed that the Chinese had paper currency, coal, gunpowder, and rockets long before the West. What they couldn't understand was the big deal about spices. Who would pay a year's wages for a tiny bag of pepper? How did simple traders parlay a camel ride across Asia into a fortune? They were asking important questions that involved geography, economics, opportunity, middlemen, and supply and demand. I wanted a simple, graphic answer. So I devised a silk route simulation called the Prices of Spices. *Simulations* are staged replications that use authentic information in a dynamic setting to help students understand a concept or event. They can be as elaborate as restaging an historic trial or in my case, as simple as passing a tin of pepper.

First I asked my students to consult their Marco Polo vintage maps and identify all the major cities between Venice and Bejing. We listed them on the board in east-to-west order. With our route set, students volunteered to be traders in each city, and I gave them a few minutes to prepare. Some made city signs or placards announcing *Spices Bought and Sold Here*. Andrew, a brilliant, quiet student dove into the coat closet and emerged with his head turbaned in a purple sweatshirt, looking like something right out of the Three Kings.

I gave each group a bundle of paper currency and a bag of coins, then I triggered the simulation by giving a small tin of pepper to the residents of Beijing. They made their way to the next city and sold the pepper. Those traders turned around and ventured west until they found the next group of traders. Then they negotiated a price and returned home. The Venice-bound pepper moved from city to city, and each time the price rose as traders tried to cover their expenses and make a profit. After each transaction, I recorded the going price on the board. At the end of its journey, the price of pepper had skyrocketed. The discussion that followed touched on economics, supply and demand, relative versus absolute values, the role of merchants in globalizing distribution of goods, price setting, danger versus profit, motives, and sales strategies. That's a lot of cerebral exercise for a Beijing buck.

Ideally simulations allow students to understand the nature of the event or have an experience similar to the people who went through it. In addition, they challenge students to exercise critical thinking, apply strategies, and hone interpersonal skills—all in an authentic historic context. Successful simulations encourage historic empathy by forcing students to approach situations from different points of view and grapple with their emotions. If you're tempted to dismiss simulations as too time consuming, bear in mind that a well-constructed simulation has the potential to authentically integrate reading, writing, oral language, and sometimes math, science, and the visual and performing arts.

Max Fischer (1997) has published several books of simulations, or you can just make up your own wherever you get to a contentious moment in history. Here are a few suggestions. Let your kids be the first settlers in Jamestown, stuck on a ship in port for three weeks arguing about where to set up the town—next to the malarial swamp or farther up river? Stage a demonstration where students represent groups supporting and opposing the 1965 strike by farmworkers led by Cesar Chavez. Act out the unfair taxation of Chinese gold miners in the 1850s. Re-create the trial of Susan B. Anthony for voting illegally. Students will beg for more.

Primary Sources in the Making

If you teach your students to log on to your town's website, and then click on the City Council Agenda and Minutes, they're likely to discover some primary source texts that are not only very close to home but also close to their hearts. City council members routinely discuss issues that have a direct impact on students—renovating parks, animal regulations, extending curfews, school budgets, support for the arts, restrictions on noise. Students can track issues of interest and have a conversation with their city officials via email. If a topic is very important to kids, such as construction of a skateboard park, encourage them to attend the meeting and speak directly to the council. It's very empowering for students to learn that they don't have to be voting age to be heard.

Multiple Perspectives

Choose a single event in history, such as the assassination of a president, the beginning of a revolution or end of a war, the funeral of a famous person, or passage of landmark legislation. Find accounts of the event from different newspapers, magazines, websites, and electronic archives, including newspapers or journals from other countries. For example, read about civil rights legislation in newspapers from the North, South, Canada, and England. Compare and contrast the versions. Ask, *What accounts for the differences in reporting? Do you detect any bias in the writing? Are some facts left out? What might be the reason?* Now look up the same event in a history book. Ask students to consider, *How does the coverage differ? Why do you think newspapers and history books are written so differently?*

Time Capsule

Prepare a community time capsule with the class. What primary sources—documents, images, and objects—will you include to describe your life, school, friends, and community to future generations? What important message do you want to convey? Which documents or artifacts will get your message across? When should your time capsule be opened? How will you ensure that it is recovered and opened?

The Learning Ledger

The Learning Ledger is a tool for regular, focused self-assessment. Learning Ledgers help students account for their day, like diary or journal with the expressed purpose of capturing concrete descriptions of their work with primary source texts and the effect on them.

Basic Three Questions for the Learning Ledger
* What did I do?
* How did I do it?
* What did I learn?

Questions Related to Primary Source Documents
* What type of documents did I examine?
* What was the most interesting thing about the documents?
* What did I learn about life in that time?
* What did I learn about the person who wrote it?
* What did I learn about reading texts written in another place or time?
* How did I use documents to answer my questions?
* What questions do I still have?
* What other documents or sources could help me answer my questions tomorrow?
* What do I still wonder about?
* What else do I want to find out?
* What could I teach someone else about _____?

Additional Questions for the Learning Ledger
* What did I enjoy most about my work today?
* What do I want to try next time?
* What did I learn about how I am smart?
* What did I learn about myself?
* What's the best thing I did all month?
* Who do I enjoy working with?
* Who helps me learn?

- What helps me learn?
- How do I help other kids learn?
- What did I do with other students?
- How did I do it?
- What did I learn about working as a group?
- How did I help the group?
- How did I get help from the group?
- What did I do well?

In Closing

Get yourself an armful of primary sources documents and learning in your class takes a quantum leap from lounging to interrogating. Students can eavesdrop on conversations and rub elbows with people from different times, places, and cultures without ever leaving home. They're handling the tools of historians, and in the process they realize that their textbook is only one historical interpretation of past events, but not necessarily the only interpretation. Primary sources force students to realize that any account of an event, no matter how impartial it appears to be, is essentially subjective. By using primary sources, students get to act like historians. They'll debate you and their classmates about the interpretation of the documents. They'll challenge other students' conclusions and hunt for evidence to support their own. Your classroom may be transformed into a lively arena where students test and apply important analytical skills.

4

Informants

How to Make Dead People Talk

*After my return from the Canoe camp nothing worthy of remark took place
until the arrival of the steamer, St. Peters, late in June 1837. The mirth usual
on such occasions was not of long duration, for immediately on the landing of
the boat we learned that smallpox was on board. Prompt measures were adopted
to prevent an epidemic . . . but they proved fatal to most of our patients. About
15 days afterward there was such a stench in the fort that it could be smelt at a
distance of 300 yards. It was awful—the scene in the fort, where some went
crazy and the others were half eaten up with maggots before they died. Those
who recovered were so much disfigured that one could scarcely recognize them.*

—Lawrence Larpenteur, *Forty Years a Fur Trader
on the Upper Missouri, 1833–1872*

Thematic Strands:
Individual Development and
Identity
People, Places, and Environments
Global Connections

Learning Layers: Geography, history, deciphering historic texts,
Internet research skills, language arts, biography, autobiography, psychology,
sociology, cultural anthropology, economics, analytic and inferential thinking,
contextual analysis

What's the Big Idea About First-Person Documents?

Bill Coate is a teacher in Madera, California, whose idea of a great field trip is to
take his students to a graveyard, followed by junkets to the coroner, tax assessor, and
newspaper morgue—any place they can track down dead people. Cruising graveyards has become an academic tradition in Bill's class. Early in the year, he and his
fifth graders go to the local cemetery where they wander among the headstones,
reading names, dates, and the engraved sentiments of grieving loved ones until they
find an intriguing grave. If the stone is fancy and the epitaph tantalizing, Bill
announces, "Let's dig 'im up!" and the adventure begins.

The long-dead resident of Madera is adopted by Bill and his students, who vow to resurrect the person in the only way humanly possible: by researching his or her life and writing a biography for the entire town to read. Using the information from the tombstone as a starting point, the students follow the paper trail—a death certificate at the county recorder's office, an obituary from the newspaper morgue, the U.S. census reports. Then they search for wills and inventories, letters, diaries, military records, tax rolls, and land deeds, using the raw material to bring this person's story to light.

Our Town Had Amnesia

Like many good learning adventures, this one started accidentally, when Bill took his class out for some *al fresco* academics. While exploring along the banks of the Chowchilla River they came upon three old graves, all bearing the last name Minturn. Only one had an epitaph. "Her Children Shall Arise and Call Her Blessed." Bill and his kids were intrigued. Who was this Abby West Minturn?

So they began to snoop, but no one in town remembered a Minturn family. The name didn't even ring a bell at the local historical or genealogical societies. The Minturns had been erased from local memory. The way Bill saw it, "our town was suffering from a case of historical amnesia." So his class embraced the Minturn's like long-lost relatives. They became Minturn magnets, scouring the town for anything remotely connected to Abby and her children. The Minturn mystery became the central feature of their days and occupied them after school and on weekends, too.

Soon they were regulars in offices around town that rarely saw a child, much less a gaggle of twelve-year-olds intent on examining obituaries and titles to land. Slowly they began to resurrect the story of a struggling family, transplanted from New England, plagued by suicide, sudden death, and the harsh realities of frontier living. The Minturns were gone but no longer forgotten, and Bill's kids were on their way to becoming published historians.

The Stuff of Gossip

At first glance, Bill Coate may seem to be teaching in another universe. But don't despair. You can capture the essence of what he accomplishes with his students, even if you're confined to a classroom the size of a modest living room, without a single field trip, much less the freedom to roam from graveyard to newspaper archives. What Bill teaches his kids is how to make dead people talk. How to get to know someone who walked the planet years, decades, or even centuries before they were born. And you can do that, too, even if you use a textbook to carry most of your lessons along—providing you're willing to engage in a bit of gossip.

It's hard to suppress the gossip gene because we're social beings, born with an inordinate interest in each other. If you doubt this, just consider the publishing fortunes made from hawking supermarket tabloids and national weekly magazines focused solely on our species—at work, at play, in court, intoxicated. The same thing that draws crowds into theaters makes social studies irresistible—characters, conflict, drama, inspiration, and heartache. We're fascinated with ourselves. And you can leverage that obsession to drive learning in your classroom by zeroing in on the *who* in social studies—stories from yesterday or yesteryear about people— what they did and why they did it. Sometimes an intensely private tragedy, like the Minturns', will hook students on history for life. So when you're putting together a list of people your students should meet, be sure to go beyond the good ol' heroes club. Give equal time to the daredevils, dunderheads, and scoundrels. Put women, immigrants, expatriots, and children on center stage. When looking for informants, round up every flavor of humanity and make 'em talk.

Basically you want to set up a kind of dating service between your students and the people they really should meet—except that they're dead or living on another continent. So how do you make that connection? Time machines and "Beam me up, Scotty" come to mind. However, if you're fresh out of human relocation devices, your next best bet is primary sources, of the first-person variety.

Some of the most enlightening documents in history were written either by participants or bystanders. For example, most of us think of *Magellan* and *circumnavigating* in the same breath, but do you realize that Ferdinand himself never crossed the finish line? He went berserk in the Philippine Islands, insisted on mass religious conversions, and was hacked to death in the surf by a tribe who remained aggressively impervious to the charms of Christianity. How do we know? The story of Magellan's fate comes from the diary of Antonio Pigafetta, an Italian who was not a member of the crew, but an adventurous tourist who paid for his passage, and kept a diary in which he told the whole tragic story from his front row seat.

With a handful of stories like that, you become the purveyor of juicy details that rarely make it into the textbooks, and your students are hooked. Tantalize them with the fifteenth-century beauty rituals of Elizabeth I, who, as a young queen, drank carefully measured doses of poison to drain the blood from her face because pale was pretty. With gossip like that, students will be dying to get acquainted with the first woman to rule England. Hint that historians suspect there was cannibalism in Jamestown—a man salted his wife and packed her in a trunk for secret winter suppers. I'd put money down that your students will spend the day scouring their colonial documents for evidence of man-eaters. Ask your students to reflect on the bitter end of General Custer, who boasted shortly before the Battle of Little Big Horn, "Hurray, boys! We've got them. We'll finish them up and then go home to our station" (Cerf and Navasky 1984). Hours later he ordered his soldiers to shoot their horses and pile their carcasses into a bulwark in a final doomed effort to stave off defeat and death. His men died sheltering against the bodies of the beloved steeds.

First-person accounts are powerful primary sources because they speak in a direct voice. Their details create a sense of you-are-thereness that erases the tens, hundreds, or thousands of years that separate writer and reader. This very personal category of documents includes: diaries, eyewitness accounts, autobiographies, travel narratives, interviews, correspondence, journals, oral histories, and radio and television broadcasts. It includes such marvels as Edward R. Murrow's radio broadcasts during the blitz of London, the diary of Anne Frank, Pliny the Younger's account of the eruption of Vesuvius, slave narratives, and the travels of Marco Polo.

To sample the lure of first-person documents, turn to any page in *Roughing It* by Mark Twain (Clemens 1872), an hilarious but information-packed account of traveling across America in the 1860s. Twain chronicled his trip west to dig for wealth in the silver mines of Nevada. Instead, he found fame and fortune as a writer and entertainer. The following section describes sleeping in a stagecoach filled with mail as it presses west through the darkness over rough terrain.

We began to get into country, now, threaded here and there with little streams. These had high, steep banks on each side, and every time we flew down one bank and scrambled up the other, our party inside got mixed somewhat. First we would all be down in a pile at the forward end of the stage, nearly in a sitting posture, and in a second we would shoot to the other end, and stand on our heads. And we would sprawl and kick, too, and ward off ends and corners of mail-bags that came lumbering over us and about us; and as the dust rose from the tumult, we would all sneeze in chorus, and the majority of us would grumble, and probably say some hasty thing, like: "Take your elbow out of my ribs!—can't you quit crowding?". . . Still, all things considered, it was a very comfortable night. (12)

Or read this 1614 version of a what-to-eat-in-the-new-world travel article, "A True Discourse of the Present Estate of Virginia," written by Ralph Hamor to encourage potential colonists:

Now, least any man should be discouraged because as yet no mention is made of any other provision of victuals, save only of bread-corn, which will afford but a bare, and miserable living, the Land is stored with plenty and variety of wild beasts, Lions, Bears, Deer of all sorts. Beavers, Otters, Foxes, Raccoons, almost as big as a Fox, as good meat as a lamb, hares, wild Cats, muskrats, Squirells flying, and other of three or four sorts, Opossums, of the bigness and likeness of a Pig. Of each of these beasts, the Lion excepted, my self have many times eaten, and can testify that they are not only tasteful, but also wholesome and nourishing food. (Hamor 1957)

One of the most unexpected acquaintances your students can make is with children who wrote about their lives. There is a substantial body of first-person narratives written by children who were on-lookers or participants in major events in the past and present. They've documented their experiences in diaries and journals, websites and blogs that range from innocent to heartbreaking. This passage is from the 1864 Civil War diary of Carrie Berry.

Aug. 3. Wednesday.

This was my birthday. I was ten years old, But I did not have a cake times were too hard so I celebrated with ironing. I hope by my next birthday we will have peace in our land so that I can have a nice dinner.

Students are fascinated to discover that children their age rode for the Pony Express, shouldered a musket, suffered the deprivations of war, or openly defied a repressive government. It's unfortunate then that our textbooks so rarely include these poignant passages, and it may account for our students feeling that history is something that happens without them.

This chapter focuses on instructional strategies using first-person accounts and literature as tools for truly capturing the human faces and experiences that are at the heart of an engrossing social studies program. You will learn how to examine first-person documents, develop questioning strategies for different types of primary sources, use literature as an historic resource, and create original writing based on research.

What About Standards?

When you decide to incorporate first-person accounts into your social studies programs by using diaries, eyewitness accounts, autobiographies, travel narratives, interviews, correspondence, journals, biographies, and historic fiction, your students will develop and demonstrate skills that are fundamental to a rigorous standards-based approach to social studies. The following list suggests the range of learning challenges students will face as they try to view human development and dilemmas through the eyes of individuals who were there.

Students will:
- Understand that history is a record of human experiences that links the past to the present and the future.
- Develop an understanding of how events influence the lives of individuals, including children.
- Develop a sense of historic empathy with people of the past.

- Read a wide range of literature, both fiction and nonfiction from many periods in many genres to build an understanding of the many dimensions of human experience.
- Compare different stories about an historical figure.
- Learn to analyze historical fiction.
- Distinguish between historical fact and fiction by comparing documentary sources on historical figures and events with fictionalized characters and events.
- Apply a wide range of strategies to comprehend, interpret, evaluate, and appreciate texts, including prior experience, interactions with other readers and writers, their knowledge of other texts, word-identification strategies, and their understanding of textual features.
- Develop historical research capabilities, including the ability to formulate historical questions, interrogate historical documents, and obtain historical data.
- Synthesize knowledge of an historic time and place from first-person accounts to construct a story, explanation, or historical narrative.

Awareness

Assessing Prior Knowledge About First-Person Documents

The goal of these Awareness activities is to find out *what* your students know about people associated with major events, either past or present, and *how* they know about them. First, you'll simply prospect for the names of people who stuck in your students' memory because of their fame or infamy, ingenuity, or tragedy. This is a bit of an adventure in itself because you never know what will emerge. A budding social activist might mention Susan B. Anthony's fight to gain the vote for women, or Nelson Mandela's struggle against apartheid. Or Iqbal Masih and his campaign for schools in Pakistan. Wait a minute. You've never heard of Iqbal? He was a Pakistani, sold into child-bonded labor in 1987 by his father for the equivalent of twelve dollars. As a modern slave, he worked twelve-hour days, sometimes chained to a carpet loom. He was four years old.

Now you're aware—and maybe a little curious. There's more. Iqbal escaped from his owners when he was ten years old and began to speak out against child slavery. In two short years, he organized children in Pakistan and around the world to campaign for freedom and schools for all Pakistani children. For his efforts Iqbal received the Reebok Human Rights Youth in Action Award 1994. On Easter Sunday, 1995, he was murdered. He was twelve years old.

Now think. In nine short sentences, you've probably covered the ground from *Iqbal who?* to grabbing your mouse and Googling his name. Over two hundred thousand citations are waiting in cyberspace to help you explore the legacy of this amazing child, but that can only happen because now you're aware and curious. That's the challenge you face when introducing your students to the faces in your social studies program. This section has two activities to help you, beginning with open-ended questions about people in history. They can be done in pairs, small groups or as a whole class. Working collaboratively is a boon to all students because it provides modeling, scaffolding, and creates opportunities for dialogue and debate.

You Are Here: Who Do We Know in History?

So let's get started. Ask your students to name anyone, living or dead, who did something important enough that they are remembered or considered to be a famous, influential, or historic figure. The person could be a scientist, inventor, cowboy, president, architect, religious leader, sports figure, musician, artist, educator, union organizer, explorer, poet, astronaut, or civil rights activist. Take a minute to think about the names your students might generate: Madonna, Hitler, Babe Ruth, John Glenn, John Lennon, Mother Teresa, Bill Clinton, Kofi Annan, Mark Twain, Picasso, the Pope, King Tut, Walt Disney, Marie Curie, or Tom Cruise. No matter who they suggest, don't wince. If the person fits one of the previous descriptions, acknowledge the contribution and ask for more. Let's continue:

1. As students share the names, list them on the board or a chart. Be patient but exhaustive in your questioning. Give them lots of thinking time because each name they harvest will stimulate the neural networks in other students, causing more memories, associations, and names to emerge.
2. When you are finished, give each student an index card or strip of paper. Ask them to choose one person from the list and write one thing they know about that person.
3. Have students share their information with each other, then ask them as a group to figure out a way to organize all the information. They could make generic categories, such as *leaders*, or the categories could be name-specific, such as *Martin Luther King Jr. facts*. Post the clusters of information on a bulletin board or chart.
4. Review all the facts aloud so that students can appreciate how much they already know.

How Do We Know This?

Now you want your students to think about how they acquired all this information about people they've never met or who've been dead for hundreds of years.

Ask, *How do we know this?* Have students brainstorm all the ways that they came by their data. List their ideas. Then ask, *How could we learn more?* Student responses indicate their knowledge of the historic sources they can access to learn about the lives and accomplishments of individuals.

Waking Magoun's Brain

By now you should have a fairly good idea of who your students know and how they met. The next step is to stoke their curiosity about the intimate details that won these people a place in the history books, newspaper headlines, tabloids, or their brains. Somehow you want students to experience what it would be like to live side by side with people in another place or era. In an ideal classroom, you could manipulate the time-space continuum, and in the blink of an eye, you kids could be shaking hands with Napolean, Dorthea Dix, Anne Boleyn, Mother Teresa, or Chief Joseph. Then they'd hang out together and chat. Your students could shadow these luminaries, see what they ate, meet their friends, go through their closets, check out the sanitation facilities, so that ultimately they could become experts on one significant person. Since that's probably not an option without making a major contribution to the Psychic Hotline, I strongly suggest you investigate the world of time-machine literature.

Time-Machine Literature

This may seem an unlikely suggestion for a chapter on primary source documents, but time-travel books are exceptional transporters. The stories usually open with one or more inquisitive or discontented kids, living in the present, minding their own business, worried about homework or boyfriends, or making the cut on the Little League team. Then suddenly, without warning, they're thrust, scooped, sucked, or catapulted into the middle of a Civil War battle, a medieval joust, or an outing with the Knights Templar. In an instant, they're aware at a cellular level of a wholly different way of life. Awareness is accompanied by fear, confusion, a scramble for survival, and of course, intense curiosity. Magoun's brain is on red alert.

Time-travel books capture the eyewitness perspective found in first-person documents but with the added bonus that the characters, abruptly dislodged from their century and homeland, react with contemporary eyes and emotions. They're outsiders. Rubberneckers. That makes them keen observers of differences in clothing, laws, customs, vocabulary, punishments, disease, mortality rates, occupations, and eating without a fork. As they struggle to adjust, they provide a running commentary about what's intriguing, offensive, or unjust about their new existence.

These books are written to entice readers into another world—they're high interest and loaded with explicit details. Without so much as a whimper, history-hating students relinquish their resentment and begin to soak up details about politics, economics, and cultural life. They notice the effects of geography on the action and characters, witness the origin of inventions, compare levels of technology and observe the accoutrements of daily life. Granted, these characters are fictional, but the authors of time-travel adventures do vast amounts of research so the characters experiences are largely authentic, and therefore, instructional. But it's instruction embedded in narrative. So it sticks. Here's a sampling of this intriguing genre.

Some Time-Machine Titles to Read Aloud

Middle Ages and Renaissance

Max and Me and the Time Machine by Gery Greer. New York: Harper Collins, 1988.
When Steve brings home a time machine he bought for $2.50 at a garage sale, Max is suspicious. "There's no such thing as time travel. *Or* time machines." Then they both end up in the year 1250 in medieval England—Steve as Sir Robert Marshall and Max as his horse!—and Max must admit the machine works.

Happily Ever After by Anna Quindlen. New York: Viking, 1997.
When a girl who loves to read fairy tales is transported back to medieval times, she finds that the life of a princess in a castle is less fun than she imagined.

Stranger in the Mist by Paul McCusker. Colorado Springs: Chariot Victor, 1996.
Why has King Arthur returned in the 1990s? Can he help a world so different from the one he knew?

The Kid Who Got Zapped Through Time by Deborah Scott. New York: Harper-Trophy, 1988.
Twelve-year-old Flattop Kincaid touches a spot on his computer marked *wizard*, and suddenly he's in medieval England, where the peasant family who finds him thinks he's royalty because of his red satin baseball jacket. The peasants take him in and share their crowded dirty little home, full of bugs and animals. They try to teach Flattop not to offend the local lord, or they'll all be killed. Flattop is horrified by the way they live and terrified he won't find his way back to twentieth-century California. With no modern conveniences, including the computer that zapped him back, he may be stuck in this terrible era in history.

Connecticut Yankee in King Arthur's Court by Mark Twain. New York: Charles L. Webster, 1899.
A Connecticut Yankee is a fantasy about how Hank Morgan is knocked unconscious in nineteenth-century Connecticut and awakens in King Arthur's England

in the year 538. Over a span of ten years, Morgan introduces profound changes into this society.

Trolley to Yesterday by John Bellairs. New York: Dial, 1989.
Johnny Dixon and Professor Childermass discover a trolley that transports them back to Constantinople in 1453 as the Turks are invading the Byzantine Empire.

American History

Qwerty Stevens, Stuck in Time with Benjamin Franklin by Dan Gutman. 2002. New York: Simon & Schuster Books for Young Readers.
After accidentally sucking Benjamin Franklin into twenty-first-century New Jersey with his Anytime Anywhere machine, thirteen-year-old Qwerty Stevens and his best friend almost wind up stuck in Philadelphia on July 4, 1776, when they try to send him back.

The Humpbacked Fluteplayer by Sharman Russell. 1994. New York: A. A. Knopf.
While on a school field trip, May and Evan find themselves transported back in time and made slaves by one of the warring Indian tribes who lived in the Arizona desert long ago.

Vision Quest by Pamela Service. 1989. New York: Atheneum.
Kate finds life dreary in her small Nevada desert town until contact with an Indian artifact sends her visions of a restless shaman from the past, visions which eventually drag her and her friend Jimmy Fong into that far distant Nevada.

Civil War

A Boy Called Girl by Belinda Hurmence. 1982. New York: Clarion Books.
A pampered young black girl who has been mysteriously transported back to the days of slavery, struggles to escape her bondage.

The Root Cellar by Janet Lunn. 1983. New York: Atheneum.

Window in Time by Karen Weinberg. 1991. Shippensburg, PA: White Mane.
While exploring the basement of his new house in Westminster, Maryland, Ben puts on an old jacket and boots that he finds and is suddenly transported back to the time of the Civil War.

19th Century

Three Rivers Crossing by Robert Lytle. 2000. Spring Lake, MI: River Road.
After a fishing accident, seventh grader Walker Morrison finds himself transported back in time to the nineteenth century of his village of Stony Creek. There, he becomes friends with the Taylor children, his ancestors, for whom he risks his life.

The Edison Mystery by Dan Gutman. 2001. New York: Simon & Schuster Books for Young Readers.
Thirteen-year-old Robert "Qwerty" Stevens uses the time machine he finds in his backyard to visit Thomas Edison's workshop in 1879, and there helps develop the electric lightbulb, but then needs his sister's help to return to his own time.

Time Out by Helen Cresswell. 1990. New York: Atheneum.
Twelve-year-old Tweeny and her parents, servants in a London house in 1887, use a book of magic spells to travel forward in time one hundred years and find the England of 1987 to be an astonishing place.

The Switching Well by Peni Griffin. 1993. New York: Margaret McElderry.
A twist of magic sends Ada Bauer, a native of San Antonio, Texas, 100 years into the future, from the late nineteenth century to the present. Simultaneously, Amber Burak, a teenager in contemporary San Antonio, travels 100 years back, to Ada's time. Struggling to return home, each is almost lost in the social service network of the other's era. Griffin's story is especially fascinating in its exploration of changing mores and folkways.

The Orphan of Ellis Island by Elvira Woodruff. 1997. New York: Scholastic.
During a school trip to Ellis Island, Dominick Avaro, a ten-year-old foster child, travels back in time to 1908 Italy and accompanies two young emigrants to America.

Thinking and Writing About Time Travel

The characters in time-machine books are frequently discontented with their lives before their adventures begin. Once transplanted, they face hardships and peril that lead them to conclude, like Dorothy, that "there's no place like home." The following activity encourages kids to ponder the lure of time travel. Ask your students to make two lists:

- Things I like about my life now.
- Things I dislike about my life now.

Then ask them to imagine that they were transported with the main character in the book you read. How would life be better? How would it be worse? Ask students to write a response to this question: *If you had a fully operational, fail-safe time machine, where would you go and why?*

Great time-machine books are so fanciful and engrossing that eager listeners can barely suppress the urge to shout, "I want to go there!" That surge of enthusiasm launches them into the Exploration phase of learning.

⊕ Exploration

Discovering More About First-Person Documents

Once you succeed in stimulating your students' curiosity about how people lived in other times and places, it would be excellent to give them some hands-on time with first-person primary sources. The goal in this Exploration section is to acquaint your students with a variety of documents and the people who took the time to record some aspect of their lives.

Firsthand accounts of any period in history are so plentiful that the hardest part will be choosing. Like other primary source documents, they're widely available on the Internet. Simply Google using keywords such as *diary, journal, letters, historic,* and you'll have hundreds of choices. Digital History (www.digitalhistory .uh.edu/) is a huge website with a major section that includes journals and diaries. For one-stop convenience, you can go to Repository of Primary Sources (www .uidaho.edu/special-collections/Other.Repositories.html) for a listing of more than five thousand websites describing holdings of manuscripts, archives, rare books, historical photographs, and other primary sources for the research scholar. There may also be some useful excerpts in your textbook.

While you yourself may spend hours looking at primary sources on line, the most practical approach for your classroom may be to print out copies of interesting documents that your kids can examine, compare and contrast, even annotate as part of their exploration. Try to find selections that will appeal to different student interests—diaries from children caught up in wars, journals from botanists combing American's unspoiled forests for plant samples, letters from prison, travel journals from the Westward movement, letters from the Court of Spain, speeches by presidents, union leaders and student activists. Then guide your students through their interrogations so that they learn to extract every morsel of information using curiosity and critical thinking skills.

First-Person Primary Source Documents: A Sampler

Here's a list of first-person documents you can locate simply by clicking your mouse.

Diaries: Diaries are day-to-day records of events. They're frequently terse and practical, containing little more than lists of expenditures, miles traveled, chores completed, weather conditions, animal sightings, and meals. For example, this 1847 wagon-train diary of James Coon contains many entries like this: *Thu Apr 22nd, 6 miles to Clinton. Cold rane. Fri Apr 23rd. 6 miles to Parris. Pleasant.* Diaries may also function as a listener for the writer who pours out intimate, stream-of-consciousness conversations that may never be read by another living soul. Some writers think of their diaries as a special friend—Anne Frank called her diary Kitty.

Journals: A journal is usually written less regularly than a diary to record events that strike the writer as significant or interesting. They have a certain quality of storytelling in them that is often missing in diaries, but lack the big-picture hindsight of memoirs or autobiographies. Journals have a direct, in-the-moment perspective. Blogs are the electronic version of paper journals with the advantage of being instantly published.

Travel Journals: For thousands of years, curiosity seekers, outcasts, merchants, and pilgrims have been leaving home and returning with colorful stories for envious homebodies. The most serious brand of traveler—explorers—brought back artifacts, maps and navigational information, diseases, and treasure. Many of these footsore wanderers took notes in diaries or journals that were subsequently shared or published. As a result we can read about Ewart Grogan, the first person to walk the length of Africa from the Cape to Cairo in 1898. You can read the reverse journey, from Cairo to Cape Town, written by Paul Theroux in 2003. Like all travel journals, they give details about the climate, geography, local inhabitants, flora and fauna, cities, and cultures.

Letters: Human beings have been sending each other letters for a long time—in China, the same service has been delivering mail continuously for over two thousand years. And while the invention of the telephone threatened to relegate letter writing to a dying art, emails and blogs seem to have revived the urge to correspond in writing. Letters are unique in that they have an interpersonal intention not found in diaries or journals. Many famous letters chronicle turning points in history, and thousands are available on the Internet, including Martin Luther King Jr.'s famous Letter from a Birmingham Jail.

Interviews: Recorded interviews are an excellent way to bring living history into your classroom, as they allow students to hear the actual voice of the person. They're a livelier form of primary source document that provide tone of voice, accents, and emotions, not just words printed on paper. Many interviews are now available on the Web. For sound bites from the civil rights movement, visit *Voices of the Civil Rights Era* (www.voicesofcivilrights.org).

Autobiography and Memoir: The word *autobiography* means self-life-writing. This type of writing differs from a journal or diary because the writer has been through his or her life, or a good portion of it, and is looking back over the whole. It's the story of a life, told from the inside out. *The Autobiography of Benjamin Franklin* is a classic piece of Americana originally written for Franklin's son William. The work portrays life in Philadelphia, as well as shrewd observations on the literature, philosophy, and religion of the time.

Oral Histories: Oral histories are the oldest method of capturing the history of a group, originating when tribes designated people to pass their stories down from one generation to the next. This is also one of the most modern techniques, adopted in the 1940s with the advent of tape recorders. Oral history is not folklore, gossip, hearsay, or rumor. It is a systematic collection of living people's testimony about their experiences as participants in past events and ways of life. There is an excellent collection of slave narratives recorded after the Civil War that captures daily life before emancipation. See *American Slave Narratives: An Online Anthology* @ http://xroads.virginia.edu/~HYPER/wpa/wpahome.html.

Wills: Wills may be the last documents people create before passing on, yet the writing is typically impersonal, more like a shopping list than a good-bye. But wills can provide students with valuable information about material culture, class, family size, personal relationships, and what people valued enough to bequeath to the next generation.

Speeches: Reading speeches can give your students a front row seat at some of the pivotal moments in the life of a leader—be it a queen, union organizer, or tribal chief. Speeches tend to synthesize in a very compact and compelling way something that's very importance to the speaker, whether it is a call to arms, the redirection of a nation, or an anguished farewell, as in the last speech of Chief Joseph of the Nez Perce, when he declared: "Hear me, my Chiefs. I am tired; my heart is sick and sad. From where the sun now stands I will fight no more forever" (Beal 1963).

First-Person Documents as Informants

Once you have gathered an intriguing selection of first-person documents, you'll need to give your students plenty of getting-to-know-you time. If the document is antique or from another culture, their first encounter can be akin to listening to someone speaking a foreign language that you have studied but never road-tested, so they may need to do a bit of deciphering before they can concentrate on the content. The following activities provide examples of strategies that allow students to practice decoding first person documents.

Letters as Informants

Letters are a unique form of personal narrative because they represent one side of a written conversation. Readers glean details about daily life and the current situation of the writer, but they also gain insights about the person to whom the letter is addressed. The tone of the letter, the questions, and the requests hint at the relationship between the correspondents and the condition of the world in which they live. You may have students in your class who've never written an authentic letter to a real correspondent, so it will be interesting for them to read the following letter to the then First Lady Eleanor Roosevelt, in 1936, from a child who describes the reality of her life during the Depression.

Nov. 6, 1936

Dear Mrs. Roosevelt

I am writing to you for some of your old soiled dresses if you have any. As I am a poor girl who has to stay out of school. On account of dresses & slips and a coat. I am in the seventh grade but I have to stay out of school because I have no books or clothes to ware. I am in need of dresses & slips and a coat very bad. If you have any soiled clothes that you don't want to ware I would be very glad to get them. But please do not let the news paper reporters get hold of this in any way and I will keep it from geting out here so there will be no one else to get hold of it. But do not let my name get out in the paper. I am thirteen years old.

Yours Truly,
Miss L. H.
Gravette, Ark.
R #3
c/o A. H.

Read the letter and ask:

- What does this letter tell you about living in Arkansas in 1936?
- What does it tell you about this child's life?
- Why was the child concerned about her name being revealed?
- How do you think this child felt about the First Lady?
- How do you think Mrs. Roosevelt felt when she got a letter like this?
- What were economic conditions like in the United States during the 1930s?
- If you lived during the Depression, how would your life have been different from the way you live now?

Activity

Your students may not need clothes to wear to school, but they probably have some concerns that they could share with the current First Lady—about the environment, war, peace, their neighborhood, family, unemployment, or education. If they decide to send letters to the First Lady, they'll probably receive a reply from her staff. It's quite exciting for kids to open an envelope with a return address from the White House. Send their letters to the First Lady at 1600 Pennsylvania Avenue, Washington, DC.

Diaries as Informants

Some diaries are written in a staccato style, almost like shorthand, but they're packed with details of events and daily life. So, while they reveal little about the writer, there is much to learn about the context in which they were written. The following passage describes the reality of trekking across the United States to pursue a dream of wealth in California's gold fields.

Tuesday April 30, 1850
Started the morning about $\frac{1}{2}$ past 5a.m. Captain's thigh is better. Went about 10 miles and camped on account of high winds. At 9a.m. saw a dead horse. Very cold. Very large prairies. Don't like the country. Come to a log house where there is 3 men. They have 2 barrels of liquor to accommodate the emigrants. Killed a rattlesnake near one of our tents. Passed a dead horse. 12 p.m. Struct tent. Went 13 miles. Land rolling prairie. Pitched tent at 5p.m. Saw elk horns along the road and some deer. Wind high.

The Gold Rush Diary of George Bonniwell

War Diaries of Two Children

Many people write diaries when confined to a small space, sometimes by circumstances beyond their control. Their diaries are the place where they can safely reveal their thoughts and emotions about their plight. The following excerpts were written by children caught in two different conflicts, fifty years and a continent apart. Yet they have many similarities. These entries remind your students that children are eyewitnesses and often victims of historic conflicts and calamities, in this case the war in Bosnia-Herzegovina and the internment of Japanese Americans during World War II.

The War in Bosnia and Herzegovina 1992–1995

That's my life! The life of an innocent eleven-year-old schoolgirl!! A schoolgirl without a school, without the fun and excitement of school. A child without games, without friends, without the sun, without the birds, without nature, without fruit, without chocolate or sweets, with just a little powdered milk. In short, a child without a childhood. A wartime child.

—*Zlata Filipovic, Sarajevo, Bosnia (1994)*

Japanese Internment Camp

We now have oil stoves in our homes and school. But it does little good because you have to be near the stove in order to receive any heat. By keeping all the windows closed the room may become warm, but we were warned against it. Several people have been sent to the hospital because they did not leave any windows open—they inhaled the fume which comes out of the stove. In school the stove is in one corner and I am in the opposite corner so the warmth does not come near me. It certainly took a long time to get the stoves because of too much red tape involved. We still have no books to study out of. We are taught the progressive way. It is like a lecture form. The teacher talks and we take notes. When test time comes we have to study our notes. I hope by next semester we will be able to study from books.

—*Louise Ogawa, from Poston, Colorado, Internment Camp, January 6, 1942*

Read these passages and ask:

* What is similar about the experiences of these two children?
* What is different?
* What did these children miss in their lives? Why?
* How do you think they feel about their situations?
* What would you ask these children if you could meet them?
* What do you wonder about children involved in wars?
* Have you read about any other children caught in wars?
* How could you find out more?

Activity

Through the Library of Congress, you can view "Suffering Under a Great Injustice: Ansel Adams' Photographs of Japanese-American Internment at Manzanar" (http://memory.loc.gov/ammem/collections/anseladams/). This collection features 209 photographs taken by Adams in 1943. They portray the Japanese Americans who were relocated from their homes during World War II and interned in the Manzanar War Relocation Center in California.

Wills as Informants

Students rarely get a chance to see contemporary wills and adults may be reluctant to discuss them, but there are many historic wills on the Internet, including those of Adolph Hitler and Elvis Presley. The following excerpt is from Will's will. Shakespeare had money and some interesting items that he bequeathed to his family members and the poor.

In the name of god Amen I William Shackspeare, of Stratford upon Avon in the countrie of Warr., gent., in perfect health and memorie, God be praysed, doe make and ordayne this my last will and testament in manner and forme followeing, **Item**, I gyve and bequeath unto the poore of Stratford aforesaied tenn poundes **Item**, I gyve and bequeath unto my saied sister Jone xx.li. and all my wearing apparrell, to be paied and delivered within one yeare after my deceas; and I doe will and devise unto her *the house* with thappurtenaunces in Stratford, wherein she dwelleth, for her naturall lief, under the yearlie rent of xij.d. **Item**, *I gyve unto my wief my second best bed with the furniture*, **Item**, I gyve and bequeath to my saied daughter Judith my broad silver gilt bole. All the rest of my goodes, chattel, leases, plate, jewels, and household stuffe whatsoever, after my dettes and legasies paied, and my funerall expenses dischardged, I give, devise, and bequeath to my sonne in lawe, John Hall gent., and my daughter Susanna, his wief, whom I ordaine and make executours of this my last will and testament.

Read the will and ask:

- What did you learn about William Shakespeare from this document?
- What did you learn about his family?
- Why do you think he said he was in perfect health and memory?
- What did you learn about the kinds of things that people valued in 1616, when this will was written?
- Was there anything that seemed unusual to you about the will?
- How do you think wills are different now?
- What else did you notice that is different from documents written today?

Interviews as Informants

Recorded interviews are like having a guest speaker without all the time-consuming arrangements. Plus, the recorded voice can be replayed over and over until students extract every bit of useable information. Many interviews are now available on the Internet, including conversations with presidents, war veterans, musicians, artists, protesters, inventors, and everyday people talking about life in their hometowns. For sound bites from the civil rights movement, visit *Voices of the Civil Rights Era* at www.voicesofcivilrights.org. After listening to an interview, ask:

- What did you learn about this person?
- What did you learn about his or her family?
- What did you learn about his or her job?
- What were some important or tragic events in his or her life?
- Was there anything unusual about the way this person lived or died?

Activity

If you were a journalist chosen to interview this person, what questions would you ask? Stage a mock interview in which students take turns being interviewed, using information gleaned from historic documents to answer the questions.

Autobiographies as Informants

Autobiographies can play a key role in your social studies program, either as class sets, independent reading for individuals, or as read-aloud books that you share with your students. Consider books that have been produced as books-on-tape to bring in another voice, particularly if the book is read by the author. An excellent example of this genre is *Stride Toward Freedom* (1958), written by Martin Luther King Jr. It is his story of the Montgomery bus boycott, 381 days of peaceful resistance that became the turning point in the civil rights movement.

Read the autobiography and ask:

- What did you learn about civil rights laws from this autobiography?
- What did you learn about how people can challenge injustice?
- What would you have done if you were in Martin Luther King Jr.'s position?
- What would you have done if you were living in Montgomery at the time of the boycott?
- What skills did Martin Luther King Jr. have that helped him succeed?
- Who helped Martin Luther King Jr. succeed?
- If Martin Luther King Jr. was living today, what do you think he would be doing?
- How could we be more like Martin Luther King Jr.?

Keeping Track of Who's Who

When I was studying the Renaissance with my students, we kept bumping into new names—friends of Michelangelo, another Medici, an obscure mathematician. So I designated one bulletin board as *Who's Who in the Renaissance*. Whenever we came across a new name, we'd add it to the list, along with pictures, etchings, letters, paintings, and documents. This device creates something like a class picture or yearbook of the era you're studying.

Once you cue your students to hunt for people who have valuable things to say about your social studies theme, you can use a similar idea to keep track. Let your students know that as they identify the names and faces of the important players, or locate diaries, journals, or letters that provide information, they need to add their research to the *Who's Who* board. They can post pictures, photographs, or downloads from the Internet. Challenge them to decide how to organize the material, perhaps using categories such as writers, leaders, explorers, rulers, artists, thinkers, and rogues.

Writing Prompts

First-person narratives are excellent starting points for writing prompts because of the human-to-human connection. Students can relate to people who are lonely, frustrated, trying to solve a problem, or celebrating a triumph. Even a few sentences lifted from a longer document can stimulate rich, thoughtful writing about social studies. When you're constructing writing prompts to help your students think about social studies, it's important to use verbs that explicitly convey the purpose of the writing task. The following prompts can be modified to elicit students' thoughts and assess their comprehension of first person documents.

- *Explain* how wagon trains crossed the mountains, using information from this travel journal.
- *Tell* about the last days of Chief Joseph and the Nez Perce tribe.
- *Defend* Harriet Tubman against the charge that she was breaking the law when she helped slaves escape to freedom.
- Write a statement to *persuade* a judge that Rosa Parks should not be arrested for sitting in the front of the bus.
- Use the information from this diary to *describe* the dangers pioneers faced when crossing the plains.
- *Summarize* the most important ideas Hammurabi included in his laws.
- *Define slavery* and give examples of how and where it is practiced in the twenty-first century.
- *Express* your feelings about the plight of children in internment camps based on their diaries and letters.
- *Evaluate* the success of the bus boycott lead by civil rights leader Martin Luther King Jr. based on his autobiography, *Stride Toward Freedom*.
- *Analyze* the skills needed to organize the bus boycott in Montgomery.

Show Me: Checking Comprehension

When you're reading first-person documents, it's vitally important to incorporate comprehension checks to make sure your kids are pulling the critical information from these sources. The standard approach is to ask questions, such as *What was it like to be a soldier with George Washington during their winter at Valley Forge?* The problem with this approach is that it's slow—only one reply at a time. The other students are in suspended animation—unraveling a sweater cuff or prospecting for lint to pass the time.

Show Me is an alternative approach to checking comprehension that lets your kids move, gesture, and make faces to show what they understand about a text or story. You tap directly into kinesthetic and spatial intelligence, and all your students can respond at once. That includes your second language learners, who can demonstrate their receptive language levels without ever saying a word. It's simple. Just say something like, "Show me what the soldiers were doing during their winter at Valley Forge." Appropriate responses would be huddling together, shivering, building fires, cupping their hands around a warm drink, lying on the ground moaning and dying. Kids move, mime, gesture and mug—all dramatic skills—with the single purpose of showing what they know. It's so much fun that they return to the text with increased focus, waiting for the next round of Show Me. Repeat these pauses at irregular intervals during the reading. Here are some other examples of prompts:

* Show me how the main character felt when . . .
* Show me what the boy did when he saw Queen Elizabeth for the first time.
* Show me what happened to Marco Polo during the wind storm in the desert.
* Show me the shape of the Coliseum.
* Show me how you think the judge looked during Ethel Rosenberg's testimony. What about the jury?

> Reading history is good for all of us. If you know history, you know that there is no such thing as a self-made man or self-made woman. We are shaped by people we have never met.
> —David McCullough

This brand of drama is spontaneous and takes a matter of seconds. All of your students can be active and creative, but they're focused on your learning goals, not on performance for its own sake. At the end of the lesson, you can work together to develop a list of verbs that describe their actions, and post it as part of your word bank.

Inquiry

Digging Deeper into First-Person Documents

While studying the Renaissance with my students, I decided it was the perfect time to take a biographical approach to social studies, since that period is loaded with high profile, heavily documented superstars. First, we concentrated on the setting—architecture, city life, clothing, diet. We tried to imagine the atmosphere of the times—the foment of new ideas, the urge to explore, and the scramble for power. Finally, it was time for them to fan out into the crowd and get to know one Renaissance figure. In effect, to go from a casual handshake to a serious conversation.

Any time you're studying an issue or an era full of personalities, your students have a chance to get to know one person in depth. Certain periods spring to mind as likely candidates—the Revolutionary period and the civil rights movement both have a rich trove of dynamic characters. There are also many outstanding leaders your students should meet among contemporary Native Americans and social justice activists. Your students can wring a huge amount of crisp, detailed information out of first-person narratives simply by asking thoughtful questions. Think of this process as a blind date with a document.

How to Make First-Person Documents Talk: Blind Dating

We all know that the goal of a blind date is not to have fun. It's all about information. In a few short hours, maybe a cocktail or two, you need to size up the person you've just met to decide if there's a relationship in your future or it's back to solitary meals in front of the television. In this section, you're going to teach your students to take a primary source document on a blind date.

First, they'll just give the document a close look. This is usually the stark terror moment of an actual blind date, but first-person documents rarely generate that level of anxiety. The getting-to-know-you phase follows as they consider, *What am I seeing? Hearing? What's being said? What does it mean? What are the interests and issues motivating this person? What else is going on that may be an influence?* And finally, *what do I think about this person? Do I want to know more? How would I find out?* Or in the case of a spectacularly bad blind date, *how soon can I feign a migraine or induce projectile vomiting so I can get the hell out of here?*

Extracting all that information on a real blind date can be as easy as lending an ear if the object of your curiosity is nervous or narcissistic, babbling on without drawing a breath. But you can't count on that level of conversation from a shy person, and certainly not one who's dead. So as good blind-daters, your students need to be armed with an abundant supply of penetrating questions. Here's a four-step questioning process to make first-person documents talk.

What Is It?
* What type of document is this? Letter, diary, journal?
* When and where was it written? What are the clues?
* Is it handwritten or machine printed? What does that suggest?
* What do you notice about the typeface or design?
* Can you identify the author?
* What do you know or can you guess about the author? Age, profession, interests, education?
* What type of person do you think the writer is? What words tell that?
* Do you think the author is writing for himself or herself or to others?
* Can you identify the audience?
* How could you find out more?

What Does It Say?
* Who or what is the story or information about?
* What do the words say?
* What do they mean?
* What's unusual about the language?

- List any important facts you learned from the document.
- Does the author have first- or secondhand knowledge about what he or she has written?

What's the Point?
- Why was this document written?
- Was it written for a public audience or a specific group?
- Is it personal or for a few people?
- How do you know who it is for?
- What does the author hope to do with this document? (Inform? Argue? Persuade?)
- What phrases or words indicate the author's intent?
- What biases might the writer have?
- Why might the writer have that bias?
- What ideas, words, or phrases suggest bias?

What Else Do I Want to Know?
- What do I wonder about this document?
- What else do I want to know about the author?
- What guesses (inferences) can I make from this about the author?
- What other primary or secondary sources might help answer my questions?
- How can I find information on the internet?
- Who still knows about this event?
- Who else could give me more information?

Meet Annie Burton: A Conversation with an Autobiography

The first time you model this blind-date inquiry process, it's a good idea to start with something short, captivating, and easily accessible to all students. I've chosen a very brief but moving paragraph from an autobiography, *Memories of Childhood's Slavery Days* (1909) by Annie L. Burton. The entire book can be read on the Internet, but with four sentences, you can introduce your students to Annie as a child, and stimulate their imagine about what it was like to live under the institution of slavery. But first, a bit of background.

Annie Burton was born into slavery in 1858 on a plantation outside of Clayton, Alabama, and raised by her mistress after her mother ran away. She grew up during the Civil War and remembers fondly her early days on the plantation. After Emancipation, Burton's mother returned for her children. Annie was hired as a nanny by Mrs. E. M. Williams, who taught her how to read and write. After her mother died, Annie took responsibility for her three younger siblings and moved to Boston. In 1888, she married, and together she and her husband ran a boarding house. She began taking evening classes at the Franklin Evening School, and the headmaster, Frank Guild, suggested that each of the students write their life story. Burton embraced his idea and produced her autobiography.

The following excerpt is taken from Section One, called "Recollections of a Happy Life," in which she describes life on the plantation:

> We children had no supper, and only a little piece of bread or something of the kind in the morning. Our dishes consisted of one wooden bowl, and oyster shells were our spoons. This bowl served about fifteen children, and often the dogs and the ducks and the peafowl had a dip in it. Sometimes we had buttermilk and bread in our bowl, sometimes greens or bones.

In preparation for this activity, you may want to download a picture of Annie Burton from the Internet as well as some images of plantation life. Give your students copies of the paragraph from *Memories of Childhood's Slavery Days* and have them read and discuss it in pairs or small groups. Then let the questions begin.

What Is It?
* What type of document is this?
* What can you guess about the author?
* What type of person do you think the writer is? What words tell that?
* Do you think the author is writing for herself or to others?
* Can you identify the audience?
* How could you find out more?

What Does It Say?
* Who or what is the story or information about?
* What do the words tell about this childhood in the south?
* Why do you think this section of the book is called "Recollections of a Happy Life"?
* How does it sound to you? Why might she think it was happy?
* List any important facts you learned from the document.
* Does the author have first- or secondhand knowledge that she has written?

What's the Point?
* What do you think the author hoped to do with this autobiography (Inform? Argue? Persuade?)?
* What do you think the effect was when people from the North read this?
* Why do you think it was important that Annie Burton wrote her autobiography?

What Else Do I Want to Know?

- What do I wonder about this document?
- What else do I want to know about Annie Burton?
- What guesses (inferences) can I make from this about the author?
- How can I find information on the Internet?
- Who else could give me more information?

On Their Own

You'll need to model this inquiry process numerous times with a variety of documents until students have acquired an appetite for inquiry. Gradually, they'll gain the skills and confidence to tackle documents on their own. Each time you lead students through this comprehensive thinking activity, you're reinforcing strategies they can use across the curriculum—in literature, economics, ethics, for substantive essays and standardized tests. Paramount among these are the abilities to extract information and interpret its meaning, draw conclusions or inferences from evidence, and compile, organize, and evaluate information.

One way to encourage investigative independence in your students is to introduce the element of choice into your curriculum. As you teach your way through any era, you teach and discuss general information with the whole class, but let your students choose one personality from the period that they want to investigate on their own. For example, if you're studying the Renaissance, your students may be interested in the writings of Laura Cereta, a fifteenth-century feminist. There is a summary of her letters on the Internet, in which she writes about the life and roles of women in her time and culture (www.pinn.net/~sunshine/book-sum/cereta.html). Other persons of interest include: the architects Brunelleschi and Inigo Jones; the artists Sofonisban Anguisola, Lavinia Fontana, Artemesia Gentileschi, Botticelli, Ghirlandiao, da Vinci; the writers Dante, Petrarch, Francis Bacon; the leaders Isabella d'Este, Elizabeth I, Lorenzo de Medici and William the Silent; the scientists Copernicus, Galileo, Paracelsus, and Pedro Nunes.

They'll need to scour text documents for information, but they can also extract valuable information from images, objects, and biographies. And remember, this isn't about becoming a Thomas Tallis expert, just for the sake of being an expert. Esoteric knowledge is interesting, but it's not the goal. The point is to hone in on a research target, gather relevant information, and synthesize it so they can bring that person to life for a listener. Then they've mastered what it takes to learn anything they want, from motorcycle repair to gourmet cooking—and that's the goal. Eventually you'll set aside time for them to present their expert findings to the class, and everyone gets smarter.

Guiding Questions for Biographical Research

Students can use the following questions to guide their research and shape their presentations:

- What attracted you to this person?
- Name three of this person's major accomplishments.
- What advantages and disadvantages did your person have over other people who lived at the time?
- What point of view, attitudes, and values does your person have? Be able to explain them.
- What's one quotable quote from (or about) this person that will help your classmates know him or her better?
- What do you admire most about this person?
- What mistakes did this person make? What was the result?
- What were the strengths and weaknesses of this person?
- Do you think this person would have been a success if he or she lived in the twenty-first century?

Annotated Visual Biography Time Line

Students with strong visual skills may want to create a time line of the person they've researched, using sketches, collage, drawings, or images from the Internet. They should include personal accomplishments and important events taking place in the surrounding world that influenced their subject. They can annotate the time line with keywords and phrases to capture the important information about their person.

Annotated Life Story Map

Students interested in the visual arts and narrative can show the main events and locations in their person's life using a map format. Drawings, collage images, text, dates, and geographical details indicate the highlights. Students annotate the map with keywords and phrases to capture the important information about their subject.

Using Biographies to Inquire About Social Studies

In addition to first-person primary documents, reading biographies either as a class text or a read-aloud selection, builds content knowledge while exposing students to the art of good storytelling. Biographies are often superior to primary source documents because they provide in-depth information about many aspects of a person's life not found in primary sources. Most biographers go well beyond simply retelling the high points of a life, letting readers eavesdrop on thoughts and conversations that reveal a character's motives, fears, disappointments, and triumphs. Although most biographies are about famous people, living or dead, the life of an ordinary person can also provide essential information about a specific time and place. Biographies let readers see:

- The human side of history. The setting and characters provide a context for understanding important events.
- How real people handle challenges and how their actions influence other people and history.
- That characters demonstrate virtues such as courage, persistence, honesty, and respect for human rights, providing role models for readers.
- Effective strategies for handling peer pressure and opposition by reading about situations that the character handled successfully.
- How people use their beliefs as a foundation to improve their world.

The following are the three approaches that authors take to telling a person's life story, and each delivers important factual information embedded in prose pictures that increase comprehension and retention.

1. *Authentic biographies* are the purest form of history stories. The author documents all the facts using eyewitness accounts, written documents, letters, diaries, and more recently, audio and videotape recordings.
2. *Fictionalized biographies* are also based on careful research, but the author turns primary source documents into drama by imagining conversations that the main character might have had related to the action.
3. *Biographical fiction* is a variation where the author begins with the known accomplishments of the subject of the biography, then works more in the style of a novelist to fill in the blanks of the story using invented dialogue and fictional secondary characters. These books tell what the characters might have been doing when they weren't performing memorable feats.

There are countless biographies that can take your students to any period in history without a passport. Just ask a good children's librarian and soon your arms will be stuffed with great titles. But here's one book you simply mustn't miss—We Were There, Too: Young People in U.S. History by Phillip Hoose (2001). This unique book describes the roles that young people played in history, from stories about the boys who sailed with Columbus to today's young activists. Based largely on primary sources—first-person accounts, journals, and interviews—it contains more than seventy young people from diverse cultures. Your students will be entertained and enlightened, but mainly they'll be thrilled to discover true-life tales about kids that never appear in the history books. The author, Phil Hoose, is a warm and gentle man who truly loves kids and history. The book is crammed with anecdotes, and it is written in a style that will have your students fighting over who gets it next. Invest in several copies and tell parents that it makes a dandy gift.

If you have second-language learners, capitalize on their visual intelligence by choosing picture books that convey important content through illustrations and simple condensed text. Preview the content by showing the pictures, summarizing action, and identifying the major characters. After reading, have students draw pictures, make lists of relevant words, or retell a part of the story that they like.

Dialogues During and After Reading Biographies

The following questions can be used as the starting point for class discussions or as journal prompts.

- In what ways was this person's life different from most other people?
- What adjectives would you use to describe this person?
- If you lived at the same time as this person, do you think you would have been friends?
- What characteristic did this person have that helped him or her survive and overcome obstacles?
- Do you agree with most of this person's decisions? What would you have done differently?
- What lessons did you learn from this person's life?
- List the skills this person had that helped him or her succeed. Put a check in front of any skills that you possess. Now make a second list of additional skills that you have.

Action

Using Knowledge About First-Person Documents

If students collect lots and lots of data, but are never challenged to use it by processing what they've learned into a product, their knowledge is vestigial, like your appendix. It's there, but it serves no purpose. The activities in this section encourage students to use the skills and knowledge they gained while exploring first-person documents to actually work as historians—to contribute original material to the historic record, and to teach other students about people who've made a difference.

The Madera Method: Learning Through Research

Let's get back to Abby Minturn, Bill Coate, and his fifth-grade history buffs from the beginning of the chapter. They spent a good six months tracing Abby Minturn and her children through primary source documents. Then their challenge was to turn a pile of raw data into a story that would awaken the same curiosity and awe they felt standing on the banks of a river, staring at three tiny graves.

How did they do it? When they had located every available document related to their person, they tackled the task of making sense of what they'd unearthed. Each primary source was analyzed and the information was used to construct the chronology of the Minturn's life, including genealogical information from New York and Rhode Island, their home before the ill-fated trip to California. Then the students filled in the story around them by researching what was going on politically, socially, and economically during their lives, including national and local events that should be part of the story. When they felt that they had a firm grip on the facts, it was time to write.

They experimented with various approaches to writing the Minturn story, tested and rejected the traditional third-person narrative, and finally settled on first-person voice. They adopted an approach that has become their trademark and claim to fame. They decided to write an historic biography in the form of a fictional diary. Each student took a year in the life of Abby Minturn and assumed her identity. Then they wrote a diary that could have been Abby's, filled with the solid facts of their research.

With every new project, Bill urged his students to show everything they know in diaries, so crammed with details about the person and the times that you can fairly hear the sound of wagon wheels and church bells. The following is a passage from a subsequent book they titled, *The Captain*, where the Captain, who began as a gold miner and graduated to tavern keeper, says:

> I stared at my reflection in the stream, depressed to the depths of my feelings. Each day I notice Chinamen downstream. The Chinamen are easy to tell from the other miners. They wear large, oversized day shirts with baggy pants, a coolie hat made of straw and a long black jacket. I don't wish the Chinamen ill; it's just that I feel they are taking all the gold I should be getting.

In the process of writing their historical diaries, these students strengthen their skills in grammar, history, anthropology, economics, research, critical thinking, and cultural awareness. When the writing was complete, their book was published and presented to the community at a Young Authors' Reception.

This annual adventure in historic research and writing was dubbed *The Madera Method: Learning Through Research*. The goal of the Madera Method is to teach students reading, writing, and history through authentic historical research projects, then publish their original biographical works. Bill's students begin as curiosity seekers, and end the year as accomplished historians.

Bill Coate has created a portal through which the citizens of Madera can experience the rich and lively history of the town. Each year his students capture a piece of the ebb and flow of small human dramas, one pioneer at a time. Irving Stone expressed the importance of their quiet enterprise in the preface he wrote for their books. It reads,

> This is the greatest adventure of mankind: to find something that was never known before or understood. Each new piece of knowledge does not need to have a specific or functional use, at least not at the moment. It is sufficient triumph that we have learned something and proved it by documentation, that had been formerly part of the darkness.

Here are some other ideas for using knowledge gained from studying first-person documents.

Renaissance Dinner Party

It became a tradition in my class to culminate and assess major social studies units with a Learning Fair—like a bazaar or exhibition of student projects. After my students had successfully staged a Santa Monica History Fair, Colonial America Fair, and Mesopotamian Fair, I started looking for a different way to culminate our Renaissance unit. We'd taken a biographical, who's-who-in-the-fifteenth-century approach to this period in history. In addition to our whole-group social studies and literature lessons, each student became an expert on one of the Renaissance superstars. So I began to wonder what it would have been like to have a dinner party for the Renaissance A-list. With all those giants in the same room, the conversation should have been dazzling. So we found the menu from one of Leonardo da Vinci's parties—pasta, bread, and grapes. Then we transformed our classroom into a fifteenth-century dining hall with murals, ivy, velvet drapery, and candles. On the day of the event, students showed up dressed as Queen Elizabeth, Galileo, Leonardo da Vinci, his two apprentices, Michelangelo, Genevra de Benci, Lorenzo de Medici, Brunelleschi, Joan of Arc, Pope Julius II, Martin Luther, and many more of their contemporaries. But more important than their costumes was the fact that they were prepared to converse, debate, even quarrel *in character* to convey all they'd learned about the Renaissance. This culmination combined art, drama, historic research, architecture, dramatic monologues, and spontaneous dialogues. Queen Elizabeth presided over our table and the Pope made a surprise entrance, bursting out of the coat closet in a flurry of red robes.

Family History

Investigating family origins and stories can be a powerful incentive for students to practice research skills, while addressing standards in geography, history, and language arts. You may want to take a generic approach via ethic origins—my family is from Cuba—or have your students hone in on a particular ancestor or living family member. Here are some ideas.

Trace Your Ancestry

We are a land of immigrants and any classroom could embrace students whose families came from a dozen different countries. Tracing family roots is an excellent way for students to explore ethnic identity, while you are promoting cultural awareness for all of your students. Encourage students to research customs, language, dress, foods, and cultural traditions of their ancestral homes. Their presentations can include artifacts, maps, recipes or prepared foods, holiday customs, and current events in their country of origin. Be sure students describe how their family came to your community.

Who's Who in My Family

You may want to give your students the opportunity to do a modified version of Bill Coate's Madera Method, focusing on digging up their own ancestors, and recovering family stories. First they'll need to find out who's in their family and who's gone. This may be recorded in a family bible, on a family tree computer program, or in grandma's head. Some of the best conversation-starters about family history are primary source documents: photographs of grandparents, uncles and cousins, letters, souvenirs, recipes, items of clothing or jewelry, and personal papers. Children ask *Who's that standing next to grandma in this picture?* and the adventure begins. If your students' families have lived in the community for generations, they'll probably find ancestor evidence at the cemetery, local historical society, or genealogical group. Once students have decided on the subject of their investigation, they need to gather the basic facts, guided by these questions:

- When was this person born?
- Where was he or she born? City, state, country?
- Where else did he or she live during his or her lifetime?
- Why did he or she move?
- Who was in the family? Brothers, sisters? Mom and dad?
- Where did he or she go to school?
- What types of jobs did this person have?
- What else did this person do that was special? Musical talent, art ability, sportsperson?
- Who were the presidents when he or she was growing up?
- Were there any wars?
- Was life hard for families and children?

- When did this person die? Where is he or she buried?
- What was happening in the world when this person was a child or adult?
- How did those events affect your family members?

Putting It Together

As your students collect bits and pieces of their family stories, they'll need a way to organize their discoveries. The goal is to find a format that will preserve the information for future reference, and make it easy to share with others. This is exactly what historians do—collect, preserve, and convey information. So do people who write memoirs, biographies, autobiographies, and historic fiction. They're all telling a story about people, but using a variety of approaches to get the job done.

Writing is only one way—and perhaps not the most effective—for students to present their family stories. Likewise, the typical family tree is a limiting format for the simple reason that it reinforces a singular notion of family and emphasizes chronology and DNA over human stories. Instead, encourage formats that highlight relationships, memory, anecdotes, and important individuals as the organizing principle. The following section describes some alternative formats for sharing family research, combining text, illustrations, visual materials, and artifacts. Demonstrate several formats and let your students choose the one that showcases their work best, but let them know that they're also free to create their own unique frame for telling their family stories.

Family Pocket Map

The pocket map creates a gallery of who's who in a child's life, without the traditional chronology. It's perfect for students being raised by a grandmother and two aunts or a single-parent family with lots of important cousins. It's just a long piece of paper folded up along the bottom to form a pocket. When it's fan-folded, each important person has his or her own pocket in which students store pictures, notes, and keepsakes. It's user-friendly for younger students because the primary organizational technique is sorting. They can easily revisit and add information every time they discover a new element in their family story. To make a pocket map:

1. Take a long piece of sturdy paper, ten inches wide and as long as you want.
2. Fold up three inches along the long edge to form a pocket.
3. Draw up-and-down lines four or five inches apart from one end to the other.
4. Fold along the lines like an accordion to create pockets. Staple or glue the edge of the end pockets so nothing will fall out.

5. Have students put their name on one pocket and then assign pockets to all the other important people in their family story. They can deposit pictures, cards, momentos, and their own writing in the pockets.

6. For storage, fold the pocket map like an accordion and tie it with ribbon or put it in an envelope.

Family Picture Book

A plain scrapbook or looseleaf binder can be a good starting point for telling a family story. This format works well for documenting individuals who are important in a child's life, but are not related. Students may want to assign one page or section to each person, then attach pictures, maps, letters, postcards, wedding announcements, and newspaper clippings. Then they can add their own writing and illustrations to each section, blending documents and text. Or they can organize the book chronologically, by year or annual events such as vacations and family celebrations.

Collage

A collage can be the perfect format for a child with strengths in graphic design or drawing. It's also great for kids who have lots of memories but few physical artifacts to document their lives, as is often the case with students who are homeless, itinerant, in foster care, or recent immigrants. Using a collage technique, they can select generic images from magazines to represent their family stories and augment them with watercolor, line drawings, colored paper, fabric, poetry, and prose. The overall impression may be more like a dream than a strict family tree, but more satisfying in that it is both beautiful and emotionally evocative.

Writing Ancestor Biographies

Students can use a strict chronological narrative for their ancestor biographies, focus on a short period in a person's life, or write the story of a whole family, telling what became of all the brothers and sisters. Or they can adopt a fictional approach—making up a story about their great-grandmother's life, using all the data they've collected and imagining the setting for her childhood or adult years. At the end of your family history investigations, ask your students what they learned about how to investigate people who lived in the past. You want them to focus on: skills they used or had to develop, insights about the challenges of the process, what they liked best, what they still wonder about. This provides a model for diving into more remote history and making it as personal and compelling as their own family stories.

Keeping a Personal Journal

Encourage students to begin keeping a diary or journal of their own lives with the thought that in fifty or one hundred years, this could fascinate a descendant or history buff interested in early twenty-first-century life. Some of your students may already be closet journalists, so they'll pounce on the opportunity to have their passion count as schoolwork. Others may need some models to get them started. You could use the writings of Laura Freeman, a Vermont schoolgirl who lived in Royalton, Vermont (see www.vermonthistory.org/educate/diaries.htm). On January 1, 1893, she began her diary, in which she describes her experiences in school, her chores, the books she reads, her family's activities, and her bout with scarlet fever.

Laura Freeman's Journal, 1893

January 1	Snowed pretty hard. Went and read to West a while. Lizzie is 8. Had slivered beef for breakfast and cranberry short cakes for dinner. Skated a lot yesterday on the river.
January 2	Warm. West went out doors for the first time since he took sick.
January 4	15 below zero. Slid a lot this morn. West went outdoors a lot today. Had a written exercise in arithmetic and grammar.
January 5	Cold. Took our skates to school. Got to have compositions tomorrow. Mine is about fishing. Not good skating. Too much snow on the ice. Feel awful tired.
January 6	Very cold. All of us stayed in the house. Had rice pudding for dinner. My head aches. Don't believe I shall go to school tomorrow.

Have students work in pairs or small groups to develop a list of topics that would capture typical aspects of childhood in twenty-first-century America. As students write, they should think about the kind of details that would help a reader from centuries in the future picture life now. Ask the historic society if they have any children's journals, and would they be interested in adding to their collection with some newly minted one.

The Learning Ledger

The Learning Ledger is a tool for regular, focused self-assessment. Learning Ledgers help students account for their day, like a memoir, diary, or journal with the expressed purpose of capturing concrete descriptions of their work with first-person documents and its effects on them.

Basic Three Questions for the Learning Ledger

- What did I do?
- How did I do it?
- What did I learn?

Additional Questions Related to First-Person Narratives

- Who did I learn about from these documents?
- What was interesting about his or her life?
- What did I learn about living in another time?
- If I could meet this person, what would I say? What questions would I ask?
- What else do I wonder about this person?
- Have I changed my mind about _____? Why?
- What did I learn about researching people in the past?
- How did I use documents to answer my questions about _____ (person)?
- What questions do I still have?
- What other documents or sources could help me answer my questions tomorrow?

Additional Generic Questions for the Learning Ledger

- What did I enjoy most about my work today?
- What do I want to try next time?
- What did I learn about how I am smart?
- What did I learn about myself?
- What's the best thing I did all month?
- Who do I enjoy working with?
- Who helps me learn?
- What helps me learn?
- How do I help other kids learn?

In Closing

If you want history to come alive for your students, tap into the human elements and then drill deep. Look for adventure, conflict, invention, heroism, competition, and heartbreak. Insist on a complete who-was-there role call. Root out the runaways and high-society suffragettes, the informers and the also-rans. Resurrect the oppressed, the marginalized, and the faceless cogs that drive the history machine in any era. Then you have a story worth telling and one that students will love.

5

Getting the Picture

Thinking with Things

Because the artifact reflects the values and influences which were important to the individual who made it and the society and time in which it was manufactured, it can be viewed as making an important cultural and historical statement. Both oral and written history may reflect judgments that are inaccurate and biased; the artifact does not lie.

—Dorothy Duncan, *The Artifact: What Can It Tell Us About the Past?*

Thematic Strands: Science, Technology, and Society Global Connections	**Learning Layers:** Geography, history, visual literacy, media literacy, literature, language arts, sociology, cultural anthropology, economics

What's the Big Idea About Thinking with Things?

Twenty-first-century children live in a world awash with visual stimulation, from their first colorful baby toy to the miles of billboards that line city streets and highways. Times Square in New York City—followed closely by Las Vegas—is probably the apogee of ocular excess, with thousands of square feet of screaming, building-high video screens streaming nonstop, and neon displays that make you squint at midnight. But even a modest suburban mall or big box store gets an A for effort in filling every inch of useable space with a kaleidoscope of images—all begging for attention.

But exposure to visual material does not equal visual literacy. Bombarded with visual input and blessed with 20/20 vision—a cause of constant envy in teachers with aging eyes—nonetheless, most students don't know how to see. Specifically, they seem to be severely visually challenged when it comes to looking at a *still* image or object—a photograph, etching, painting, or chunk of pottery. And I say, blame television! After years of nonstop exposure to television, videotapes and

DVDs, many kids simply have no talent for scanning an image, taking a close look in the corners, zeroing in on minor details, then linking eyeball and brain with a string of queries, starting with "What is this?" And understandably so. Those behaviors are useless—even distracting—to a serious TV viewer because the medium adheres almost religiously to a bull's-eye format. All the important images are right in the center. They move or emit sound every three or four seconds, so the viewer receives a constant flow of prompts about where to look in order to extract information from the screen. Physically and cognitively, television is an extremely low-effort event.

Now fast-forward to the classroom. Hoping to inject some variety into her lessons, an enthusiastic teacher tells her students to retire their textbooks for the morning. She pulls out a painting of the Boston Tea party. They're stumped. The image doesn't move or make noise. It has important information in all four corners, background, and fore. This is tough. They lock on to the biggest, most central image—the ship—and it's all over. They've looked. They're done. Bring on the next picture.

That's a real scenario, but not a pretty picture. When shown a painting of that famous tea party, most fourth-grade respondents were unable to identify the reason for the protest. Despite the men in colonial dress dumping boxes into a harbor, they couldn't nail the right answer even when presented with four choices. Students face the same challenge when looking at inanimate objects such as leather buckets, carved masks, iron tools, or familiar historic buildings. At first they see only the broad outlines or the brightest colors. And that's partially our fault.

Learning Through the Material Culture

We tend to be word oriented when we teach social studies, relying on textbooks to do the heavy lifting, with worksheets, core literature, primary source documents, encyclopedias, and websites occasionally pitching in. We forget that many students think in pictures and do their best work when handling concrete objects. Neglected or completely overlooked are the rich learning possibilities offered by things made by people—the material culture—such as, household utensils, furniture, buildings, works of art, photographs, clothing, and numerous other items. Students can learn about their own society or people in other places, times, and cultures from these pieces. These artifacts are the tools that professional historians, archaeologists, and anthropologists use to conduct their investigations. They provide clues about survival strategies, inventions, art, rituals, religion, ingenuity, luxury or humor, and acquaint your students with the individuals and societies that created and used them.

Despite the real benefits of lessons based on the material culture, actual objects make rare appearances in classrooms, and like an Elvis sighting, they can cause quite a stir. Present your students with a porcupine quill basket, a shell ladle, or a shard of colonial tile and they may react as if you ducked out into the corridor and returned with a moon rock—something wholly unexpected but worthy of their interest. They quickly discover that examining a colonial auger, a Sioux quiver, or a sod house is a lot of fun. The tactile experience alone perks students up. But sensation alone is not sufficient. Artifacts aren't meant to be a holiday from learning. You need to insist that your students link their eyes and fingertips with the frontal lobe of their brains, so they actually use tactile information to understand social studies concepts, and make explicit connections to the world in which they live.

To access information from the material culture, your students must learn how to read images and objects, just as they would read an historic document such as the Constitution or the diary of a Civil War soldier. *Reading* in this case means describing, analyzing, and interpreting. That takes patience and close attention to detail—the antitelevision skills—because artifacts can be enigmatic, and that's one of the very reasons to include them in your lessons. The most puzzling ones— like the crank for a Model T Ford or a shoebutton hook—force kids to scrutinize, wonder, and speculate. That's the lure but it's also the work. The result is a boost in vocabulary, oral and written language, analysis, synthesis and evaluation—the stratospheric levels of Bloom's taxonomy. How do you make that happen? Ask and ask and ask. Pelt them with questions like: *Who might have used these objects? For what? How are the objects in your life the same as the ones used two hundred years ago? How are they different? Why did they change? What replaced them? How might they be different in the future?*

With skillful questioning and coaching, students can amass impressive amounts of information about social studies simply by looking at objects from the material culture and decoding the stories they can tell. Coupling objects with open-ended questions is a powerful technique for transporting kids to the past, and making them think their way home. Cognitively speaking, this is leagues ahead of reading the chapter and answering the questions at the end.

Why Is This an Effective Way to Learn Social Studies?

Objectifying your social studies lessons using visual materials can lower barriers and accelerate the learning process for a broad range of students. Handling artifacts such as old tools appeals to kinesthetic learners who use their hands and eyes to gather information about shape, size, texture, weight, material, and function. Students who are visually intelligent are finely tuned to colors, patterns, shapes, symbols, graphic designs, and pictures. These students also snap up heavily illustrated reading material, scouring the pictures for details. With a little encouragement, they can extract as much information from a painting, etching, or picture book as other kids glean from an entire encyclopedia entry.

Visual materials are also important tools for ensuring equal access to curriculum content for second-language learners and students with reading disabilities or weak auditory processing skills, allowing them to use their eyes and brain to access information directly, vaulting over their language and learning challenges. Artifacts and images provide a concrete context for social studies concepts that would otherwise simply be words on a page, no different from a paragraph about Mars or cell division. As an added bonus, visual materials are surprising to kids. They expect pictures during art time—if you still have art time—but not during social studies.

Objects can also create a connection with the rich and complex cultures that have no written language—no manifestos, autobiographies, or caches of correspondence to inform us about daily life among those people. This is particularly true if you're studying the early history of North America, when the continent was blanketed with Native American tribes. Our only source of information may be the oral tradition—if there are survivors—and items such as clothing, weapons, cooking instruments, jewelry, religious accoutrements, funerary items, statuary, furniture, armor, tools, and musical instruments. In many cases, our most tangible connection to these people is through their surviving handcrafts—a beaded-blanket from the Osage tribe, Kwakiutl masks, Apache medicine bags, buffalo robes, and weapons.

Paintings, etchings, and photographs bridge time and space. Looking at a photograph of teenaged Civil War soldiers puts a human face on that tragic national upheaval. So whenever you're planning a social studies lesson, ask yourself how you can include *things* as well as text. The time you spend foraging for paintings, drawings, etchings, maps, photographs, and artifacts will be well worth it when you see your students pounce on these treasures as if you'd raided the candy aisle.

What About Standards?

When you decide to use household utensils, furniture, buildings, works of art, clothing, advertisements, maps, photographs, and other objects as instructional materials in your social studies program, your students will develop and demonstrate skills that are fundamental to a rigorous standards-based approach to social studies. The following list suggests the range of learning challenges students will face as they examine images and objects to learn about the past and present.

Students will:

- Draw upon data in historical maps.
- Extract information from photographs, paintings, cartoons, and architectural drawings.

- Describe how science and technology have changed the lives of people and the physical environment.
- Use artifacts as sources of historical and cultural information.
- Apply a wide range of strategies to comprehend, interpret, evaluate, and appreciate visual materials and artifacts, including prior experience, interactions with other students, and their understanding of visual symbols.
- Develop historical research capabilities, including the ability to formulate historical questions, and obtain historical data from visual materials and artifacts.
- Synthesize knowledge of an historic time and place from visual materials and artifacts to construct a story, explanation, or historical narrative.

Awareness

Assessing Prior Knowledge About the Material Culture

The goal of the Awareness stage of the learning cycle is to find out what your students know about artifacts. The activities in this section use literature and actual objects to help students identify the kinds of things that are part of the material culture and see how they provide clues to historians, archaeologists, social scientists, and anthropologists. As your students share what they already know, they can feel smart before you present any formal lessons. As you assess their comments, you build an authentic foundation from which to launch the Exploration and Inquiry stages of the learning cycle.

You Are Here: The Town Dump—Exploring Personal Artifacts

So let's get started with a touching piece of literature called "The Town Dump," written by Wallace Stegner. As a child, Stegner frequented the dump with his brothers and friends, gleaning treasures from the heaps of trash. This essay demonstrates that one way we can learn about people is by studying what they discard. This is an eloquent piece of read-aloud literature that specifically addresses the topics of history, civilization, relics, and what artifacts reveal about a community, all through the eyes of a child who haunts the town dump.

> I remember the dump better than I remember most things in that town, better than I remember most of the people. I spent more time with it, for one thing; it has more poetry and excitement in it than people did . . . If the history of our town was not exactly written, it was at least hinted, in the dump. Rummaging through its foul purlieus I had several times been surprised and shocked to find relics of my own life tossed out there to rot or blow away.

Read "The Town Dump" (available on the Internet at www.stanford.edu/~jonahw/ATE-F05/Stegner.doc) to your students, if only to give them a close encounter with superb writing—the descriptions are vivid and lyrical.

1. Before reading, prompt students to try to visualize the town and the dump as you read. After reading, ask them to share their favorite images—the leeches, the hobos, the colt—and reread those sections to emphasize the descriptive power of the writing.

2. Discuss the events and locations in the story and then ask your students to sketch a story map showing the town, the river, the flume, the dump, and the many artifacts the author treasured.

3. Ask students to think about artifacts that they could gather to represent their own childhoods, and discuss formats for display. When students share their personal artifacts with the class, have the group discuss what they reveal about the student's daily life and the historical period in which they live.

A Footnote on What We Throw Away

After your discussion of "The Town Dump," it may interest your students to look at some statistics on what Americans throw away these days. In just one year, Americans generate 236 million tons of garbage. While about 30 percent of it gets recycled or composted, 164 million tons are tossed away, including:

26,800,000 tons of food
8,550,000 tons of furniture and furnishings
6,330,000 tons of clothing and footwear
5,190,000 tons of glass beer and soda bottles
4,200,000 tons of plastic wrap and bags
3,650,000 tons of junk mail
3,470,000 tons of diapers
3,160,000 tons of office paper
3,070,000 tons of tires
2,820,000 tons of carpets and rugs
2,230,000 tons of newspapers
2,060,000 tons of appliances
1,520,000 tons of magazines
1,170,000 tons of wine and liquor bottles
970,000 tons of paper plates and cups
840,000 tons of books
830,000 tons of beer and soda cans

780,000 tons of towels, sheets, and pillowcases
540,000 tons of telephone directories
450,000 tons of milk cartons
160,000 tons of lead-acid (car) batteries

Waking Magoun's Brain

The biggest challenge to reading artifacts accurately is that we see them through twenty-first-century eyes, stripped of the original context that could provide clues to their ancestry or use. Eventually your kids will discover that decoding artifacts can be guided or misguided by comparing antiquities to familiar objects. For example, a Roman toilet looks remarkably similar to the contemporary version, but a colonial butter churn can really stump them.

Is This Anything?

To sharpen your students' observation skills and give them some batting practice with identifying artifacts, bring in some odd objects, such as an apple corer or a peeler, garlic press, coal burning iron, industrial-sized bobbin, potato masher, curling iron, ice cream mould, tea ball, shoe last, sausage maker, cigar cutter, or any other unfamiliar objects cluttering up your garage or kitchen drawers. Put each object on a separate table and have students move from table to table in small groups to examine each to see if they can guess what it is. Post the following questions to guide students in their investigations:

* How would you describe this object?
* What is it made of?
* What do you think this object might have been used for? Why? (You may have more than one idea.)
* Who do you think made or used it?
* What does this object tell us about the life of the person who made or used it?
* What would you like to know about this object? (You may have more than one question.)
* How do you think we could find out more?

When they've examined all the objects, ask the groups to explain what they thought the object was and the clues that helped them arrive at their conclusion. Compare and contrast ideas before you reveal the actual purpose of the object. Encourage students to bring in other curious objects for the class to identify.

⊕ Exploration

Discovering More About the Material Culture

Once you succeed in stimulating your students' curiosity about artifacts, and how they help us construct pictures of the past, it would be excellent to let them take a closer look at artifacts and the people who examine them. These Exploration activities use literature and real objects to help students think about artifacts—what they are, who uses them, and how they can teach or trick us about other people, times, or cultures.

Motel of the Mysteries

David Macaulay, author, illustrator, and recipient of a MacArthur Genius award in 2006, has spent most of his life studying the Top Ten List of things made by people, and producing hundreds of detailed drawings to tell their stories. First he published *Cathedral*, then went on to share his passion in *City*, *Pyramid*, *Underground*, *Castle*, *Mill*, *Mosque*, *Ship*, and *Unbuilding*.

Macaulay is an expert at investigating things made in the past, so he was the perfect person to write *Motel of the Mysteries* (1979), a spoof on the discovery of the tomb of Tutankhamon. This book recounts the expedition of a forty-first-century archaeologist investigating the remains of the Usa culture. He mistakenly believes that a long-buried twentieth-century American motel is a sacred tomb, and interprets all the objects in it to match his theory. The *Do Not Disturb* sign on the doorknob is the sacred seal, the television set is the Great Altar, and the toilet is the focal point of the burial ceremony. This is a quick and lively way to open a discussion about artifacts and how we make inferences to explain their meanings. This book helps students understand that our hunches—shaped by our beliefs and the way we use objects—can be wildly inaccurate.

Trash Bag Archaeology

After you read and discuss *Motel of the Mysteries* with your students, it's time for some application. You need to do a bit of preparation for this activity by collecting trash—not garbage—but receipts, food containers, product boxes or wrappers, magazines, junk mail, movie ticket stubs, newsletters, business, correspondence, toiletry containers, a calendar, a shoe with sand inside or mud on the outside, fishing weights, coupons, sections from newspaper, a battery, water bottle, vitamin bottles, and pet supplies. Divide students into small groups and give each a bag of trash. Their task is to examine the contents and make some guesses about who generated this trash. Use the following prompt, *Who do you think discarded this? What evidence can you find to support your hunches about the person's:*

- age
- gender
- occupation
- interests
- health
- residence
- marital status and family
- class/socioeconomic status

Have each group present their person and defend their hunches based on the evidence provided by the trash. Encourage the class to suggest other interpretations for the artifacts.

Inquiry

Digging Deeper into the Material Culture

When you introduce your students to the idea of the material culture in social studies, you're essentially redefining images and objects as safety deposit boxes, stuffed with valuable information about other times, people, places, and cultures. The activities in this Inquiry section are designed to help your students discover the conversational potential of artifacts by modeling how to scrutinize, analyze, and discuss two- and three-dimensional materials. As they examine these artifacts, they learn to formulate questions, pursue hunches, make discoveries, and compare their impressions with other students. You can use these ideas to conduct a series of short inquiry lessons, or as the starting point for in-depth research projects, presentations, and authentic assessments. Let's take a look at how you can guide your students through a thorough investigation of three items from the material culture: a painting, an object, and a building.

How to Make Images Talk

Images are perfect tools for getting to the past—fast. They provide a window through which your students can witness the turning point in a war, the arrival of the railroad in your town, or the coronation of a queen. They can even discover esoteric fashion trends—the Dolce and Gabbana of the Renaissance. Did you know that some men wore shoes two-and-a-half feet long? Walking in them was only possible by yanking the toes up off the ground with chains attached at the knees. Not to be outdone, Venetian women of a certain class towered over the crowd in *chopines*, satin-lined shoes nailed to wooden stilts as much as two feet high. These fashionable giants could only get around town if steadied by two servants. Sumptuary laws put an end to both of these extravagant styles, but thanks to some antique etchings, the story lives on.

What else can your students learn by looking at images? Egyptian murals show mortuary priests removing the corpse's brain with a hook shoved in through the nostrils. Urban students can study rural life through the landscape paintings of George Innes, and rural students can glimpse city life in the lithographs of George Bellows. Portrait painters put a face on historic names like King Henry VIII, Queen Marie Antoinette, Ibn Battutu, the explorer, and Sylvia Pankhurst, the hunger-striking suffragette.

Taking a Peek at the New World

In 1585, Queen Elizabeth's courtier Walter Raleigh sponsored an expedition to the New World. The venture failed to establish a lasting colony, but thanks to the artist, John White, we have a valuable visual record of the land that would be called Virginia. White was hired to accompany the expedition and make paintings that gave the people in England, particularly the Queen and other anxious investors, a glimpse of a world they had never seen. White's paintings serve a similar purpose in the twenty-first century, letting us study a world that no longer exists.

White documented his discoveries much as a photographer covers a news story. His instructions were to "Draw to life one of each kind of thing that is strange to us in England . . . all strange birds, beasts, fishes, plants, herbs, trees, and fruits . . . also the figures and shapes of men and women in their apparel, as also their manner of weapons in every place as you shall find them differing" (www.vahistorical.org/cole/overview.htm). White created an entire series of portraits—tattooed men and women, fishing parties, and tribal leaders. Studying them makes your students eyewitnesses to the moment of contact between England and the indigenous populations of North America.

Exploring the Indian Village of Secoton by John White

Thanks to White's talent and diligence, your students can get a bird's-eye view of life in a Powhatan village at the time of contact with English explorers and settlers. You can locate the painting of The Indian Village of Secoton on the Internet (www .virtualjamestown.org/images/white_debry_html/white35.html). One very effective way to use rich historic material such as White's image is to construct a lesson as a visual scavenger hunt. Decide beforehand those things you want your students to find in the painting. While they examine the picture of the village, hand out the following to guide their viewing:

Welcome to the Village of Secoton. Imagine that you are an English explorer and this is your first visit to a Powhatan community. Look carefully in all areas of the village. See if you can discover:

- *People eating*
- *A type of weapon*
- *Evidence that they grow their own food*
- *Two different kinds of clothing or body adornment*
- *Two different kinds of shelters*
- *Architectural details similar to our houses*
- *A source of water*
- *A type of fence or barrier*
- *Three different kinds of activities*
- *A method for cooking food*
- *List any other interesting observations or discoveries.*

Print out or make copies of White's paintings so that students can work in pairs or small groups to scour them. Provide magnifying glasses to emphasize the idea of close, systematic scrutiny. When they have had time to really look, help them discover what they've learned by asking open-ended questions like the following to promote description, analysis, synthesis, and interpretation.

Questions to Prompt Description
- Tell me what you see. What else? What else? List items on the board.
- What's going on in the picture?
- What's in the background? Foreground?
- Who do you see?
- What are they wearing?
- Where are they?
- Describe the setting. What's man-made? What's natural?
- What are they doing?
- How are they doing it?
- What tools or instruments do you see?
- What animals or plants do you see?

Questions to Prompt Analysis
- Who do you think these people are? What gave you that clue?
- What do you think the people in the circle are doing? What made you think that?
- What about the people crouching in the line? What's your idea about that?
- When do you think these events happen? How can you tell?
- Where do you think this is? What clues are in the picture?
- How do you think these people fed and clothed themselves?
- Is this like any other scene you have seen or read about in history?

117

- Is there anything in this scene that was similar to life in England at the same time?
- Is there anything in this scene that is similar to our own lives?
- Is there anything that is different from our lives today?
- What can you tell about men and women?
- What can you tell about natural resources?
- What can you tell about beliefs or ceremonies?
- Is this image related to any other primary source documents that we have seen?
- Is it related to anything in our textbook?

Questions to Prompt Synthesis and Interpretation

- Why do you think this painting was created?
- What did the painter want to tell the viewer?
- How do you think the painter felt about these people?
- What can we learn about life in the past from this image?
- What guesses can you make about these people from this image?
- What guesses can you make about living in this time from this image?
- What is the most interesting thing in this image?
- What do you wonder about life in the Village of Secoton?
- How do you think you could find out more?

That's how you teach kids to look. Be sure to solicit multiple answers to each question—there's no one right answer in this type of exploration. Before you know it, your television-dazed students will be scouting for details like a bargain hunter riffling a sale bin.

What Else Can You Do with This Image?

- Choose a person in the picture and make him or her come to life and talk about the village.
- Pretend you could walk into the image. Where would you go? What would you do?
- Choose two people in the image. Write a dialogue between them.
- Imagine you are an art critic. What would you say about this image as a work of art?

Sources of Images

Your school or district may no longer have the slotted, wooden bins stuffed with art prints that used to be standard fare for classrooms, so where can you go for images that function as primary source documents for history lessons? Many art and natural history museums have slide libraries that lend slides to teachers for a nominal weekly fee—something like five dollars for fifty slides. Their collections typically include images of paintings, medieval manuscripts, buildings, monuments, sculpture, and even prehistoric tools and ritual objects. If you can beg or borrow a slide projector, the visual world, historically speaking, is yours for five bucks a week. Other inexpensive sources of images:

> Internet sites have images that can be projected with an LCD or printed out
> postcards for small-group work
> old calendars
> used art and history books (cut apart)
> copies of etchings or paintings

How to Make Objects Talk

In the recent past, young children spent their time outdoors building forts, digging in the dirt, throwing rocks, and making snowmen. Now we have two-year-olds camped out in front of the television or massaging a plastic mouse and experiencing the world virtually, so touching real objects can be a unique experience for kids who live electronic, flat-screen lives. Your students may be excited at the prospect of handling objects that have weight, texture, color, and dimensions. They may even act a bit silly, like people encountering a formal table setting for the first time—four spoons, three knives, umpteen drinking vessels. They're not sure what's expected, but just keep guiding them back to the task of gathering information with their eyes and fingers.

You can launch a serious social studies discussion with a few artifacts—either authentic or reproductions—including coins, beads, buttons, nails, thimbles, tiles, pottery, jars, musical instruments, arrowheads, toys, candlesticks, quilts, doorknobs, farm tools, eyeglasses, pipes, kitchen implements such as a strainer, meat grinder or potato masher, medical instruments, cameras, measuring devices, or scales. If you can get outdoors with your students, the range of items grows to encompass gravestones, monuments, statues, markers, fences, signs, stone walls, bridges, plaques on buildings, manhole covers, farm machinery, old or antique vehicles.

Providing magnifying glasses encourages close scrutiny and is a real help if students are looking at coins or similar small objects with embossed or engraved text or symbols. Give them plenty of time to look, then prompt them to look harder and think using the following questions:

Questions to Prompt Description
- Tell me what you see.
- Describe the material, size, color, and weight of the object.

- Describe the texture of the surfaces. Are they smooth or rough?
- Describe any decoration on it.
- Does it have any moving parts? What is their function?
- Does it have any compartments or hidden parts?
- Look inside and on the underside. What do you see?
- Does it look new or worn?

Questions to Prompt Analysis

- What do you think this item is?
- Do you know what it is called?
- How do you think it was used?
- Is the texture or size related to the function?
- How do you think it was made?
- When do you think it was made?
- Where do you think it was made?
- What does this item remind you of?
- Do we use similar objects today?
- Is this item related to any other primary source documents?
- Is it related to anything in our textbook?

Questions to Prompt Synthesis and Interpretation

- Why do you think it was made?
- What else could it be or mean?
- What does it make you wonder?
- What guesses can you make about the people who made or used this?
- What does it tell about the relationship between nature and the person who made it?
- Does it tell anything about the beliefs of the people who used or made it?
- What do you think is important about this item?
- What is unique or unusual about this?
- Where could I find more information about this artifact?

What Else Can You Do with Artifacts?

- Group the artifacts in categories according to appearance, function, and materials.
- Line the artifacts up chronologically from oldest to most recent.
- Make a pencil drawing or watercolor painting of an object in the style of John White.
- Find pictures in magazines of contemporary objects that look similar or serve a similar purpose.

Sources of Artifacts

Our Natural History Museum has an amazing lending library of stuffed animals, mineral and rock collections, antique bowls, weapons, and textile samples. The more delicate items are enclosed in Plexiglas boxes, so kids can look to their hearts' content without fear of harming the specimens. To discover other sources for artifacts try:

artifact reproduction companies
local natural history museum
local historic society
antiques stores
secondhand and thrift shops
garage and tag sales
collections of parents, grandparents, and colleagues

The HistoryWired (http://historywired.si.edu/about.cfm) website offers a virtual tour of a large collection of objects from the Smithsonian's National Museum of American History. Browsing on this site will give you dozens of ideas for additions to your collection.

How to Make Buildings Talk

One of the easiest material culture lessons you can plan is a walk around the block. Discovering the brick-and-mortar history in your community can be as simple as strolling through the historic neighborhood and sketching leaded windows, Dutch doors, and stone foundations. Or it can be as elaborate as passing through the gates of a restored village like Sturbridge, Williamsburg, New Paltz, or Deerfield and entering another century, complete with historic interpreters. What can kids learn about the past through architecture? How tall people were. Building materials. How public and private space was divided and decorated. Who lived where in town. How the size of structures reveals status. The number and kind of religions represented by historic churches.

Here are some questions you can use to help your students learn more about people and activities in the past by looking at buildings.

Questions to Prompt Description
- Tell me what you see.
- Describe the materials used to make this building.
- Describe the texture of the surfaces. Are they smooth or rough?
- Describe the size and shapes of the windows and doors.

- Describe any decoration or inscription on it.
- Does it look new or old? What are the clues?

Questions to Prompt Analysis

- How is this building different from structures that are built now?
- How is it the same? Why?
- When do you think it was built? How can you tell?
- Why do you think it was built?
- Do you think it is being used for the same purpose today?
- For whom might it have been built?
- What do the patterns in the bricks look like?

Questions to Prompt Synthesis and Interpretation

- Who do you think built this?
- Who else might have lived here or used this building?
- Was it always in this place or was it moved?
- Is this how it looked originally or has it shrunk or grown?
- What do you notice about the gardens and landscaping?
- Does it have outbuildings and how are they used?
- What can we learn about the people who made or used this building by looking at the size, shape, doors and windows, materials, decoration, and location?
- What appeals to you about this structure?
- Would you like to live or work in this building? Why?

Sources of Information About Buildings

But what if you don't know anything about architecture? Can't tell the difference between Beaux Art and a bungalow? It's not a problem. You can learn right along with your kids because the main ingredients for this lesson are sharp eyes and curiosity. As for learning more about vocabulary, architectural styles, and historic periods, go directly to the website of Architeacher (www.architeacher.org/historic/historic-styles1.html). It has a huge section of photographs and explanations of various periods in American architecture that you can use as a crib sheet for spotting architectural styles in your town. While you're there, you'll get a view of preservation efforts nationwide.

But closer to home, there are plenty of real-life experts who will help you and your students get smarter about the built environment, and what it has to say about people and the past. Your local historic society probably has a list of the oldest or most historically significant structures in your area. Some organizations promote historic appreciation by publishing self-guided walking tours, complete with maps and brochures full of historic information, dates, and stories. All you need to do is ask.

There are undoubtedly people in your town whose sole purpose in life is to preserve and protect historic landmarks. They might be members of the local Landmarks Commission, the neighborhood historic association, or the Historic Conservancy, and they'll happily take you on a walking tour of who's-who in the architectural history of your town. They'll also know the names of preservation architects who can give your kids a course in First Aid for Historic Buildings in the hopes of breeding a new generation of people willing to go to bat for elderly buildings. Contact your local AIA (American Institute of Architects) and they can point you in the direction of more resources for studying the built environment, with a perspective on how and why architectural styles and building methods have changed over time.

 ## Action

Using Knowledge About the Material Culture

If students collect lots and lots of data by examining the material culture, but are never challenged to process what they've learned into products, the knowledge soon becomes irrelevant and is easily forgotten. The activities in this section encourage students to use the skills and knowledge they gained while exploring artifacts to preserve a small corner in their community, contribute original material to the historic record, and teach other students about the built environment.

Studying the Silent City

Gravestones are important items in our material culture, functioning as memorials, objects of art, genealogies, and expressions of cultural beliefs and rituals. Depending on the age of your cemetery, the headstones, monuments, and buildings may be deteriorating, erasing a rich source of historical and genealogical information about the people who lived in your town. Some students are fascinated with graveyards and may want to do a study that combines data gathering and preservation. Suggest that they consider the following ideas in their research:

- Identify and classify types of memorials.
- Analyze the change in memorials over the decades or centuries.
- Analyze the placement and design of the grave markers to determine issues of socioeconomic status, association, or family.
- Analyze the inscriptions for clues to religious or cultural beliefs.
- Identify who is buried there.

- Research some of their stories.
- Document historically important or unique markers by making detailed drawings, rubbings, or photographs.

Students can document their research using photography or make a video documentary of their project. Have them determine who is responsible for the maintenance of the cemetery, and interview that person or group. If the cemetery is overgrown and neglected, or simply showing signs of deterioration that could be prevented, your students can create an action plan for preserving or restoring the cemetery. If they are granted permission to carry out their plan, it could be the basis for service learning and community organizing.

Archaeology and Ethics: Researching the Story of Kennewick Man

One of the dilemmas that arises with the discovery of artifacts from the past is *who they belong to* and *how they should be treated*. This is a particularly thorny issue for archaeologists who discover burial sites. They're eager to get their hands on the remains so they can study the past. The descendants of the dead often protest that the scientific action desecrates their ancestors and disrespects their culture. These disputes are frequently settled in court, as in the case of the Kennewick Man.

Kennewick Man is the name given to the remains of a prehistoric man found on a bank of the Columbia River near Kennewick, Washington, on July 28, 1996. The discovery was accidental: a pair of spectators at the yearly hydroplane competition found a skull while watching the races. The remains became embroiled in the inherent conflict between Native American religious rights and the interests of archaeologists. Based on the Native American Graves Protection and Repatriation Act, five Native American groups claimed the remains and asked for a traditional burial. In 2004, the United States Court of Appeals for the Ninth Circuit ruled that a cultural link between the tribes and the skeleton was not met, opening the door for more scientific study. In 2005, scientists from around the United States convened in Seattle for ten days to study the remains, making many detailed measurements, and determining the cause of death. This case can be an interesting research project for students who are interested in Native American cultures, issues of law and ethics, and the interests of science versus the rights of individuals and groups.

Helping Out with Local History

The local Historic Society is like the family album for the whole town. The members—usually volunteers—keep alive the records of who did what and why, and they're always looking for an extra pair of helping hands for mailing flyers, organizing exhibitions, or cataloguing images and objects. Students can get involved in local history by joining the brigade of volunteers. But if their real intention is to spread the word to citizens who will never darken the door of the Historic Society, your students can reach out by mounting their own historic presentations, such as a *Who's Who* in the history of your town. They can download or borrow images from the local archives, then present to parents, members of the public, and other students to increase awareness of local history. Finally, students can undertake their own documentation project by photographing disappearing buildings, signs, views, or venues. Be sure that they label and date the images. They may want to talk to the archivist at the Historic Society to determine what other information should be included, then give copies of the town archives.

Creating Personal History Documents

Your students can use photography to document their own lives, creating a contemporary archive of a twenty-first-century childhood. The photos can be used as the basis of a memoir project studded with family photos. Ask the local library or historic society if they would be interested in providing a temporary exhibition space.

Giving History Back to Your City: A Block Study

The goal of this activity is to focus on a small part of a neighborhood and assemble its history through careful observation of the buildings and information gleaned from primary source documents. You might choose the block on which your school is located, one block of the original Main Street, or a block where history was made. Students should try to determine:

- when the area was developed
- where the residents might have come from
- where they worked and shopped
- typical buildings and their use
- famous or distinctive buildings in the area

Families of Buildings or Structures

Another approach is to focus on one kind of building in some detail to produce a short history of that type of structure in your area. In my town, this would definitely include piers, amusement parks, roller coasters, and elegant hotels from the 1920s. Your students may choose to focus on schools, apartment buildings, parks, shops, early skyscrapers, auto showrooms, drive-in theatres, early fast-food establishments, mansions, religious structures, or buildings shaped like objects such as doughnuts or hotdogs. Students should try to determine:

- dates of the buildings
- reason they flourished
- builders or architects associated
- trends or changes reflected by these structures
- survival, use and historic status in the present
- future trends for this type of structure

When students are ready to present their research, be sure to invite local experts and interested amateurs, including architects, historians, university staff, long-time residents, Rotarians, librarians, and museum staff. Inevitably they will come bearing stories or recollections of their own, adding rich details to the research projects.

The Learning Ledger

The Learning Ledger is a tool for regular, focused self-assessment. Learning Ledgers help students account for their day, like a memoir, diary, or journal with the expressed purpose of capturing concrete descriptions of their work with the material culture in the classroom or the community, and its effects on them.

Basic Three Questions for the Learning Ledger
- What did I do?
- How did I do it?
- What did I learn?

Questions Related to Using the Material Culture and Artifacts
- What did I learn from looking at _____(objects, paintings, photographs)?
- How did I learn it?
- What did I learn about life in another time?
- What do I still wonder about?
- What else do I want to find out?
- What could I teach someone else about _____?

Additional Questions for the Learning Ledger
- What did I enjoy most about my work today?
- What do I want to try next time?
- What did I learn about how I am smart?
- What did I learn about myself?
- What's the best thing I did all month?
- Who do I enjoy working with?
- Who helps me learn?

- What helps me learn?
- How do I help other kids learn?
- What did I do with other students?
- How did I do it?
- What did I learn about working as a group?
- How did I help the group?
- How did I get help from the group?
- What did I do well?

In Closing

I'm a big fan of taking the remote out of education by getting kids as close as possible to real things. My classroom closets were always stuffed with beautiful junk because I've witnessed how visual and tactile materials can transport students across time and space. Exquisitely rendered paintings, drawings and etching, such as medieval harvest scenes, can be a virtual window on the prephotographic past, providing a rich context for social studies content, while developing aesthetic appreciation. In a glance, objects simplify complex ideas, and make abstract notions concrete.

Artifacts can challenge or refine our preconceptions about ancient culture, as in the recent announcement about the Antikythera Mechanism. This mesmerizing artifact is an ancient Greek calculator about the size of a shoebox, with dials on the outside and a complex assembly of bronze gear wheels within. By winding a knob on its side, the first-century-BC operator could calculate the positions of the sun, Moon, Mercury, and Venus for any chosen date, rather like a perpetual calendar for tracking the heavenly bodies. Newly revealed inscriptions also appear to confirm that the device could also calculate the positions of Mars, Jupiter, and Saturn—the other planets known at the time.

But I didn't fully realize the importance of using real objects and images until I read *Thinking in Pictures* by Temple Grandin (1995). Dr. Grandin is a noted author, speaker, video producer, and expert in animal handling, and she is also autistic. In her book she confides,

> I think in pictures. Words are like a second language to me. I translate both spoken and written words into full-color movies, complete with sound, which run like a VCR tape in my head. When somebody speaks to me, his words are instantly translated into pictures. I create new images all the time by taking many little parts of the images I have in the video library in my imagination and piecing them together. (19)

No doubt many of your students are visual thinkers, just waiting for the day when a teacher will speak in their primary language—pictures. Try it—and what a conversation you'll see.

6

Community as Classroom

Place-Based Explorations and Discoveries

*From the standpoint of the child, the great waste of school comes from his
inability to utilize the experiences he gets outside of school in any complete
and free way within the school itself; while, on the other hand, he is unable
to apply in daily life what he is learning at school. When the child gets to the
schoolroom, he has to put out of his mind a large part of the ideas, interests
and activities that predominate in his home and neighborhood. That is the
isolation of the school—its isolation from life.*

—John Dewey, *The School and Society*

Thematic Strands: Time,
Continuity, and Change
People, Places, and
Environments

Learning Layers: Geography, local history, literature, sociology,
cultural anthropology, economics, environmental studies, historic
preservation, architecture, social studies, ecology, language arts, logic,
fine arts, politics, economics, urban planning, government

What's the Big Idea About Place-Based Learning?

On a warm October evening in 1992, when most youngsters in Tucson, Arizona,
were settling down in front of their television sets, thirty elementary school students
filed into the City Council chambers and took their seats. But this was not your
usual let's-visit-city-hall field trip. These kids were on the agenda, and they meant
business. Serious business. When they rose to speak, the city fathers listened
intently as these fifth graders discussed, in Spanish and English, the economy, ecology, zoning, and property values—subjects near and dear to politicians' hearts, but
rarely included in the elementary curriculum. Their request was simple and direct—
would the council members donate a city-owned, trash-strewn lot to the school
district for educational purposes?

These students, and scores of others across the country, were hard at work,
learning *about* their communities, *in* their communities, so they could improve

their communities, and just possibly change a little piece of the world. In a neighboring state, a huddle of kindergartners graphed information about shelters and food banks gleaned from a series of phone calls. Then they compared the amount each facility spent on blankets and meals, trying to determine the best way to invest their bake sale money to help the homeless. In a former mill town, third-grade students stood before the Landmarks Commission and explained the architectural features on their model of an abandoned manufacturing building, hoping to postpone its demolition and convince the commissioners to protect it under the town's historic preservation ordinance. In a sunny tourist magnet by the sea, sixth-grade students testified at a community meeting convened by the Army Corps of Engineers. The topic was restoring the breakwater in the bay to create a boat basin. The students requested a line-by-line clarification of the Environmental Impact Report—*what does minimal disruption mean?*—trying to pierce the veil of bureaucratic language to determine for themselves the potential harm the project might inflict on the ecology of their bay.

Researching, lobbying, writing, PowerPointing, and testifying in public—it's all in a day's work for these students because their teachers have learned the value of *place-based learning.* John Dewey had a simple explanation for this approach to education. He believed that "ordinary contacts with day-to-day community life, whether social, economic, cultural or political," provided real and significant learning opportunities for students of all ages (1899, 80). Instead of the unending stream of unconsciousness that occupies many a schoolchild's morning—thirty-minute helpings of science, followed by history, followed by writing—students get to sink their brains and fists deep into real-world learning.

Place-based learning is a like a collective jailbreak for eager kids and their intrepid teachers. Formerly sentenced to 180 days in a well-lit box, they suddenly find themselves heading for the streets to get smarter about local history, architecture, taxation, ecology, politics, economics, and with a little luck, the mysteries of waste management. The community is their classroom.

When teachers adopt place-based education, whether they're in a prairie town, a big city, or a suburban neighborhood, on an island, an archipelago, or a reservation, their local setting becomes the context and content for learning. In the process, students gain a deep understanding of the place they call home, including the cultural, natural, political, and economic processes that make it work and give it its character. Riding a city bus, interviewing the mayor, analyzing traffic accidents in the vicinity of the school, pulling water samples from the stream near an industrial site, recording the number of fast-food containers littering the beach on a Monday morning, monitoring bird sightings during migration season, testifying at a Recreation and Parks Commission meeting, surveying recycling stations—these personal, sensory experiences help students embrace their community as a classroom, the likes of which they have never experienced. Even the simplest community outing can bring students face-to-face with complex social issues that lead them to ask questions like, *Why are there no parks on the poor side of town? Why are there so many liquor stores in our neighborhood? Why are the beautiful old buildings being torn down? Why are taxes spent on street furniture but not on schools? What happened to the feeding program at City Hall?*

Al Fresco Achievement: Why This Works

Even if you find the best social studies book in the country, well written, lavishly illustrated, provocative, at best it provides a generic approach to the world your students inhabit. Try as they might, it's hard for students to grasp complex notions about history, culture, economics, and the environment by reading a chapter and answering the questions at the end, which inevitably drive them back into the text. It's a closed-loop activity, performed in a featureless space the size of a modest living room. Is it any surprise that kids hate social studies?

But exploring in the community stimulates a high degree of interest. Even indifferent students, with a limited record of academic success, tend to thrive when their work is connected to a real context—their own environment. Students who get their arms around a chunk of community-based curriculum can be as tenacious as a dog with a chew-bone. Seized by the novelty or urgency of their personal projects, they become producers, rather than simply consumers, of knowledge. So what is it about a walk around the block that can be so compelling?

Social Studies and Life are Connected

Firsthand experiences in the community make it clear that there is an authentic connection between what you talk about in social studies and what's going on right outside, whereas, even the best textbook lessons rarely translate into a visceral, *Oh-my-god!* moment when kids understand that there is a link between the goings-on in their town and the standard social studies curriculum. For example, take the idea of democracy. You can lecture until you're blue in the face about this noble invention, or you can head for your next city council meeting. Slap a toga on those people and you could be watching a re-enactment of a Roman senate meeting in the time of Julius Caesar. No joke. Our founding fathers cribbed heavily from the Roman Republic when designing a kingless government. The senate, along with separation of powers, checks and balances, voting, debates, and the occasional impeachment—all Roman ideas. So if you're studying early civilizations, get thee to city hall, and let your kids witness how this antique institution is faring after twenty-five hundred years.

Students Co-Create the Curriculum

Explorations in the community begin as adventures. No one knows what will be uncovered. There are no right answers. As teacher, you set the basic direction of the investigation—local history, the built environment, environmental protection, contemporary economic or social problems—then students sharpen the focus by asking questions and identifying their personal interests. The more students pursue their ideas—water pollution, homeless services, healing the bay, dog parks, skate parks—the more ownership they feel for the work, which is why many community explorations turn into crusades.

Real-World Tasks Are Multidisciplinary

Place-based learning compresses many academic subjects into a single integrated whole. Community activities typically include: researching land deeds, debating with politicians, challenging outdated municipal codes, writing letters to the editor about bicycle or fishing ordinances, designing a website on community service opportunities for kids, organizing a traveling exhibit on community history, or synthesizing pollution data to present to students, parents, and community leaders. These activities often encompass subject matter, academic, and social skills commonly seen in high school or even college.

Learning Is Active

If you decide to trade your classroom for the adventures of the street, you will certainly be busy, but so will your students, particularly as they shift into the role of investigators. There are countless opportunities for them to observe, draw, read and write, interview, photograph, and generally poke their noses into anything with learning potential.

Life and Learning Are Fused

Place-based learning catapults students into a world they may have only glimpsed on television or from the window of a car or bus. They go from neutral spectating to scrutinizing every nook and cranny, and occasionally, agitating for change. They pester the local historian, have City Hall on speed-dial, call the mayor by her first name, enjoy after-hours tours of private facilities, and are regulars at archives generally frequented by scholars and dozers. Research becomes recreation and their newly discovered passion is community improvement. In the process, they experience a direct and powerful connection between the skills you teach in the classroom and their ability to influence life in their neighborhood or town.

What Do Kids Get from Place-Based Learning?

One of the reasons students drop out of school, physically or just mentally, is that they don't believe school means anything to anyone, except perhaps the teacher. And some teachers are so robotized by the relentless sameness of the job that even they don't seem to care. Taken from either point of view, it's hard to imagine getting yourself all in a lather, or even investing an earnest effort in, say, your ninety-seventh pop quiz. It simply doesn't matter. Whereas placed-based learning has protoplasm. It's a kinetic, continually morphing arena in which your students mix with preschoolers, war vets, decision makers, do-gooders, homeless people, charity workers, neighbors, nobodies, busy-bodies, protesters, and civic leaders. Working to expand a community garden or boycott the sale of imitation guns, students can see their direct, positive impact on the community, which confirms that they're valued contributors. Kids don't drop out when school delivers a message like that.

Many kids would drop out of their hometowns, too, if they could escape to some exotic clime. They dismiss their surroundings as too poor, too rural, too traditional, or too dull. Familiarity, lack of curiosity, and a scant amount of specific knowledge can make even a vibrant city seem laughable as a topic for serious investigation. In effect, ignorance alienates kids emotionally and intellectually from the place that should nurture and sustain them. But place-based learning creates an attachment that can last a lifetime. As students gain a feel for their town, they can appreciate its pleasures, examine the problems, and speculate about potential. Potential begs for action, so they can pitch in to help a worthy cause, or organize some blood-sweat-and-tears volunteering of their own. You could end up with a room full of activists who are educated, empowered, and engaged.

What About Resources?

In place-based learning, the community is one throbbing three-dimensional resource. Just outside your classroom door you can find elaborate demonstrations of science, sociology, engineering, politics, art, and anthropology in living color; and the built environment is a three-dimensional history lesson in itself. Museums and historic societies are obvious resources for learning about social studies, but pick any nursing home and you're sure to find people who can deliver oral histories that will have kids hanging on their every word. Two of my students took a video camera to a retirement center and came back with amazing stories about the era of giant roller coasters, told by two ninety-year-olds who shared their recollections with the giddy glee of kids with a handful of quarters.

Don't forget City Hall. You may think it's just for politicians, but no. It's a think tank full of experts who are also public servants. Every department has specialists, many of whom would kill for the opportunity to escape their offices and mix it up with a gaggle of inquisitive youngsters. In a quick tour of my city's website, I found contacts for an archivist, an arborist, an environmental scientist, meals-on-wheels, Heal the Bay, commissioners for the arts, architecture and landmarks, litter and debris removal specialists, homeless shelters, librarians, sustainable plants, affordable housing, animal shelter, ride sharing, visitor information, and voter registration—all potential resources for miniseminars in the field, or in your classroom.

What About Standards?

But you're worried about those tests—the lists and lists of skills or morsels of information your students are supposed to digest by the end of the year. Hopping on a city bus with your class may not look like a winning strategy for producing smarter kids or higher test scores. It may seem downright anarchistic. But fear not. When you decide to incorporate place-based explorations into your social studies program, your students will develop and demonstrate skills that are fundamental to a rigorous standards-based approach to social studies. The following list suggests the range of learning challenges students will face as they undertake a thorough exploration of the place they call home.

Students will:
- Demonstrate how to use maps and other geographic representations, tools, and technologies to acquire, process, and report information from a spatial perspective.
- Understand the history of the local community and how communities in North America varied long ago.
- Identify the people, events, problems, and ideas that were significant in creating the history of their community.
- Understand the physical and human characteristics of places.
- Describe the processes, patterns, and functions of human settlement.
- Apply geographic knowledge to interpret the past.
- Understand how to apply geography to interpret the present and plan for the future.
- Conduct research on issues and interests by generating ideas, formulating questions, and identifying problems that they can address.
- Gather, evaluate, and synthesize data from a variety of sources to communicate their discoveries in ways that suit their purpose and audience.

- Examine the role of local government to determine its purpose and most important functions.
- Develop historical research capabilities, including the ability to formulate historical questions, interrogate historical documents, and obtain historical data.
- Synthesize knowledge of an historic time and place from primary source documents to construct a story, explanation, or historical narrative.
- Create learning materials and opportunities so other students and adults learn about your community.

An Inspirational Footnote

I have an intense and abiding belief that place-based education not only promotes academic achievement but also contributes to long-term community development—that students who investigate the alleys and archives of their town with an eye toward improvement have the skills and motivation to be good stewards of their neighborhood and the environment. I realize you have to take that on faith, since you can't hit fast-forward to witness what your students may tackle in the decades after they leave your classroom. But let's take a look at one of the possible outcomes of place-consciousness—what it looks like when adult citizens understand the history of their town, and are motivated to fight for its well-being.

Saving Paducah from Itself

When the big shopping malls opened on the outskirts of Paducah, Kentucky, they dealt a near-fatal blow to Lower Town, the historic heart of the city. Like many small towns across the country, it might have succumbed but for a local artist with a sense of place that told him his blighted neighborhood was special and should be saved.

Lower Town had been placed on the National Register of Historic Places in 1982, but many of its historic houses had been left to deteriorate by negligent landlords. Mark Barone, a long-time resident, thought Lower Town had possibilities. It had good housing stock built in the Victorian, Italianate, Greek Revival, and Queen Anne styles. Barone had an idea—*The Artist Relocation Program*. It was simple, chic, and cheap. What if Paducah's city government and financial establishment could lure artists to become residents of the neighborhood? The hook? Buy a house for one dollar, fix it up, set up your studio and open your doors occasionally for public art walks.

Barone's proposal was deemed brilliant. The city gave him a salaried job, a small advertising budget, and Paducah now has sixty artists in residence in Lower

Town, an elaborate mural project along the riverfront, and a booming down-town that has become a magnet for mall-hating shoppers and art lovers. It's the fastest growing artists' colony in the country, thanks to a man with a vision and place-consciousness.

Awareness

Assessing Prior Knowledge About Your Community

Many kids have never thought about the fact that they live in a community. They don't have a clue that stop lights, libraries, playgrounds, mailboxes, even sewers and dumpsters are all part of an elaborate system created and maintained for the public benefit. If they're young, their experiences largely consist of home, school, and the back seat of a car. Seatbelted in, they experience the community as a blur from the window, with no interaction or narration. For older kids, the territory may expand to include a subway or school bus, city streets where one must be careful, a park or playground, the corner market, but it's a giant step to picturing the complex human machine that is a community, and a quantum leap to defining their role within that world. But that's where you're headed when you decide to use the community as your social studies classroom, so it helps to have a working definition of your new daytime address.

The goal of the Awareness stage of the learning cycle is to introduce your community as the topic, find out what your students already know about it, and peak their interest thereby transforming them from passive observers to eager explorers. The activities in this section raise awareness by encouraging your students to dredge up their prior knowledge, so they can feel smart before you ever hit the streets. As you flush out that information, you build an authentic foundation from which to launch the Exploration and Inquiry stages of the learning cycle.

You Are Here: Street Smarts

All students approach new learning tasks with rich funds of knowledge, and this is never more true than when you are talking about your community. Kids are tuned in to certain aspects of their town that escape adults—off-limits adventures in gloomy alleys, cyber anything, hobby stores, who has the best donuts and the most intriguing dumpsters. But have they ever consciously processed their observations, or had a conversation about the ways that they're street savvy? That's where you come in. Use the following questions to start a dossier on your town. Ask:

- What do you know about our town (city, neighborhood)?
- What's the most interesting part of our community?

- Who lives here? Who doesn't? Why?
- What kind of work do people do?
- What do people do for fun?
- What would you tell a first-time visitor about our town?

List all of their answers on the board. Tell students that all the information they provided is beginning to paint a picture of their community. Now pause and ask your students to consider the word *community*. What does it mean to them? Use the following questions to produce a beginning definition that you will revisit and refine over time. Ask:

- What do you think the word *community* means?
- What does a community need?
- What makes people want to live in a community?
- What discourages them?
- What words would you use to describe our community?

With older students, you might want to probe a bit deeper. Ask:

- Is a community just a physical space and the built environment or is there more to it?
- Is it everyone living within certain boundaries?
- Can a community be certain groups of people?
- Are there several different communities within our town? What are they?
- What does it take to belong to one of these communities?

Before and After Maps

Before you actually leave school to go exploring, ask your kids to draw a map of the school and the surrounding area, just using the images in their heads. This is a freehand creation. It's not scaled. It can be pictorial or symbolic, bird's-eye view or multiple perspectives. Some students may annotate their maps with words and symbols but that isn't necessary at this point. To prime the pump, ask them to think of places in the community that are important to them: school, where relatives and friends live, a favorite store, park, pond, movie theater, or bike trail. Encourage them to show the routes or pathways they use to get to these places.

When students are finished, display their maps so they can identify similar features but also appreciate the uniqueness of each. Make a mental note about what students include on their maps, what's ignored, what's prominent, and the level of detail. Assess their general familiarity with cartographic conventions, and specific geographic or man-made features of the community. They can revisit their maps after your first community walk to add details, or make changes based on their discoveries.

If you have students who are reluctant to draw anything, including maps, try this no-fail process. Rather than frightening them with paper and pencils, lure them with a dollop of shaving cream. Squirt a shot on their tabletops, and let them smear it around until they've created a silky, fragrant surface on which to experiment with map-making. If they make a mistake or change their minds, they can simply erase by smearing, and start over. Using this no-risk format allows kids to limber up and concentrate on the task, visualize their environment, remember details, translate spatial experiences into two-dimensional lines, make choices, and edit without worrying about the final product. Kinesthetic kids will be ecstatic. Perfectionists are liberated because it's impossible to get it wrong.

Waking Magoun's Brain: Curiosity Begins at Home

Now ask your students if there's anything they wonder or that puzzles them about your community. From the moment you ask that question, you're on your way to a great adventure. They may say things like *I wonder who made that statue in the park. I wonder how old the merry-go-round is. I wonder why we don't have a zoo. What's inside the observatory? Why is the rollercade closed?* One of my favorite responses in this category came from a first grader who asked with great sincerity, "What does the Hollywood sign say?" Their list may be short at first, but it's the starting point for your investigations and research. Post it in a prominent place and encourage your students to add more questions along the way.

A Peek at the Past

One of my favorite ways to stimulate curiosity about our town was to beguile my students with a gallery of old photographs. I live in a beach town with a long history of amusement piers, so I'd start with prints of roller coasters looking like x-rays of giant mountains and piers battered to a skeletal state by winter storms. There are men in high silk hats strolling on the boardwalk and overdressed ladies wading in the surf. You could also use posters or advertisements from any period in your town's history. Give your kids plenty of time to notice all the details, then ask some open-ended questions to launch the conversation. Here are some suggestions:

- What do you notice?
- Describe what you see.
- What people and objects do you see?
- What is the setting or season?
- What can you tell about the place and time when this was created?
- What do you think you would hear or smell if you were in this picture?

- Does it seem to be posed or candid?
- What does the picture make you wonder?
- What do you already know about this time period, place, or event?
- What can you conclude from what you see?
- Who or what seems to be missing from the photograph?

Ask students if their families have any old photographs of the town that they would like to share, including high school sports or class pictures, holiday celebrations, or family vacation shots. I try to photocopy any contributions and return the originals immediately.

Let Your Fingers Do the Walking

Another way to generate curiosity about your neighborhood is to bring in copies of the *Yellow Pages* or any of the other behemoth directories that pile up on your doorstep every few months. These hefty volumes represent a goldmine of community information. Most of them include local maps, pages of human resources, emergency information, and the advertisements for hundreds of businesses. Tear one apart and give each student three to five pages to inspect. Students are often surprised to discover that their town shelters a yachting club, exfoliators, tree surgeons, pushcart manufacturers, private detectives, and morticians. You'll get questions like, *What's a bail bondsman? An image consultant? What are occult supplies?* When they're finished browsing, ask a few questions of your own: *Where could I buy ice? What about bricks? How many magicians are in town? Do we have a large animal vet?* If you have access to city directories from forty or fifty years ago—or can photocopy old directories from the library archives, let your kids compare local businesses now and then. Ask them to figure out, *Which are extinct? Which have survived relatively unchanged, perhaps even retaining the same name and owners? Why?* The evolution of business can tell a lot about the history and economic life of your town.

Hometown Tourist

Do you ever wonder what tourists do when they visit your town? Drop by the tourist office or Chamber of Commerce and pick up some maps and brochures, then have your students do the research. They may be surprised to find behind-the-scenes tours of bakeries, the newspaper, fish market, farmers' market, dairy, lumber mill, or brewery. Rehearsals of the local symphony and star-gazing at the college planetarium are also possibilities. If you live in a large city, scoop up the commercial travel books in your library, read sections aloud, and put sticky notes on anything your students want to add to their community itinerary. Then use the maps to plan a walking tour or bus adventure.

Exploration

Discovering More About Your Community

If you really want your kids to examine the gears and levers that keep a community moving or condemn it to stagnation, you need to go exploring. Field trips are essential information-gathering excursions that announce to your students that there are many ways to learn. A close inspection of a construction site raises questions about stability, gravity, density, earthquake codes, zoning, lumber versus metal, skills, and careers. A guided tour of the community garden involves vocabulary development,

> *Anyone can look for history in a museum. The creative explorer looks for history in a hardware store.*
> —Robert Wieder

botany, sustainable environments, water cycles, ecology, and the link between farmer and consumer. Some students can learn more on a twenty-minute walk than during a whole morning squirming in their desks.

This was certainly true for that group of South Tucson ten-year-olds you met at the beginning of this chapter. The year was 1992. Their school was at the bottom of the heap in standardized achievement, yet the principal, teachers, and parents knew their kids were smart. Enter Dr. Paul Heckman and Dr. Viki Montera, researchers in the Education and Community Change Project (ECC). They were convinced that the students at Ochoa Elementary had knowledge, abilities, and interests that would translate nicely into some important learning, but so far that wasn't happening. So Dr. Heckman urged the teachers in the project to put down their textbooks just long enough to discover what fascinated their students. One teacher decided to take a leap of faith, which is how she and her kids ended up exploring in the neighborhood, inventorying trash-strewn lots, liquor stores, and abandoned houses that were havens for criminals.

Back in their classroom the students asked the blunt questions that adults, even their well-meaning teachers, tended to avoid. *Why are there so many liquor stores right down the street from our school? Where does all the trash come from and who keeps dumping it on the lot? What can we do to improve our neighborhood?*

It could have been a misery marathon, but instead of being discouraged, they'd found a

> *We shall not cease from exploration,*
> *and the end of our exploring will be to arrive where we started,*
> *and know the place for the first time.*
> —T. S. Eliot

cause. Students and adults in the community joined forces for a clean-up day, but soon the trash was as plentiful as ever. That's when the students decided that the only way to make progress was to adopt the lot and make it an extension of their classroom. "I invited my kids to write speeches to present to the Tucson City Council, pointing out that we should have the lot for educational purposes," reported Linda Ketcham. "That was on a Friday. On the following Monday, ten students returned to school with diagrams and speeches." Hence, the trip to City Hall.

Learning About Your Community by Exploring

The first time I took my students on a field trip, I returned to school with a headache the size of Montana and parts of Wyoming. The sense of responsibility was absolutely crushing, but with a bit of practice, community junkets became my favorite part of teaching. I looked forward to a day on the loose as much or more than my students. But the following are a few essential rules of the road that you must address before leaving. Take plenty of time to plan for success, get some comfortable shoes—and don't forget the ibuprophen.

1. *Where are we going?* Whenever possible, do a trial run alone to thoroughly consider your route and destination. What are the transportation issues? Is the area used to having kids as visitors? Do they need advanced warning? How long will the whole trip take? Don't forget to factor in time to stop, discuss, and collect data. An idyllic community walk becomes a punishment if you force-march your kids back to school in time for dismissal.

2. *Why are we going?* Have clear learning objectives in mind, and state them as questions to emphasize the investigative nature of your outing. For example, *How many kinds of transportation do we have in our community, who uses each, and why?* Every student should be able to explain the purpose of the trip and what they are expected to do, produce, research, collect, or observe.

3. *How will we gather information?* Students can use words, phrases, drawings, graphs, or sketches to collect data in their Explorer's Journals (see pages 142–43). You can also document with photos, audio or video recordings. If your students are very young, you may just have them observe, then debrief and record their impressions when you return to class.

4. *How will we be safe?* Be very explicit about safety rules, and warn students about any hazards they'll encounter. Take along plenty of adults and be sure they know that their role is to supervise, not play mommy-and-me or socialize with other parents while you keep thirty kids in line. Give the office your route and estimated time of return, so if you fail to turn up, they'll

know where to start the search. Take a cell phone and emergency contact numbers.

5. *What about permission?* Whenever you leave the confines of your school campus, you should have written permission from parents or guardians. Check with your administrator for specific requirements.

What's the Goal?

Announcing your learning goal distinguishes your social studies excursion from recess or hanging out at the mall with friends, and gives students clear expectations from the minute you depart. There are hundreds of solid reasons why you should sally forth, but here are some goal-setting questions that could frame your neighborhood outings.

- What types of businesses are in our neighborhood/town? What kinds aren't? Why?
- What types of entertainment? Where? Why?
- Where is the oldest section of town? What evidence of the past can still be seen? Who lives or works there? Why?
- Where is the newest part of town? What's going on there? Who lives or works there? Why?
- What kinds of public services can be seen? Where are they located? Why?
- What types of jobs are most people doing? Who's doing what?
- What kinds of architecture can we see?
- What's the explanation for the styles and locations?
- What problems can we see in our community? Who's in charge of finding solutions?

Scavenger Hunt

On any block in your town, there are hundreds of items to capture kids' attention— dog droppings, graffiti, a cloud of urine fumes wafting from a stairwell, a revealing underwear ad on a bus bench, or a decrepit telephone booth with the receiver dangling like an outlaw in a western movie. These discoveries fascinate, if only for the opportunity to groan and squeal. The same block embraces a cast-iron building façade in the Baroque style, the date June 1924 pressed in the sidewalk, a For Rent sign with data on prices in the housing market, the last barber pole twirling in your community, a cyber-cafe, a twenty-four-hour urgent care facility, and a library. Not to mention words, words, words: parking restrictions, shop signs, neon Don't Walks, newspaper headlines, movie marquees, and street names. Plus a thicket of numbers and symbols.

Kids can absorb an immense amount of valuable community information in a hundred yards, especially when their sensory gateways are wide open. Your challenge is to corral their attention, without curbing their impulse to explore. The solution? A scavenger hunt. Give your students a list of things you want them to search for as they amble along the sidewalk or gaze out the bus window. It could include fire departments, police stations, fire hydrants, libraries, clinics, banks, food stores, mailboxes, bookstores, parking signs, and anything else you want them to notice. Or you could organize the list by themes such as: things our taxes pay for, public safety items, social service venues, or recreation opportunities. If your focus is local history, challenge them to spot clues to the past—old buildings, dates on buildings or embedded in sidewalk, plaques, statues, monuments, or memorials. They check off the items that they spot, note their locations for mapping activities, or comment on unusual features. With a checklist and pencil in hand, kids spend their time visually scouring their environment, instead of kicking rocks or prospecting under a bus bench for small change.

After your walk, divide them into teams and have them compare their data, then have a whole-group discussion about what it means. For example, if students saw nine banks and no libraries, what might that mean? If they saw no grocery stores on the whole walk, what are the implications for older people who live in the area? Did they see a lot of police cars or very few? Were the streets in good condition or pot-holed? Is the area crowded with pedestrians or just cars? What does that say?

Documenting Discoveries

The following section describes five formats for collecting community data.

Community Explorer's Journal

Journals have long been havens for artists, naturalists, explorers, and inventors including Thoreau, da Vinci, Einstein, Darwin, and Lewis and Clark, as a place to record their observations and experiences, using words, sketches, diagrams, or graphs. But journals can also function as scrapbooks, containing articles from the newspaper, flyers, bits of informative trash, locations of buildings, names of people and landmarks, data on traffic jams, and or progress on graffiti removal projects.

Help your students understand that their Community Explorer's Journal is not a writing assignment. It's more like a backpack in which they stash images and ideas about things they see and think on their excursions—notes about smells, snatches of dialogue, funny signs, strange people. Words can mix freely with sketches and printed material like bus transfers—anything that helps them remember the details once they get back to the classroom. After each foray, encourage them to share their observations with a partner.

Since journals are personal, shouldn't they look unique? Instead of buying a case of blank notebooks or commercial journals, why not let your students design their own? Give them a few days notice about the journal-making project, and encourage them to bring in any materials they'd like to use. Journals don't need to be rectangles or even squares. They can be shaped like a bridge, a tennis shoe, a boat, or your famous lighthouse. The cover can be made of cardboard, cloth, tin, or wood. You provide the innards—plain or lined paper, scissors, glue, string, and staples. Add a pile of old magazines and colored paper for the covers. Talk a bit about the creative possibilities and then turn them loose. Here are a few more ways to collect community data.

Photography

Digital cameras are an excellent way to document your community investigations because the images can be used for websites, PowerPoint presentations, or downloaded as print material for classroom use. But disposable cameras are a great low-tech alternative. They're terrific for young students because they can be thoroughly manhandled and still take a decent picture. You can write on the outside of the box who's shooting what, and then ration the number of shots for each student. Photos make great conversation starters, provide graphic information for experience charts, or they can jump-start drawing projects. Glue a photograph in the center of a piece of paper and let students expand the image by adding what lay beyond the edge of the frame. The photo acts like the first piece in a puzzle, and they fill in the rest. For example, if you have a picture of passengers disembarking from a bus, they complete the drawing by adding the bus bench, street signs, the road, traffic, exhaust, and stop lights.

Videotaping

Videotaping is a documentary device that capitalizes on the skills of visual learners, challenging them to collect and organize ideas and images, write narratives or scripts, and speak persuasively. With a few technical cues and a good neck strap, they can collect dynamic data—footage of a congested intersection, the scene of an accident, farmers arriving at the weekly market, the holiday parade, the firehouse, interviews with experts, a dangerous corner near school, or a sign announcing the library restoration. Back in class, they can replay the tape to study images or transcribe testimony. Edited footage can provide evidence of problems or solutions when applying for grants, making presentations to the city council, petitioning funders, or launching a safety campaign. Students can present their information in on-camera commentaries, just like news reporters working on location, narrate off-camera or lay down sound tracks. Put together a team of visual, verbal, and interpersonal learners for this type of work. They can host screenings to teach other students or enlist their support. Students who catch the camera bug can log on to the Film Festival Watch List to find a wider audience for their work (www .withoutabox.net).

Audiotaping

Audiotapes are excellent for capturing oral histories or conducting man-on-the-street interviews to survey citizens about local problems and solutions. But here's another idea. Students with musical intelligence may be acutely sensitive to the sounds in your environment—anything from three-hundred-year-old church bells to the drone of freeway traffic. Construction noises, playground voices, concert music, the roar of the surf or a waterfall, the call of a foghorn or train whistle can be interspersed with their own narration to create a sound portrait of your community.

Experience Charts

If you are working with very young children, you're already familiar with the importance of being their scribe. Take a tape recorder along on your walks and stop periodically to record their comments and any interesting sounds—such as jackhammers or street cleaners—that will make interesting topics for discussion. Back in your classroom, ask them to describe the things that caught their attention or raised questions. Record their remarks on charts as graphically as possible, using a mixture of words, symbols, and sketches. Don't worry if you can't draw well—neither can they. Just stick with simple lines that capture the essence and add a splash of color. For example, if you saw a fire engine on your walk, draw a long rectangle, add two wheels and put a ladder on the side. With a splash of red, you're in business. Act confident and your kids will understand that this is just a symbol. Write the words *fire engine* next to the drawing to reinforce the concept that words are also symbols that represent ideas. Pictures help nonreaders and second-language learners follow the discussion, and access the information on the charts for subsequent conversations or project work. Everyone will be more attentive and engaged as they watch their thoughts take on a visible form.

Processing Explorations and Discoveries

Let's take a minute to consider one big difference between fresh-picked data from a community walk and textbook lessons. Equal opportunity. When you tour the neighborhood with your students, you level the playing field for subsequent lessons. All of your students have a shared experience, with you providing vocabulary, narration, emphasizing concepts, pointing out subtle details, and asking questions to make them think. All have a common core of information, with lots of visual impressions and ideas to take back to the classroom. This may be in marked contrast to classroom lessons that begin with a major gap between students—some of them have *no* prior knowledge and others have been on a half dozen trips with their families and have a small library of books at home. They're already well informed on the subject and ready to share.

The next challenge is extracting that material from your students to use for discussions and projects. But not all students are great talkers, so you need to invent multiple ways for them to demonstrate what they've learned while rubbernecking in the neighborhood. For example, using concrete objects such as blocks or stackable containers, students with strong visual, spatial, and kinesthetic intelligence can construct physical models of the neighborhood, or think with their hands about complex urban planning problems and solutions. The following activities encourage analysis of community data using maps, three-dimensional models, discussion questions, and writing prompts. But let's start with a graphic organizer—the Community Central bulletin board.

> *In Chicago I began my practice of urban tourism, which continues to this day. I wandered everywhere, walking for hours—took buses to the end of the line, just to see where they would go—prowled around strange neighborhoods—and studied maps of the city.*
>
> —Daniel Pinkwater, *Chicago Days, Hoboken Nights*

Community Central: Maps as Graphic Organizers

Each excursion beyond the playground adds to your inventory of information about the community: three bus benches, one new convenience store, ten For Sale signs, two new restaurants, seven newspaper boxes in three languages, one mailbox, seven fire hydrants, three video stores and a boarded up shoe store. Kids need time to digest and synthesize all this before they can articulate hypotheses and concerns. So you need to keep the data in front of their eyes. One solution is to post a big, clear community map on a bulletin board. Have students develop a set of symbols for city services, schools, libraries, retail stores, entertainment venues, names in the news, playgrounds and parks, and crimes listed in the paper. Flank the map with space where students post their questions or observations. Stick question marks on areas that are puzzling. Seeing the big picture is a real boon to students who excel in recognizing visual and numeric patterns. Pause periodically to let everyone study the map, analyze the data, and share their hunches about what it reveals. For example, *Where is the biggest concentration of fast-food restaurants? Gas stations? Apartments? What do you notice about the relationship between socioeconom-ics and housing patterns, the location of parks and services, the number and distribution of crimes? Where are most of the new building projects? Who is being unhoused in the process? Who will replace them? How will that change the community?*

There's No Place Like Home—Reading Maps

After a single field trip or a series of walks, give students a local map—talk to your Chamber of Commerce or visitors' center for free, visitor-friendly versions. You don't need a map for each student, but it's good to have one for three or four students, because map reading really is a contact sport. First encounters with maps can be daunting, like staring at the electrical diagram for Las Vegas, because even the simplest map has hundreds of words and numbers, symbols and colors scattered over a grid. Initially, students may not recognize a single element in this sea of information. Don't intervene. As their eyes swim and dart across the surface, they're reading, and fine-tuning visual discrimination and spatial-relations skills. Ask students to locate all the landmarks that are familiar: the school, their homes, parks, plus trace the route of your explorations. Eventually someone will sing out, "I found my street!" Several kids who live in the same neighborhood will flock to get their orientation. More discoveries will follow, and soon they're finger-traveling around the town. Now it's time to ratchet up their thinking by asking questions that combine observation, analysis, and logic. Here's a starter list.

- What do you notice about the shape of the city border?
- Find the natural landforms in our city—bluffs, islands, valleys, hills.
- Describe the pattern that was used to design our town? Grid? Natural contours? Central square? Riverfront strip? If you have students from other countries, ask them if their cities look the same. How are their cities arranged?
- Are the city blocks long or short? What is the effect on people? Traffic?
- What are the major streets? Which way do they run? Why do you think that's the case?
- Which streets are wide? Which narrow? Why?
- Is our town foot-friendly? Can people walk easily and safely to get the things they need?
- Where are the public gathering places?
- What transportation systems are indicated on the map?
- Does the map give clues about which neighborhoods are more prosperous?

Tablecloth Topography

Maps can be very deceptive. Mountains, ravines, mesas, and foothills are all reduced to the topographic equivalent of Iowa. This world-is-flat perspective may

146

be totally out of synch with the actual landscape of your town. Who hasn't set off on a short hike, only to discover that it was a grueling two hours toiling up terrain better suited for mountain goats? What if your town is rumpled with hills or cascading down the side of a mountain? These topographic features have a significant influence on the character, layout, and functioning of a town. So invite your students to make a three-dimensional model of the local topography, using common classroom objects, recycled materials, and cloth. Here's how it works. Clear off a large table or space on the floor. Give your kids tablecloths, towels, cloth remnants, ribbon or yarn, buttons, small blocks, tissue boxes, milk cartons, and polystyrene containers. Ask them to use the materials to make a three-dimensional map of where they went and what they saw. For example, if your town is nestled in a valley, kids can stuff books, towels, or boxes under the table-cloth to make the hills. Ribbons or yarn can indicate streets, streams, or rivers. Found objects can represent buildings or bridges. With very little preparation, students can re-create and study your town, and when you're done, it disappears in a matter of minutes.

Paper Bag Mapping

Another three-dimensional approach to mapping lets students create the buildings they saw on their walks using paper bags of various sizes. Working from memory, photographs, books, or their journal sketches, they transform the bags into specific buildings, drawing doors, windows, and signs. Now clear some floor space and have them arrange their bag buildings to make a three-dimensional model of the town. They may need to grid off the streets with chalk or tape to get their bearings. This activity requires considerable cognitive effort, particularly in the areas of memory, visualization, and estimating scale and distances. Language and social skills also get a workout, as students negotiate placement of their buildings and adjust the map. Future engineers and urban planners can lead the way. When you're finished, pin the bags onto a bulletin board to create a relief map of the town, or fold them up and re-use them to work out urban planning problems. For example, your kids can redesign their city putting schools near parks for shared green space, creating auto-free zones, or clustering businesses at the perimeter to decrease traffic. They can pose and solve some very high level urban problems with a single set of bag buildings.

Writing Activities

Writing is a lot more fun when kids are brimming with fresh sensory impressions, so you may want to link your writing curriculum to your community studies and focus on sharpening observation skills and descriptive writing. Have some fun with topics such as, *smells in the city, what I saw in the gutter, who's who at the bus stop, my favorite place in town, if I could live anywhere in town, if I was mayor, I'd. . . .* Students can also write about their concerns: *What scares me about my community, what makes me sad, what's ugly, who needs help, what needs to be changed?*

A Day in the Life of City Furniture

After a community walk, ask your kids to imagine that they're a piece of street furniture—a bus bench, bus shelter, streetlight, trashcan, stop sign, mailbox, fire hydrant, crosswalk, parking meter, or billboard. Encourage them to describe what they see, feel, smell, and hear all day and night, in various seasons. Remind them that these objects overhear lots of conversation fragments as pedestrians pass by, and including these snippets of dialogue will add life to their writing.

 ## Inquiry

Digging Deeper into Your Community

The Awareness and Exploration activities gave your kids a working knowledge of their neighborhood. Now they're poised to discover the wealth of information that can be coaxed out of a photograph, a city council agenda, blueprints of an historic building, a demolition permit, or a lively octogenarian. It's time to focus and dig deep to resurrect your town's past or explore its contemporary structures. This inquiry work is driven by the questions: *What else do I want to know about my community?* and *How do I find out?* The activities in this section are predicated on two beliefs:

1. That students construct new knowledge—meaning, they learn—when they are actively engaged in grappling with, discovering, experiencing, or manipulating something of personal interest; and
2. That authentic work, which impacts and improves the community, is the best preparation for life beyond school.

There are dozens of potential questions that you could use as the starting point for an in-depth community investigation, all of which can yield rich adventures. You just need to decide what's the best fit for your learning goals, and take full advantage of the unique resources of your community. This inquiry section suggests three different inquiry approaches that can be modified to meet your needs.

The Used-to-Be Community: Exploring local history is a standard part of the social studies curriculum in every state. It includes history, geography, biography, economics, ethnic studies, and local heritage focusing on high-interest people, places, and events in the past. It's a particularly relevant and fertile area of investigation if your students have deep roots in the community, or are recent immigrants who will appreciate stories of people in the past who arrived, stayed, and built your town.

The Built Environment: If you are fortunate enough to live in a town with centuries of intact architecture, consider the built environment as your focus of investigation. Looking at urban planning, the physical origins of the town, architectural styles, historic buildings, zoning, housing, and the future of the town provides a very tangible structure for social studies investigations.

Contemporary People and Problems: If your town is struggling with environmental and human issues that impact your students and their families, this may be the most relevant direction to take. Looking at social systems, the infrastructure, the natural resources and environment, government, power, and the political process in your town teaches students the importance of public participation and the power of individual voices, whether they belong to children or adults.

Getting Smarter About the Used-to-Be Community

Somewhere in town, maybe squeezed into a storefront or tucked in the basement of City Hall, you have an historic society—and that's a lot more fun than it sounds! The one in my town has a stiff-spined schoolmarm who scolds naughty visitors and a Pioneers' picnic with carriage rides, antique cars, and storytellers. Your historic society is a portal to places that used-to-be and little-known local landmarks. The docents and enthusiasts who run it may lead tours of historic homes or publish a brochure for self-guided adventures, so your class can meander around town to find the original stagecoach depot or the first film studio. A closer look may even uncover traces of their ancestors. Here are some ideas for planning instruction and encouraging student investigations of the used-to-be community.

Potential Topics for Investigation

- Pastimes in times past—what did adults and kids do for fun?
- Local artists, writers, or musicians
- One-room schools
- Local holidays and celebrations
- Folklore and heritage studies
- Local historical research
- Famous storms and natural disasters in our town
- Native Americans who lived here before the town was established
- Famous people in your community
- Founders of the town
- My family's history in this town

- Immigrant stories
- Our town during various wars
- Our town in the seventeenth, eighteenth, and nineteenth centuries

Guiding Questions

- Who were the first people living in this area?
- What did they do to survive?
- Who came next?
- Did people arrive in groups or as individuals?
- Where did they come from?
- Why did they come?
- How did our town get its name?
- Who named it? Has it always been called this?
- Who are the notable people in our town's history?
- What resources attracted people? Do they still exist?
- Who lives here now? Who doesn't?
- How has the population changed?
- What was the racial and ethnic make-up of our community in the past? How has it changed? What caused the changes?
- What was our town like in the seventeenth, eighteenth, and nineteenth centuries and how has it changed?

Resources

Books on local and regional history, the historic society, photo archives, oral histories, Internet history and census sites, archives maintained by the school district, fire or police departments, university, natural history museums, the public library or city hall, fraternal organizations, and other local agencies that have their own archives are all great resources to find the answers you need.

Activities

The following activities help students dig into community history using primary source documents, artifacts, local experts, and their own investigative initiative.

Community Lifespan Time Line

Talking about your community in historic terms challenges students to consider the idea that for hundreds, even thousands of years, people have been born, labored, and died in the very spot where they go to school or play soccer. Some families may have lived in the same houses, passing property and jobs down through several generations. This activity begins with a single question: *When did our town start?* I used a ream of old-style computer printer paper to make a time line that would help my students visualize continuity and change in our town. But you can also use butcher paper or rolls of kitchen shelf paper. Mark off the decades and centuries and post it so students can get close enough to add information and study the accumulating data. At first it will be empty, except for a marker on the date when the town was founded. Each time your kids uncover an important event or person in the town's history, they can draw a picture and glue it on the time line with explanatory notes. The time line helps visual and spatial learners grasp the sequence and patterns of events over time. To emphasize a broader context, put milestones in your community history above the time line and significant happenings in the United States or internationally below.

First Nations

The town of Deerfield, Massachusetts, has a collection of authentic buildings nestled along a 330-year-old street. Yet this venerable old village is just a pup in the long life of this plot of ground. The fields surrounding Deerfield have been under continuous cultivation for ten thousand years. So in a sense, the community's history starts in 8000 BC. But many community history units begin and end with written history—white people history—taking a tabula rasa approach to everyone who hunted, tilled, and revered the land for centuries before the first saloons, stables, and boarding houses sprang up. When you're thinking about the story of your community, take the long view. Devote time to uncovering the deep roots of your town by asking:

* Who were the Native Americans that lived in our area before the town was established?
* How did they live? What did they eat?
* What were their beliefs and cultural practices?
* When did they leave the area and why?
* Are any of their descendants still living in the area?

If you can find any tribal descendants, invite them to meet with your students and share artifacts, cultural practices, and stories. Check with your local natural history museum for information or artifacts and log on to 500 Nations (www .500nations.com) for specific tribal information.

The Founding Fathers and Mothers

Once you establish the Native American heritage of your area, try to identify the next wave of occupation. Ask:

* Who came after the Native American inhabitants?
* Who started the present community?

- Where did they come from? Why?
- What was it about the location or the landscape that might have attracted them (access to water, rich soil, mountains for protection, minerals, rivers, or the sea for trade)?
- If the founders of your town could see it today, what do you think would be the most surprising to them?

Family Roots Survey

Have a discussion with your students about family roots in the community. Some students will know every relative back to the Mayflower, some won't, and a few students who are adopted or in foster care may not know their families at all. So you need to be sensitive to your definition of *family* and very understanding if students can't participate in this activity. Touch on the idea that some families move often, while others have lived in the same community for decades or even generations. Ask students to do an informal survey at home to get a picture of their family's history in your community. You may ask questions, such as:

- When did you first come to our community?
- Who came first? Parents, grandparents, great grandparents?
- Where did they come from?
- Why did they come?
- How did they get here?
- What did they do when they settled? Jobs? Business? Farming? Fishing?

Students can use words or photos to indicate their family's arrival on the community time line, along with any interesting history they uncovered. You may discover that a student's family is fourth generation in your town, with a ninety-five-year-old grandmother who tells great stories. That's a primary source treasure.

Back to the Future

It's easier for kids to think about your community in *then and now* terms if they have some pictures to get them started. So consider paying a virtual visit to the past via the archives of your local newspaper. If you can't access papers printed in years past online, pay a visit to the office of the newspaper, or look at microfilm, microfiche, or CD-ROMs at the local library. Teach your students how to do basic archival research, then ask them to find the newspaper printed on the day that they were born and see what was going on in town. Ask:

- What were the headlines? Who was in the news?
- What were some other stories of interest?
- What seems to be the same about then and now? What's different?

- Look at advertisements to see how the prices of commodities such as gas, bread, or milk have changed over the years.
- Compare rents and housing prices with the present.

Living Archives

One of the most vivid and personal ways to collect details about life in the past is to locate people who've lived in your community for a long time. The obvious resources are your students' relatives, retirement homes, senior citizens' clubs, the Rotary or Elks Club, and the volunteers at the Historic Society. Invite these living archives to your classroom. Ask them to share stories and artifacts from their childhood and life in your town. If they have photos, scrapbooks, maps, or newspapers, ask if you can make copies or scan them into your computer to build your own archives. Have your students prepare a list of questions in advance and think about ways to accurately record the answers they get. You can also arrange to meet people at local landmarks or go to the local retirement home to interview residents about their experience living in your town. If you decide to delve deeply into individual stories, your students could write biographies of the people they meet.

Rewriting History

Review all of your research and then have students pick an era or year or even a single event that fascinates them. Tell them that they're going to write a newspaper as if it was written during that time period. First, they'll need to identify all the news items, topics, events, and advertisements that should be included to give it authenticity. Then they get down to writing. Division of labor allows many students to participate by contributing their strengths as writers, illustrators, layout designers, and editors. If you're doing computer editing and layout, pick a typeface that's consistent with the period. When the newspaper is complete, distribute it to other students in your school or grade level.

Getting Smarter About the Built Environment

Wandering in a well-built city can be one of the transporting delights of community-based learning. Spying a distant steeple, penetrating the gloom of a colonial tavern, hugging the cool marble columns of a bank, gaining an aerial view from the seventieth floor of a glittering skyscraper—these are sensory experiences that can't be captured paging through a book. Every town, no matter its size or age, has structures that hold valuable clues to its past, present, and future. An abandoned Main Street may indicate a moribund economy, or a robust business center that's moved to the edge of town to capitalize on cheap, abundant farmland. Mills become condominiums; storefronts house schools. The built environment is a brick-and-mortar text about your community, *if* you teach your kids how to read it. Here are some ideas for planning instruction and encouraging student investigations of the built environment.

Topics for Investigation

* Regional architecture
* Bridges, tunnels, canals, levees
* A lighthouse
* Historic buildings or neighborhoods
* One particular building—the tallest, the oldest
* Religious structures
* "Green" environmentally sensitive buildings
* Schools
* Prominent architects
* Architectural follies
* The history of the pier, speedway, cathedral, high school, canal, opera house

Guiding Questions

* Where was the center of town? Has that changed?
* Why did building start there?
* What are the oldest buildings in town?
* What do the old buildings tell about our town's past?
* How are old buildings protected? Who is in charge of preservation?
* What's the most famous building in town?
* Who designs the new buildings in our town?
* What rules do they have to follow? Building codes? Height limitations? Density?
* Why are certain kinds of buildings clustered in one area?
* How has architecture changed over the past century? Why?
* What kind of buildings do we need? Are they being built?
* What is the future of the built environment in our town?

Resources

Photographic archives provide the most detailed, user-friendly sources of information about the built environment, particularly the evolution of architectural styles and the story of particular buildings or plots of land. Photographically you can witness a corner morph from stable, to saloon, to restaurant, to vacant lot until it is crowned with a twenty-story apartment building with underground parking, all through photos. The real estate section of your local newspaper is an encyclopedia of contemporary styles, trends, and prices. A close reading hints at areas of economic depression, gentrification, and expansion. Your city's website has information on most of the previous questions listed, including experts in many departments who are available to the public. Look for announcements of meetings by the Planning and Zoning Department, Architectural Review Board, and Landmarks Commission. These are public meetings. Anyone—including students—can attend. But you can also download agendas, minutes, municipal codes, and updates on construction projects, such as bridges, highways, and airports.

Activities

Learning to Look

The first challenge is getting your students to actually *look* at buildings. That may sound obvious, but buildings are so ubiquitous that we often notice little more than the doorknob, even when entering structures that are strikingly beautiful or uniquely designed. Your students will start to notice the architecture around them when you start asking questions, like the following:

- Why do you think this was built?
- How was it built? Why did the builders use these materials?
- Who was the architect? Did he or she do other buildings in town?
- What was it originally used for? Has that changed?
- Who lived or worked here in the past? Who does now?
- Has it been physically altered?
- Should old buildings be preserved?
- How might they be used in the future?

Once you start really looking at buildings, students develop preferences—they like the sleek glass skyscrapers or weathered wooden barns. Encourage them to compile a list of adjectives to describe the characteristics that appeal to them: *curving, plain, textured, tall, fancy, austere, open, chunky, squat, elegant, slender*, or *airy*. Help them learn the names of the architectural elements: *columns, porch, turret, gables, cornices, attic, pavilion, eaves, brackets, cupola, shingles, siding, portico* and *pediment*, just for a start. Make a list and add to it whenever they discover a new element. Then go to the Architeacher website (www.architeacher.org) and click on Architecture and Aesthetics to find more about architectural styles. Your kids can see a beautiful slideshow of buildings from a humble log cabin to a Georgian mansion, with excellent text that puts the buildings in their historic and social contexts. The site also offers more ideas about community planning, teaching tips, and model programs.

Expert Eyes

If there's an architect, an architectural historian, or a preservation architect in your neighborhood, ask him or her to visit your class and take your students through the basics of reading blueprints, building codes, architectural styles, sustainable buildings, environmentally sensitive materials, and the latest advances in green building design. Perhaps this person could lead a walking tour through an architecturally diverse area, pointing out styles, periods, use of materials, and trends in development or renovation.

Mapping Change

If you can get your hands on some older maps of your town, your students can see how times have changed. Let them study the vintage and contemporary maps side by side to determine, *What's the same? What's changed? Is your town larger or smaller? What areas grew and why?* While you're on the subject of community change, don't miss the chance to introduce the classic story, *The Little House* by Virginia Burton (1943). It chronicles the changes that engulf a small house as the open countryside is devoured by a city. In the end, the house is rescued, refurbished, and carted back out to the country. Two other great titles—*The Wump World* (1974) and *Farewell to Shady Glade* (1966) by Bill Peet deal with change and how people and animals are displaced. These stories have a strong environmental message that really resonates with kids. You could also take your kids on a virtual visit to the website of the Landscape Change Program (www.uvm.edu/perkins/landscape) where they can examine the work of Vermont K–16 students who are contributing to an online archive of historical and modern photos of Vermont documenting human interaction with the land.

What's Up with Zoning?

Building in a city is not a freelance activity, although it may feel like it when you're caught in a detour around your sixteenth construction site of the day. Every city has codes—rules—for where buildings can and can't be, how big, how close together, even how much light they can emit or reflect. The Disney Concert Hall in Los Angeles, designed by Frank Gehry, had to be draped in synthetic dulling nets because reflections from the shiny surface were overheating—not to mention blinding—nearby condominium dwellers.

Ask students to use maps, directories, and firsthand observations to analyze what types of buildings are near the school, prompting them with questions, such as:

- What's next door?
- What's not close by? Why?

- How far do we have to go to find a restaurant, a bookstore, a gas station, a laundromat, a fire station, and a shoe store?
- Why are things located where they are?
- Do you think you can build a skatepark or a liquor store anywhere?
- Can a kennel be next to a hospital?
- What about the locations of plant nurseries and preschools?
- Who decides what goes where?

Help students find zoning information on your city's website or call City Hall and ask for the zoning department. There may be someone that your students can visit on a trip to City Hall or who would be a guest expert in your class.

No-Fault Architectural Drawings

Nearly every class harbors a clutch of phobics who swear they can't draw, but almost anyone can—especially when it comes to drawing buildings. You can cure the skeptics in your class, even if you can't paint a wavy line with a wet mop. The keys to success are visual analysis and baby steps. That's easier than it sounds. To start, give your kids some low-grade paper and a pencil. Now ask them, "Can you draw a square?" Expect a few kids to look at you like you're an idiot, but on the whole you should get compliance. Keep going. "How about a circle? A little triangle? A straight line? Diagonal?" Most likely you'll have a 100 percent success rate, and can actually see the neurosis beginning to recede. Now you tell them, "That's all you'll need to know if you want to draw any building, including the ones we'll see out in the community." Now here come the baby steps. "But today we're just going to go look for interesting doors and windows." Setting such a specific topic narrows their visual focus so kids really pay attention to details. It's simple, so they don't feel overwhelmed. They'll only need those straight lines you already practiced, so their confidence grows, and slowly you begin to dismantle that stereotypic house that seems to be stamped into kids' heads at birth—a small square box topped with a triangle roof, a red chimney clinging at a forty-five degree angle, leaking a wiggle of smoke.

Now grab your clipboards—just a piece of cardboard and a large clip—and head down the street. You're just sketching doors and windows, so stop in front of the first interesting building you see and have students look—just look. Encourage them to use words to describe the shapes they see—that's visual analysis—before they draw. Help them notice that a door is sitting snuggly inside a frame. Windows, too. Have them count how many lines they'll need to draw for a frame or threshold. Keep on collecting down the street. Exclaim over unique examples. Praise efforts, excellent lines, and astute observations. On another day, repeat the process, just looking at rooflines. Your kids will discover a clutter of interesting stuff—chimneys, TV antennae, vents, shingles, rain gutters, down-spouts, and decorative plasterwork. Or you can focus on steps, porches, siding, and sidewalks. After each trip, post all the drawings in your classroom and let your students walk around and study them. They'll begin to appreciate the rich details in a simple building, and recognize the distinct drawing styles of their peers.

When they're sufficiently confident, let them choose one section of a build-ing and go after all the details: doorbells, mailboxes, building numbers, windows or peepholes in the door, doorknobs, latches, and keyholes. By this time, their eyes will be as sharp as their pencils, so your job switches to cheerleading. Later they can add color with watercolor washes, marking pens, or colored pencils. Create a small gallery exhibition and invite other classes to browse the collection.

Getting Smarter About Contemporary People and Problems

The outdoors used to be the place where kids played, but there's been such seri-ous encroachment by development, compression of housing, overcrowding, crime, and pollution, that many kids live in a world the size of their living room, with television as a lifeline. This may be one reason why many Americans feel so little connection to the land or their communities, and consequently lack a sense of civic caring and responsibility. You can reconnect your kids to their commu-nities by focusing on—rather than ignoring—civic problems. They're a perfect topic for students who, in less than a decade, will be the stewards of our environ-ment, since place-based inquiry gives them a chance to practice. In the process, they can have a surprising amount of influence on local issues. It's not easy work. They'll need to do their homework and organize. Some of their investigations will take them down blind alleys. They might ruffle some civic feathers or get disen-chanted by politicians who say one thing and do another. There will be hard ques-tions and possibly some movement toward solutions, but I guarantee they will learn indelible lessons that could benefit your community for years to come. Here are some ideas for planning instruction and encouraging student investigations of contemporary people and problems.

Topics for Investigation
- Environmental concerns: wetlands and dunes restoration, migratory bird protection
- Pollution: water, air, soil, noise, sewage treatment and runoff
- City government
- Citizen participation
- Airport expansion, homeless shelters
- Law enforcement and crime
- Education: schools quality, maintenance, overcrowding, and closing

- Recycling
- Greenspace versus development
- Transportation systems
- Waterways and maritime features
- Sustainable water and power systems
- Manufacturing and business
- Taxation

Guiding Questions

- How does our city work?
- What problems does it have?
- How do people come up with solutions?
- Who gets to decide what gets done? Who doesn't?
- What fascinates me about the community?
- Where does our city get our water? Where does it go?
- Where does all that stuff we recycle go?
- What do our city taxes buy?
- How much do we pay to have a police department?
- Why do we have parking meters in some sections of town but not others?
- Why do we have homeless people in our neighborhood?
- Who is supposed to take care of problems?
- What impact does the growing population have on the location—pollution, depletion, or destruction of resources?

Resources

Your city's website should have postings on most of these topics, including experts in many departments who are available to the public. There are regular online postings of any group conducting public meetings including the city council, commissions, or publicly funded agencies. You can download agendas, minutes, municipal codes, updates on improvement projects, job listings, and bus routes. The daily newspaper and archives are the most detailed, user-friendly sources of local information. Consider online census information and websites maintained by the Chamber of Commerce and the school district.

Activities

How Does a City Work?

It's easy to criticize municipalities for being unresponsive or dysfunctional, but it's important that students also appreciate the complexity of all the things that we take for granted every day. A great place to start is to think of the city as a very complex and delicate machine, with hundreds of visible and invisible components that make it work. Locate a copy of *Underground* by David Macaulay (1976), in which he takes curious readers on a journey through a city's infrastructure—subways, sewers, telephone and power systems, columns, cables, building foundations, and other networks. The book includes cross-sections of systems that exist underneath the surface and explains how it all works. Or visit the *How Stuff Works* website (www.howstuffworks.com/), to discover more about how many things in a city work including skyscrapers, hydroelectric plants, bridges, snow-blowers, water towers, and roller coasters. Budding civil engineers can get lost in a site like this.

Community Questionnaire

If your students are intent on investigating problems in the city, they can create a questionnaire to determine which problems affect or concern most citizens—homelessness, air pollution, traffic, few health services, meager libraries with limited open hours, poor bus service, de facto segregation. This is no easy feat. Crafting effective questions that elicit reliable data requires analysis, wordsmithing, and rewriting. But homegrown surveys allow students to tailor the data they collect to their exact research needs. Here are some questions to use as a starting point.

- When did you come to this community?
- Where did you come from?
- Why did you choose to come here?
- If you had to choose again, would you still come here or go somewhere else? Why?
- If you were born here, why did you decide to stay?
- What concerns do you have about our community?
- What improvements have you seen in our community?
- What has not improved? What needs more action?
- What is the best thing about this community?
- What's the biggest problem?

After parents and other interested adults complete the surveys, and the data is tallied, the big challenge is interpreting what it means. Then students can decide on a plan of action.

Inquiry Using the Newspaper

Another important way to monitor people and problems in the community is to become devoted newspaper readers. Think of your local newspaper as a research laboratory, crammed with community information that's fresher than gourmet greens. It's cheap, which is a plus when budgets are tight. If your town has a free throw-away paper, every kid in your class can have his or her very own copy. *Free* means just that—you can snatch thirty copies from the newspaper box without feeling guilty. Kids feel grown up when they're reading the newspaper because they're mimicking adults. And they're developing the newspaper habit, which can ultimately help them be informed citizens and voters, as well as more effective community activists. And lest you should overlook the obvious, they're reading. Real-life reading. Words, sentences, and ideas in their natural habitat. And thanks to the photos, the content is readily accessible to visual learners who are still building reading skills. So every minute your students spend with a fistful of newsprint is literacy time, pure and simple. Plus, since kids want to prowl through the newspaper, their motivation is higher, their brain more activated, and they're reading at a higher level for personal satisfaction. That's an association that you can't reinforce often enough.

What Gets into the Newspaper?

Here's the big question your kids should learn to ask whenever they're reading the newspaper: *Why is this news? Why does a fire make the front page but beach clean-up is buried in the back?* This is how your kids get to be media savvy, one article at a time. Scan the local newspaper regularly and put a colored push-pin or a paper flag on the Community Central bulletin board to identify locations of news stories. Then analyze the stories for patterns or concentrations. *Are there more pins in the high-end or poorer neighborhoods?* Cut out the articles and post them around the map with a piece of yarn linking the article to the neighborhood. *What types of stories are concentrated in which areas? Are there some neighborhoods that never show up in the news?* Rank the neighborhoods by the number of times they appear in the news, then try to come up with explanations for the data. At the end of each week or month, take the stories down and keep them in a notebook that becomes a new archive. Ask students to figure out how to organize the clippings.

Virtual Field Trips

Most cities, towns, and even little hamlets have an official city website. Log on and you'll find a menu of tantalizing and sometimes provocative topics as a starting point for your investigations. For example, I logged on to mine and it appears that on this day, the city fathers are serving up cold turkey to citizen smokers. Take a look.

City's New Outdoor Smoking Law Goes into Effect on Thanksgiving Day
The Third Street Promenade, ATM and movie lines, bus stops and other outdoor locations will soon be off-limits to smokers. Specifically, smoking is prohibited on: public

beaches, Santa Monica Pier (except designated areas), outdoor dining and bar areas, within 20 feet of any entrance, exit or open window to a public building, waiting areas (bus stops, ATMs, kiosks, movie lines, etc.) and Farmers Markets. (www.smgov.net)

That single item could lead to heated discussions about public versus private rights, municipal laws, and enforcement. You know your kids will have opinions, which is a great starting point for research and dialogue with local legislators via email, fax, and phone. On your town's website you'll find a menu or search function to help students explore where they live online. For example, the website for my town lists: construction on streets, the latest budget news, disaster preparedness, a full calendar of community events, tree removal plans, and news on Coastal Clean-Up Day. If you don't have Internet access in your classroom, download and print out the website content and use it as research material in class.

A Visit to City Hall

Students can get a glimpse of local lawmaking and even influence the process at City Council meetings. The public's welcome any time, but try to attend when there's a kid-oriented issue on the agenda—restrictions on rollerblading, curfew for teens, expanding soccer fields, for example. Agendas are posted the day before online, in the newspaper, at the library or outside City Hall. Living in a democracy means you can sit and observe or speak your mind in an attempt to influence the process. If your kids decide to go public with their ideas, they'll need to fill out a chit and wait to be called. After stating their name and address they'll have two to three minutes of air time. Kids rarely speak at public meetings, so city officials tend to sit up and take notice when a junior citizen takes the podium. It's a great civics lesson.

Action

Using Knowledge About Your Community

The first time I decided to do a serious study of local history with my students, I headed for the main library, eager to start my research. Thirty seconds into the card catalogue, I knew I was in trouble. There was exactly one children's book on Santa Monica history. Publication date—1934. After leafing through its yellowing pages and grainy photographs, all I could think was—eBay, rare book section. Classroom consumption? Only with kid gloves. In the sixty-five intervening years since its publication, the pier had been destroyed and rebuilt four times, the population swelled by fifty thousand and we elected our first woman mayor, but no one had bothered to update the story for kids.

Nonetheless, it didn't occur to me at the moment that my students could or should write a new edition of Santa Monica history. I was actually a newcomer to the town with a lot to learn, so at first I was content just to explore. I had an old plaid tin full of bus tokens on my desk and permission to roam, so my students and I prowled the neighborhoods prospecting for traces of the past. We found a cluster of historic buildings, including a squat brick structure that had been a stable, a saloon, and the first movie studio in town. We had a guided tour of City Hall, interviewed the Harbor Patrol stationed on the pier, took a spin on the 1924 merry-go-round and raided the shelves of a library built by Andrew Carnegie when he diverted his oil millions to philanthropy. We became regulars at the Historic Society and had front row seats at plenty of city meetings. In the classroom, we scoured tract maps, demolition permits, zoning ordinances, architectural drawings, the city's master plan, and local history books borrowed from the adult shelves of the library.

But our most compelling resources by far were people. I was amazed at how many citizens were willing to spend a morning fascinating thirty eager kids. We interviewed anyone with family roots in the community or personal experiences that could shed light on how our town came to be. We visited with a Native American woman who traced her roots back one thousand years to the Tongva Tribe, who inhabited a huge village on the site of our local high school. She arrived laden with artifacts, stories, and songs to give my students a glimpse of the first culture in our area. Then there was a man who came bearing his father's towering metal fireman's helmet, circa 1901. His ancestors held one of the original Spanish land grants in the area before their rancho was subdivided and sold off to developers. We spent a morning with the first African American mayor of the city, a historic preservation architect, and a local historian. We were mesmerized.

Eventually my students concluded that our small city—just eight square miles—had some fascinating stories to tell, as well as some dark periods that deserved to see the light. They were leaking local history out of every pore. We couldn't take a bus ride or stroll to the library without someone gesturing wildly toward a plaque on an old building or recognizing for the first time the origin of a familiar street name. The resource table in our room groaned under the weight of documents, photographs, and city reports. It was time for a new edition of city history for kids—and they were just the ones to write it.

Writing and Rewriting History

When my students decided to write their version of local history, the initial challenge was to translate all their sleuthing and enthusiasm into a coherent, readable, and appealing story for their peers. It was moderately daunting to contemplate the scale of this enterprise, but we just approached it as one more adventure—take the first step and see what happens. Since this was a whole-class project, I wanted all of my kids—not just the budding writers—to be involved in its creation, so I devised a low-tech approach to outlining the book that was highly visible and accessible to everyone.

The Bones

First, we needed to build the skeleton of our story. We brainstormed all the big ideas in the history of the town, and I listed them on the board in whatever order they emerged. Eventually we'd exhausted the essential topics and moved on to sequence. After a short debate, we settled on a chronological, almost archaeological approach, and numbered all the items on the board—creating a working table of contents. From prehistory to the present, it featured chapters on the Tongvas, Spaniards, missions, ranchos, colonizing, the growth of business and the tourist trade, African Americans, pastimes, childhood, architectural styles, changes, and secrets. Then I covered two long chalkboards with butcher paper, and drew vertical lines about two feet apart, creating a column for each chapter. With a topic crowning each column, we plunged into another round of brainstorming to divvy up the content: details, dates, names of experts, juicy tidbits, and memorable events. We worked on this for days, until they'd emptied their heads and the butcher paper was black with ideas. The bones were in place.

The Flesh

Now came the hard work—writing. Students volunteered for the chapters they wanted to write, forming teams of writers, illustrators, and an editor responsible for getting the team across the finish line with a terrific story to show for their labors. Using the butcher paper skeleton as their road map, they talked, argued, negotiated, and began to write. Their challenge was to weave a mountain of facts—plus dozens of priceless quotations they'd stockpiled from their interviews—into a mesmerizing tale that would throw the past into sharp relief. Like all serious writing, it was exciting and frustrating and a labor of love.

Their most original contribution to local history was the chapter examining the little-known story of segregation in Santa Monica. They included photos of *Whites Only* signs at the beach and noted that the Crystal Plunge swimming pool was off-limits to African Americans six out of seven days during the summer season. They recounted that Santa Monica High School held its prom in a neighboring town because the student body was integrated, but the local hotels weren't. These bold historians documented racial issues up to the present, including the city's decision to build a freeway that bisected the African American neighborhood, a substantial enclave, destroying housing and creating a diaspora among families who had been pillars of the community for generations.

The Polish

The writing teams labored steadily until they had their first drafts. Each day we listened, critiqued, and cheered them on, as they polished their prose until they shone in the dark. After about six weeks, they'd produced a final draft of their magnum opus, *From Villages to Verandas: A Multicultural History of Santa Monica*, ninety-eight pages of lively narrative, interviews, illustrations, and little-known facts. *From Villages to Verandas* is a little masterpiece, studded with stories of the first inhabitants, the locations of hidden architectural gems, even the former location of an ostrich farm which flourished in the 1920s during the heyday of the feather boa. It's illustrated with student drawings, historic photographs, and copies of old advertisements. With a grant from the Education Foundation we headed for the local copy shop, and we were in print!

The introduction to the book reads:

> This is not the normal Santa Monica history book, only about Baker and Jones and the pier, the trains and trolleys. We are writing about Santa Monica from its true beginning. We wrote this book because we were having trouble finding information about all the people who contributed to the history of our city. Most books only tell the perspective of the Caucasian settlers. We wanted to tell the whole story rather than just a piece of it.

And so they did. We proudly distributed copies to all the school libraries and they've become a staple for classes exploring the history of our city.

Action in Your Community

There are many ways that students can put their new knowledge about their community to work to extend their own learning and that of others. The activities in this section encourage students to process their experiences into tangible products that benefit the community.

Creating Websites

Many students know how to create websites, so you might want to suggest any of the following uses for their skills:

- *Local History Website.* Upload primary source documents, their analysis of the documents, their own expert projects, video interviews with local history experts, so that community members and other students can use this as a learning portal. Invite community members to add their recollections to the site.
- *Getting to Know Our Town Website.* Specifically designed for kids, either visitors or locals, to help them discover the attractions of your town.
- *Helping Hand Website.* Design a website telling kids and their families about all the volunteer opportunities in town, from the food bank to the animal shelter.

Video Walking Tour

Have your students reflect on all their excursions and identify the most inter-esting, beautiful, thought-provoking, or informative areas that they would like to share with other students or adults. They can film those areas with voice-over or on-camera narration that incorporates information from primary source doc-uments, oral histories, and their own discoveries.

Oral Histories

Students can interview the insiders in town who can tell some great stories from the past about catching frogs in the swamp that's now a golf course, or riding the streetcar for a nickel, or watching movie companies shoot westerns on the edge of town. There are other people who are making history in your city—fighting to preserve the wetlands, creating green space, organizing petition drives to increase coastal access, refurbishing an historic theatre. All of that is great on-camera material that instantly becomes an archives for the future.

Mobile Mini-Museum or Issue-Oriented Display

As you study, consider having your students design a temporary, permanent, or traveling exhibit of your town history or your students' point of view on current issues. Set it up in your school, at PTA gatherings, or Board of Education meet-ings. Plan an opening reception during which students can talk with members of the public about their work. Send invitations to churches, retirement homes, recreation centers, the Historic Society, and Chamber of Commerce.

Taking Responsibility

As a class, adopt a stretch of the beach, a park, playground, or a strip of highway. Sign up for clean-up and maintenance. Talk to your city officials about participating in the Great American Cleanup. Each year millions of volunteers improve the quality of life across America by cleaning up litter-strewn streets and waterways, fixing up eyesores, and beautifying their communities. Last year 2.4 million Great American Cleanup volunteers collected a record breaking 208 million pounds of litter and debris; planted 4.2 million flowers and bulbs; cleaned 176 miles of roads, streets and highways; and cleaned 10,250 miles of rivers, lakes, and shorelines. Students could design and circulate flyers, identify areas of need, and rally their families to the effort. Check out Keep America Beautiful (www.kab.org) for more details.

Utopian Dreams

This final exercise asks your students to imagine a different reality for their town, to make them think about improving the place where they live, either in the

166

present as students, or in the future as adult citizens. The premise of the activity is: *What would our community be like if . . .* And then you take if from there: *If you were in charge of our city, if you were starting over, if you had unlimited power or resources. What would it look like? What would it have for people that it doesn't now? What would you do to preserve the environment?*

Students can approach this from many angles. If you were designing a town from scratch, how would you lay it out? Straight streets, a grid? What are the advantages and disadvantages of each. What would you put in the center? What would be at the far edges? Why? What would you do with street design that might affect or control traffic in certain areas? (Ring roads, pedestrian malls, walk streets, satellite parking lots with shuttle busses, subterranean parking.) What kind of transit system? How can you make streets more interesting—plazas, crescents, walk streets? What are some things you should definitely include? Are there some sorts of buildings we could really do without? Discuss locations for the various buildings. Invite urban planners, civil engineers, or town council members from your community to speak to the class.

You may want to read sections from Thomas More's *Utopia* or show your students pictures of Arcosanti, the utopian desert community built by visionary architect Paolo Soleri. Then have students build a model of their utopian town using recycled materials and junk.

The Learning Ledger

The Learning Ledger is a tool for regular, focused self-assessment. Learning Ledgers help students account for their day, like a memoir, diary, or journal with the expressed purpose of capturing concrete descriptions of their work with the material culture in the classroom or the community, and its effects on them.

Basic Three Questions for the Learning Ledger

- What did I do?
- How did I do it?
- What did I learn?

Questions Related to Community Explorations and Discovery

- What did I do in the community?
- How did I do it?
- What did I learn about how a city works? Jobs people have? Types of buildings? History? Problems in our community? What I can do to help?
- What did I do to solve a problem? How did I do it?
- What did I learn about helping people? Helping myself? Making changes?
- What did I do that I've never done before?

- What did I learn from this new experience? About myself?
- What do I still wonder about?
- What else do I want to find out?
- What could I teach someone else about _____?

Additional Questions for the Learning Ledger

- What did I enjoy most about my work today?
- What do I want to try next time?
- What did I learn about how I am smart?
- What did I learn about myself?
- What's the best thing I did all month?
- Who do I enjoy working with?
- Who helps me learn?
- What helps me learn?
- How do I help other kids learn?
- What did I do with other students?
- How did I do it?
- What did I learn about working as a group?
- How did I help the group?
- How did I get help from the group?
- What did I do well?

In Closing

At first glance all this prodding, poking, wandering, and questioning can look easy, since it's the way kids learn when left to their own devices. But it's not. Place-based learning is hard work. Nonetheless, great teachers recognize the unlimited potential of their communities as textbook, classroom, and laboratory. When you trade the safe nest of your classroom for the wide world beyond, the rules change. Learning is spontaneous and done at far greater speed than the usual classroom format. Content is immediate, tangible, and likely to run in six or seven directions at a time. Generic texts are supplanted by real life, and sometimes that's not pretty—it's a rare city that doesn't struggle with crime, poverty, failures in leadership, and inadequate funding for social supports. Your big challenge will be hooking students up with the resources they need to answer their questions and pursue their research. It takes stamina. But here's what you get in return. Kids who are eager to come to school, chomping at the bit to plunge into their research projects. When all is said and done, you're likely to have produced a group of students with better academic and social skills, and an indelible sense of purpose as members of the community.

7

Reading Between the Lines

Cultural Perspectives, Point of View, Politics, and Propaganda

Today the world is the victim of propaganda because people are not intellectually competent. More than anything the United States needs citizens competent to do their own thinking.

—William Mather Lewis, "Public Opinion on the Campus"

Thematic Strands: Individuals, Groups, and Institutions
Global Connections
Culture

Learning Layers: History, literary analysis, language arts, logic, analysis, critical thinking, persuasive writing, sociology, cultural anthropology, politics, psychology

What's the Big Idea About Point of View?

On my first trip to England, I was fascinated by the way people ate. I'm not talking about the legendary mystery meat—it was their technique that got my attention. I stared with undisguised curiosity as my companion, an Oxford graduate, sawed a perfectly good hamburger into mouthfuls, herded a morsel toward his inverted fork, then inserted it in his mouth like a doctor going after a tonsil specimen. Peas got the same treatment, squished in twos and threes onto the tines, until there was a small battalion of green pellets clinging to the fork and a dozen more escapees rolling around the plate. So there I sat there thinking *Why doesn't someone teach this "gentleman" some manners?* In truth, *I* was the oddity, laboriously cutting my fish into ladylike bites, then transferring the fork back to my right hand before ingesting. *Ladylike* is the critical word here. In my childhood, inverted forking was rude and earned you a scolding. I had a lot to learn.

No doubt you've heard the saying that *fish are the last to discover water*. I think that image explains exquisitely how difficult it is to identify the things we do out of blind obedience to the culture in which we were raised. We're so used to our cultural water that we routinely fail to give even a passing thought to why we do, or believe or dislike or covet certain things, until we're confronted by the fact that people in other countries—and even other regions of our own country—conduct themselves quite differently. We're puzzled by people who patronize a butcher shop full of horsemeat—for humans; they're stymied by a drive-thru culture that allows us to survive for weeks or even months on food swathed in grease-stained paper and devoured at sixty-five miles per hour.

Bill Bryson, a superb, Iowa-born travel writer, brilliantly captures his first head-on collision with another culture in *Neither Here Nor There* (1992):

> One of the small marvels of my first trip to Europe was the discovery that the world could be so full of variety, that there were so many different ways of doing essentially identical things, like eating, drinking and buying movie tickets. I felt like someone stepping out of doors for the first time. I had never seen a zebra-crossing, never seen a tram, never seen an unsliced loaf of bread (never even considered it an option), never seen anyone wearing a beret who expected to be taken seriously, never seen people go to a different shop for each item of dinner, never seen feathered pheasants or unskinned rabbits hanging in a butcher's window or a pig's head smiling on a platter. It was just wonderful (35).

We're largely anesthetized to the ways that our lives are governed by cultural assumptions—sliced bread, twenty-four-hour access to goods and services, black for funerals, white for weddings—until we wander into situations where people attend funerals in white, wouldn't think of shopping on Sunday, and are confident that *their* practices are perfectly normal, too.

This notion of how we expect things to be is called a *cultural perspective*, and it colors nearly every aspect of our lives—language and dialect, food and its preparation, land use, architecture, education, slang and swear words, religious beliefs, arts and crafts, customs, celebrations and festivals, family names, occupations, traditions, stories, jokes, greetings, and music.

Cultural perspectives possess an inescapable DNA-ish quality—we're stamped by the place and way in which we are raised, and from watching people around us. Every culture has a full and rigorously enforced complement, but the particulars vary, sometimes wildly. What's considered beautiful in one—the filigree of pea-sized welts called ritual scarification in Africa—seems off-putting in another. Nonverbal forms of communication—hand gestures, facial expressions, even shoulder shrugs—are also fine-tuned by culture. In Western societies, a smile indicates happiness or friendship, but in Asia it may be interpreted as a sign of mischievousness. Direct eye contact, so prized in the United States, can be a sign of disrespect among Hispanics. Using your left hand during social interactions is impolite in India, but asking personal questions such as *How old are you? How much money do you make?* or *How much did that cost?* is perfectly acceptable. The Swedish culture has a deeply ingrained concept referred to as *logom*, which cherishes having enough for every one, not too much, not too little—averageness—a sharp contrast to the American obsession with *we're number one*, and *he who dies with the most toys wins*.

Differences in cultural perspectives are a fact of living on a big planet with distinct groups of people who have been evolving independently for thousands of years. In isolation, these perspectives are a nonissue. In fact, they contribute to the cohesiveness of a society, reinforcing expectations, and reducing chronic disorder or full-scale pandemonium. Problems arise when people equate their cultural practices with what is right, and subject people with different beliefs and practices to bias, bigotry, prejudice, discrimination, harassment, hate crimes, or genocide.

As a social studies teacher, you have two critical responsibilities related to cultural perspectives. The first is to monitor your social studies materials to detect images or ideas that promote bias. When students pick up a book—particularly a history text—they need to understand that the authors had a point of view that influenced the way they told the story. The result may be unintentional distortion, disinformation, or omissions of critical information and perspectives. Second, you need to be a provocateur, constructing conversations that flush unconscious beliefs or assumptions out into the open air of your classroom, where your students can examine what they think and why they think it. This is hard work, like combing a long stretch of beach with a metal detector to find a lost watch, but it's critical that you take the time to do it, because unexamined perspectives drive behavior and make students easy targets for propaganda. (More on that later.)

Students need explicit guidance—that's you—to be able to effectively, honestly ask the questions *Where did I get that idea?* and *Is it valid?* This chapter explores ways to help students do just that by examining:

* cultural perspectives
* point of view
* bias
* propaganda

The Tools

It's no small feat for teachers and students to get a grip on these slippery, largely invisible or deeply disguised notions; it requires mental sweat. There's really no way around it—they must think critically. I hesitate to use such a threadbare term, since nearly every instructional program served up in the last decade promises a side order of critical thinking, and then goes on to tranquilize students' brains with large doses of boredom. So what does *critical thinking* really mean? It's a specific, multistep approach to dissecting a statement, argument, or presentation, and examining its component parts. Specifically, critical thinkers:

- Test for assumptions.
- Dig for bias.
- Demand clues about context.
- Ferret out alternative points of view.
- Challenge content using additional sources of information.

But critical thinking doesn't come naturally, like breathing, or reaching for extra-dark chocolate to reduce stress, or unerringly choosing the supermarket checkout line that is short but will move at a glacial pace, leaving you near comatose by the time you arrive at the register. Critical thinking requires explicit instruction, practice, and critiques. Which means your classroom should ring with conversations featuring questions such as:

- What assumptions did the author make when he referred to the next president as "he"?
- What motive do you think the speaker had for excluding any reference to profit in his defense of outsourcing?
- How do you think the Ojibwe felt about the arrival of the Europeans in North America?
- To whom was Martin Luther King Jr. speaking when he gave his "I Have a Dream" speech?
- How can we find out if the sign at the movie box office *No Food or Drink in the Theatre* is a request or a law?

It's exhausting. That's why after a morning of hounding your students to think about their thinking, you'll understand why so many adults are AWOL when election time rolls around. Voting requires thinking—and it's just too damn hard.

But thinking critically is what students must be able to do, and do well, if they're going to recognize cultural perspectives, point of view, bias, and propaganda in social studies materials, in the media, and in themselves. It's an essential skill for citizenship in the twenty-first century where the proliferation of information-gathering and reporting has produced nonstop global news coverage on radio and TV, plus Internet sites that multiply at the rate of a virus. We are drowning in information; the roar of the deluge has become the soundtrack of life. But without the ability to determine what is reliable and relevant, we may as well be cave dwellers, staring at animal entrails for guidance.

What About Standards?

When you decide to address cultural perspectives, points of view, bias, and propaganda explicitly in your social studies programs using photographs, texts, posters, literature, and legal documents, your students will develop and demonstrate skills that are fundamental to a rigorous standards-based approach to social studies. The following list suggests the range of learning challenges students will face as they undertake a thorough examination of what we believe and why.

Students will:

- Develop habits of mind to consider multiple perspectives.
- Explain causes in analyzing historical actions.
- Challenge arguments of historical inevitability.
- Detect bias and identify propaganda techniques.
- Give examples of how experiences may be interpreted differently by people from diverse cultural perspectives or frames of reference.
- Compare ways in which people from different cultures think about and deal with their physical environment and social conditions.
- Explore and describe similarities and differences in the ways groups, societies, and cultures address similar human needs and concerns.
- Analyze a particular event to identify the reasons individuals might respond to it in different ways.
- Synthesize knowledge of an historic time and place from primary source documents to explain various points of view.

 Awareness

Assessing Prior Knowledge About Cultural Perspectives

There's one big question that students will tackle in this Exploration section: *Where do we get our ideas about what is true, right, proper, or good?* And it's not an easy one. In effect they have to start the journey from thinking that their culture is the norm to realizing that cultural values are not natural laws, though they feel very natural to us. They are simply *the way we do things*.

> *We don't see things as they are but as we are.*
> —Anaïs Nin, *The Diary of Anaïs Nin*

The following activities and discussions raise awareness of cultural perspectives by encouraging your students to reveal what they already know, so they can feel smart, while you gain a clear picture of the work you need to do on culture, before tackling the thornier issues of bias and propaganda.

You Are Here: Breakfast of Champions

So let's get started. In this activity, students will consider the things we eat—and don't eat—for breakfast, and why. They'll compare a traditional American breakfast with a traditional Japanese breakfast, and try to articulate the idea that many cultural practices began as survival strategies related to climate and natural resources, and became standard procedure, even when other options were available.

In preparation, you'll need to gather pictures of typical breakfast foods from both cultures. You can find photos of American breakfast food in cooking magazines, the food section of the local paper, or bring in the real things—boxes of cereals, egg cartons, toaster-tarts, orange juice, bread and jam. You can find pictures of the traditional Japanese breakfast—miso soup, rice, pickled vegetables and grilled fish—on the Internet, or go to your local Asian market for authentic items.

Display the American and Japanese breakfast items or pictures in random order.

Ask: Can you find something you eat for breakfast? What else?
(Let students sort items into *Breakfast Food/Not Breakfast Food.*)

Ask: What other foods do you eat for breakfast? List them.
Why do you think we tend to have cereal and products like toast, muffins, croissants, English muffins, toaster tarts, waffles, or pancakes for breakfast? (Huge country with vast middle section that is excellent for wheat production; third largest producer in the world; eat what is plentiful and cheap for daily meals.)

Focus on the Japanese breakfast items.

Ask: Do you ever eat these things for breakfast? Why? Why not?
Did you know that this is what many Japanese children eat for breakfast?
Why do you think the Japanese have rice, soy, and fish for breakfast?
(Small country but climate is excellent for rice production; produces more than United States; most large population centers close to the sea; eat what is plentiful and cheap for daily meals.)

Ask: Have you ever eaten grilled fish? When?
Have you ever eaten rice? When?
How would you feel about having grilled fish for breakfast? Why?
So what is it that makes fish fine for dinner but strange for breakfast?
How do you think a Japanese child would feel about oatmeal?
Can you think of any other food that we eat in the United States that other people might find strange?

You can replicate this lesson with any items from two cultures—clothing, transportation, sports, education systems. The goal is to have students recognize that practices and preferences vary from one cultural group to another. Our *ways of doing things* are adapted to our needs—they're right for us, but not *right* in the absolute sense of the word.

Waking Magoun's Brain

One way to grab your students' attention and hold it is to show them a real-life clash between cultural values, particularly one that involves kids. The following petition describes an actual conflict between Native American students in Texas and their school district. Read the text to your students and discuss it, using questions like the ones provided.

End Cultural Bias Toward Native American Students: Let Native Children Express Their Culture

Issue

Two Native American students at the Roeseca Middle School in Los Fresnos, Texas, showed pride in their heritage, were isolated from classmates, and spent the first days of school in In-School Suspension for wearing their hair in braids.

Student Response

Students posted a petition on the Internet and asked readers to sign in support of their cause. The petition reads:

> We the undersigned request the Los Fresnos School District to change their policy regarding length of hair when a child chooses to enter their school district who is of Native American heritage. For generations our Native ancestors were forced, through U.S. Government policy which sanctioned schools to forcibly strip Native students of their cultural identity. Part of this stripping of identity was to cut or shave the hair from Native American students who were sent to schools across the United States. To have a policy which demands that a Native student cut their hair today damages that student's sense of cultural pride, hurts their self-esteem, and spits in the eye of their forefathers who railed against policies which stripped Native children of their identity. To have a policy today which segregates Native students who have chosen to honor their traditions, who have chosen to be actively involved in their cultural identity and tribal customs is outdated, antiquated, unjust, and sanctions a cultural bias which sadly perpetuates stereotypes, while harming and impeding a child's right to learn in a safe and accepting environment. We urge the School district to think clearly and rethink this policy which is harming Native children and their right to a quality education.

Students need to think critically about the two elements of this conflict: cultural bias and assumptions. Cultural bias occurs when people embrace their own practices about language, dress, accessories, demeanor, food, rituals, gestures, posture, hairstyles as appropriate or right, and assume what other people do is troublesome, antisocial, unacceptable, or wrong. Read the petition and ask:

- Why did the students object to the school's rules?
- What cultural values were the students representing?
- What cultural values was the district representing?
- What assumptions did the school district make about long hair in school?
- What assumptions did the school district make about their power?
- Would you have signed the petition? Why?
- What do you think about the treatment of the two students?

The Court Speaks

You can continue this conversation by discussing how a court viewed the issue of long hair in schools. The Alabama and Coushatta tribes of Texas sued the Trustees of the Big Sandy Independent School District on the grounds that a school dress code, which prevented boys from wearing their hair "longer than the top of a standard dress collar," violated their First Amendment free exercise and free speech rights. Twelve students from those tribes wore their hair long, despite the dress code, and were disciplined for breaking school rules. When tribal members tried to explain to the Board of Trustees that wearing long hair was religiously based, they were informed that "long hair went out with the hippies."

The court upheld the plaintiffs' free exercise claim. It found that the Native American Indian movement is a religion, that the plaintiffs' beliefs were sincerely held and thus, entitled to First Amendment protection. They concluded that wearing long hair is a deeply rooted part of that religion because it can express the wearer's link with the universe, something the Native American religion holds sacred. Share this information with your students and then ask:

- Why do you think the school district had a rule about hair length?
- What value did their rule represent?
- Evaluate the logic of their statement about hippies. What assumptions did it reveal?
- Did it help or hurt their case?
- Why did the tribal members object to the rule?
- Imagine you were the judge in this case. Explain your ruling.
- What other school rules seem to be based on cultural assumptions?

Your students may want to research other student protests and the way the courts responded.

Exploration

Discovering More About Point of View

Suppose you woke up tomorrow morning to find an encampment of other-language-speaking strangers on your front lawn. Not just loafing around, but hacking at the shrubbery, putting up shelters, bathing in your garden hose, and looking at your dog with barbecue eyes. That's the Native American point of view on Jamestown. Although there are no text documents that record how the Algonquin felt about the small invasion, their behavior spoke volumes. In their eyes, the land that would become Virginia was already *found*. They were the rightful inhabitants, and they weren't in the market for new neighbors.

But that's not the textbook version. Our kids learn that the English settlers survived a hellish Atlantic crossing, landed in 1604, broke ground and had a spectacularly rough

> *The only way in which a human being can make some approach to knowing the whole of a subject is by hearing what can be said about it by persons of every variety of opinion, and studying all modes in which it can be looked at by every character of mind. No wise man ever acquired his wisdom in any mode but this.*
> —John Stuart Mill,
> *On Liberty*

time for the first few years, valiantly enduring disease, famine, and continuing attacks by the Algonquians, who picked off any starving colonist foolish enough to pursue a scrawny squirrel beyond the protection of the palisade fence. Same story. Very different point of view.

Social studies frameworks describe history as a story well told. Since we know that every storyteller has a point of view, logically it follows that history is the story of events told from someone's point of view. It's a selective version of what happened, which means there can be other versions of the same event, told from different angles.

Think about looking at an object through a kaleidoscope and you begin to grasp the number of interpretations that a single act, event, or even remark in history could generate. This is a hugely important concept, and one that can be tough for kids to grasp, particularly if they are in the developmental stage where they see the world in black and white. Right and wrong. No nuance. It's a big challenge for them to accept that there can be numerous interpretations for any situation, none of which earn the adjective right. The activities in this section use literature and visual images to help students explore point of view and bias.

Exploring Point of View Through Literature

A person's point of view is shaped by many things, including family, birth order, child-rearing practices, education, experience, notions of hierarchy, modesty, justice, ethnic origin, gender, age, and spiritual beliefs. So *point of view* could be defined as *the view from inside my skull*. Given how unique that intracranial mix can be from one person to the next, it's not surprising that the idea of walking a mile in another man's shoes is more of an aspiration than a daily practice. It's hard to trade places with anyone else; empathy is as close as we usually get.

But literature can be a powerful tool for exploring point of view with your students because some authors are so adept at describing their characters' experiences and emotions, that it can feel like the reader is living inside their skin. Literature can help students understand point of view by allowing them to spend time with characters who:

- Have a point of view that differs from the mainstream perspective.
- Show that events can be interpreted in more than one way.
- Learn to accept the fact that different viewpoints exist.
- Change their point of view over time.

In the process, literature can actually change the reader's point of view by providing new ways of seeing the familiar. It may be the most effective weapon you have for combating bias and bigotry in your class, while promoting literacy skills. The following sections provide ideas for using literature to help students explore point of view.

Points of View on Civil Rights: *The Story of Ruby Bridges*

In November 1960, six-year-old Ruby Bridges became the first African American child to attend an all-white elementary school in New Orleans, Louisiana. Each day she was escorted to and from William Franz Elementary School by armed federal marshals. During that walk she endured the taunts, threats, and abuse of angry segregationists rallying in front of the school, determined to prevent court-ordered integration. For an entire year, Ruby was the sole student in her class, since white parents pulled their children from the school in protest.

Ruby Bridges Hall wrote about her experiences in *Through My Eyes* (1999) and the American artist, Norman Rockwell, made a painting of Ruby called *The Problem We All Live With*. Rockwell painted what the world saw on newscasts—a small girl with braids, a crisp white dress, and white tennis shoes. Her back is straight, her eyes focused straight ahead, and she's walking flanked by burley men with yellow armbands that read "U.S. Marshal." Behind her, "nigger" and "KKK" are scrawled on the wall, and a tomato is splattered at her feet. The painting is one of Rockwell's most famous works. Find or download a copy of the painting. Let students study it closely, without background information, simply using their eyes to discover the story. Then ask:

* What do you see? What else?
* What do you think is happening?
* How do you think the child feels?
* How do you think the men feel?
* What do you think the artist is trying to tell us?

Explain to students that the child in the picture is Ruby Bridges, the first African American child to integrate a formerly segregated school in New Orleans in 1960. The men walking with her are guards. Ask:

* When do people need guards?
* Can you think of anyone who has guards when they go out in public (president, celebrities, sports figures)?
* Why do you think a child would need guards?

Read aloud and discuss *Through My Eyes* by Ruby Bridges. Remind students that many people were involved in the beginning of school integration, and they saw it from different points of view. With older students, you may want to read an excerpt from John Steinbeck's *Travels with Charley* (1962), in which Steinbeck describes the "cheerleaders," the group of anti-integration women who demonstrated outside Ruby's school for an entire year, screaming racial epithets, displaying a black doll in a coffin, making death threats, winning international attention, and bringing shame to New Orleans for their undisguised racism directed toward a child. Ask:

* What do you think about the demonstrators?
* What was their point of view about school integration?
* What was their point of view about Ruby Bridges?
* What was their point of view on the teacher, Barbara Henry?
* How do you think other citizens of New Orleans felt about the cheerleaders?

Point of View Activities

Review all the people Ruby Bridges mentioned in her story. Work with your students to complete a list of all the major characters in this pivotal year in New Orleans, including: Ruby, her parents, other students in the school, their parents, the judge, the policemen, the press, the teachers and principal at William Frantz Elementary, the neighbors who lived by the school, the cheerleaders, and the people watching this event on television.

Ask students to work in teams to investigate one group's point of view. Use this prompt to get them focused: *Try to see the situation from the principal's (policeman's,*

179

teachers', judge's) point of view. They may want to do some research online, as there are many websites devoted to this event, including The Ruby Bridges Foundation (www.rubybridges.org). The following activities will help them get inside the heads of people who were in New Orleans when the schools were integrated.

1.   There was a media frenzy outside of William Frantz School. Television was a fairly new medium and reporters were scrambling to interview many people, asking what they saw and their point of view about the court-ordered integration. If you could interview people in the group you've chosen (police, teachers, etc.) what questions would you ask? What do you think they would say?

2.   Write about school desegregation in New Orleans *from your group's point of view.* Students should try to include comments on their needs, concerns, fears, hopes, feelings toward Ruby, feelings toward the judge, feelings toward other groups, and about the changes and disruption in New Orleans.

3.   Do you agree with any part of this group's point of view? Do you disagree? Why?

4.   Have teams pair up to compare and contrast their points of view.

More Literature About Point of View

Some clever authors explore point of view by retelling a familiar story, such as a fairy tale, from an unfamiliar perspective. The following titles help students develop the skill of recognizing different points of view.

George Washington's Socks by Elvira Woodruff. 1991. New York: Scholastic.
This is an excellent book for teaching history, historical fiction, and point of view. Students see how Matt's perception of the soldiers fighting in the American Revolution changed once he actually participated in it.

The Whipping Boy by Sid Fleischman. 1986. New York: Greenwillow.
This book shows two different points of view during the Middle Ages, one of the pampered prince and the other of his whipping boy, the lower-class youngster who takes the prince's punishment for him. Students appreciate the humor and get the point about different people having different perspectives.

The Magic Circle by Donna Jo Napoli. 1993. New York: Dutton Juvenile.
This is a version of the Hansel and Gretel fairy tale, but told from the point of view of the witch. It is short, well-written, and emotionally engaging.

Freaky Friday by Mary Rodgers. 1993. New York: HarperCollins Publishers.
A mother and her daughter switch bodies and suddenly see things in a whole new light.

Talkin' About Bessie by Nikki Grimes. 2002. London: Orchard.
This is a cleverly written story about the first African American woman to become a pilot. Each page tells the story from a different person's point of view. All of the storytellers knew Bessie Coleman.

The True Story of the Three Little Pigs! by Jon Scieszka. 1989. New York: Viking Juvenile.
This classic is written from the wolf's point of view and differs from the traditional story in that the wolf claims he was framed and offers his perspective/point of view on the whole situation.

The Journal of James Edmond Pease: A Civil War Union Soldier by Jim Murphy. 1998. New York: Scholastic.
Newbery Honor–winning author Jim Murphy creates a tale of uncommon courage and personal redemption in the face of some of the most brutal fighting imaginable. James's journal brings readers into the smoke of Civil War battles to hear the sounds, experience the fears, and witness the heroism and cowardice that are a part of every war.

When Will This Cruel War Be Over? The Civil War Diary of Emma Simpson by Barry Denenberg. 1996. New York: Scholastic.
Through Emma's diary entries, readers feel the helplessness and anger of Southern homeowners when Yankee troops enter their houses, take their family possessions, and then burn the homes. They feel the constant ache Emma endures as the destruction of war becomes a part of her daily life—soldiers returning home with no legs, the awful results of typhoid fever and dysentery, and always the daily news of more deaths.

Questions to Elicit Point of View

One way to ingrain vigilance about point of view is to teach your students to willfully and persistently ask, *Whose voice is telling the story?* When reading literature, nonfiction texts, newspaper articles, and even primary source documents, listening to the radio, watching television or films, students can uncover point of view by asking the following questions about a text or presentation:

- Who's telling the story?
- What seems most important to the author?
- Does the author seem to have a motive or agenda?
- Is there another way to look at this?
- Whose point of view is included here?
- Whose is left out?

- What's missing?
- Can you think of a contradictory opinion?
- Who would agree with this point of view?
- Who would disagree? Why?
- Where could I get more information about this?

A Limited Circle of Voices

Students need to realize that one reason we get a skewed view of events in history is that they were frequently recorded by a select group of people: the winners, the educated, the powerful—those who could write and had a reason to do so, which could indicate a very specific point of view. This means there were other groups of eyewitnesses, participants, or victims whose points of view were left on the cutting room floor. So while your students are trying to detect point of view, they should also develop the habit of looking for what's *not* there by asking questions to identify the groups whose views are not represented.

- Who had the means of documenting this event or their point of view about it?
- Who did not?
- Who else was there that no one talks about?
- Who were the winners?
- Whose story survived? Why?
- What information might another version of the story include?

Pictures and Point of View

Another way to address point of view is through the visual medium: historic photographs, illustrations in newspapers, magazines, and textbooks. The front page of your daily newspaper is a regular source of timely, relevant visual material with a definite point of view. Front page photos freeze-frame the most important story of the day in the opinion of the Editor-in-Chief. They're carefully chosen to convey enough information to lure people into buying the paper and reading the full story. Editors choose those photos carefully and pay photographers handsomely for a picture that truly is worth a thousand words.

The cover photo on my local newspaper recently showed the police cleaning up Skid Row by removing homeless people, making numerous arrests, and disposing of tents, clothes, and boxes illegally stacked on the sidewalk. A discussion on point of view could simply start with, *Is this a solution to the problem of homeless people? For whom? Who benefits from this? Who doesn't?* From the point of view of the business community and newly-arrived condominium owners, this is a positive step. Ditto the mayor and police chief who campaigned on the promise of safer streets. Now think about this photo from the point of view of the wheelchair-bound homeless person who uses the portable toilets on the corner, and gets his medications from the clinic down the street? What might be the point of view of the policeman in the picture? How might he feel about being ordered to evict homeless people?

Now look through your history, social studies, or literature textbooks for pictures that seem to have a specific point of view and think: *What is it? Do students agree with the message? Who might not agree?*

Political cartoons also express strong points of view. Delete the caption on cartoons from the editorial page of your newspaper. Ask students to work in groups to determine the message of the image. *Do they agree with the message? What's another point of view?* Then have them try to create captions from two points of view.

What Is Bias?

It's fairly safe to say that cultural perspectives or point of view come with the territory—like a zip code or the weather. They're a fact of where you're raised and live. However, bias takes cultural perspectives to the next level by assigning a value to your point of view. It turns subjective into objective. For example, the point of view, *I'm used to male superintendents. I've never known a woman in that position,* turns to bias when stated, *Women can't be good superintendents.*

Bias can be positive, as when you vote for someone because his family knows yours. This is sometimes called a blind spot, soft spot, or favoritism. Bias is also at work when ideas and information are presented from a flattering point of view, rather than using an objective, neutral, or factual approach—advertising being a perfect example.

Negative bias is a preformed negative opinion or attitude toward an idea, or a group of people who have common characteristics such as gender, skin color, sexual orientation, age, religion, or national origin. Racism is a negative bias, along with ageism and sexism.

Some biases are the result of eons of evolution during which humans and their ancestors learned to fear the unfamiliar. Other biases result from cultural perceptions, as seen in the breakfast exercise—fish for dinner, not for breakfast. But the good news is that our brains are flexible—our thinking can be altered by experience. Bias can be revised in response to information, personal experiences, and the conscious effort of the will. But first your students must uncover and examine bias. They need to search for it in their school materials and in themselves.

Bias in Educational Materials

History and social studies texts were once notorious for presenting a hugely biased picture of the past. The portraits were uniformly masculine. The high points were man-type events—revolution, war, victory in battle, inaugurations—as far as the eye could see. The message was that anything important enough to qualify as history was initiated or achieved by men. Under pressure from women and minorities, publishers and individual authors have made significant progress in correcting this misrepresentation. Mem Fox, beloved author of *Wilfrid Gordon Macdonald Partridge* and many other children's books, stated that she made a deliberate effort to increase the number of female characters in her books, and points out that many of her books are intentionally "dominated by main characters who are either girls, female animals, or dynamic elderly women" (Fox 1993).

School librarians have led the charge in reducing bias on their shelves, promoting books that feature characters from different cultures, and filling the biography shelves with a wide range of role models. But there are still many classic picture books that continue to reinforce a limited range of activities and roles for women and people of color. When using books like these in the classroom, you need to explicitly address bias through activities that sensitize students to the subtle messages about who's valuable and powerful in our society, and who's not.

Surveying for Bias

The beginning of the school year is an excellent time to confront bias head-on. Before your kids start to devour their books, swallowing the publisher's point of view whole, take some time to do a visual survey for bias. Divide students into teams, assign a chapter to each and have them find all the illustrations of people, either individual portraits or group scenes. Ask them to note who's in the pictures. What are they doing? Who's missing? Use the following questions to construct a chart of their data, and then have a discussion about what they notice and wonder.

- How many pictures were there of men, women, children, and people of color?
- What percentage of pictures have men?
- What type of work or roles are portrayed for men?
- What about women? What are they doing?
- Are there any children represented?
- What races or ethnicities are represented most and least often?
- What roles are they playing?

Now go to your classroom or school library. Have each student pull one picture book off the shelf and look at all the illustrations. Have them count the number of men, women, and people of color in the book. Record those numbers on the board. Then ask them to study the pictures to see who's doing what. List the activities or occupations of men, women, and people of color in separate columns on the board. Once you've completed this chart of activities or jobs, ask your students to comment on the data and speculate about the point of view presented. How does that compare with their experience of the world? For example, most of the women in books may be busy with domestic tasks, while most of their mothers go to work each day.

Test Yourself for Bias

Finding bias in literature and history stories is an excellent intellectual activity that can make students feel insightful, while keeping themselves at arm's length from the uncomfortable question of personal bias. If you are working with older students, you may want to tell them about an online test that allows anyone to determine her or his own biases or prejudices. The test was developed by Mahzarin Banaji, a Professor of Social Ethics at Harvard University. You can view a test demonstration or, by giving some information about yourself, actually take a test. More than sixty different tests are also available at http://implicit.harvard.edu, with topics ranging from animals to politics. Tests that measure race, ethnic, sex, and age bias are also available at www.tolerance.org.

 ## Inquiry

Digging Deeper into Point of View and Propaganda

In the final sentences of his classic book, *Teaching as a Subversive Activity*, Neil Postman articulates his goal of working toward a new education that would see all learners "develop built-in shockproof crap detectors as basic equipment in their survival kits" (1969). That comment makes him the godfather of this chapter and most particularly this Inquiry section.

> *Propaganda does not deceive people; it merely helps them deceive themselves.*
> —Eric Hoffer,
> *The True Believer*

Throughout this chapter, we've examined activities designed to confront students with the question: *How do we know what we know, and how can we tell where an idea lies along the spectrum from truth to crap?* We've talked about cultural perspectives—mental structures about how things should be, which can lead to bias. Propaganda is the deliberate manipulation of both cultural perspectives and bias. The activities in this Inquiry section help students learn to recognize the major propaganda techniques by analyzing commercial and political advertising.

What Is Propaganda?

Propaganda is the systematic attempt to manipulate the attitudes, beliefs, and actions of people through the use of symbols, such as words, gestures, slogans, flags, and uniforms. It's like cognitive therapy in reverse. Cognitive therapy is a psychological technique that's used to cure irrational fear, hatred, or anger resulting from distortions. It eradicates the distortions by restructuring the language that led to them. Propaganda is the opposite. It uses language to *induce* cognitive distortions, often leading to irrational fear, hatred and anger, which is then used to justify actions—bombing a country, incarcerating the innocent, violating people's civil rights.

For many adults, the word *propaganda* is synonymous with Nazi Germany. The persecution of Jews, Catholics, homosexuals, gypsies, and the disabled under Adolph Hitler is the high-water mark for the systematic application of propaganda to further a cause.

But you don't need to reach back in history to introduce your students to effective propaganda techniques. They're already well acquainted with the phenomenon, though they're probably unaware of the role it plays in their daily lives. Twenty-first-century life abounds with well-paid, totally legal purveyors of propaganda. Advertisers. Every television, radio, magazine, newspaper, and billboard hammers a singular and seductive message—happiness is just a transaction away. Life is perfectible, *if* you just get your hands on the right clothing, food, pharmaceuticals, libations, auto, or entertaining diversion. Fire up your computer and you're hit with a barrage of pop-ups, echoing the same purchasable promise. Getting your kids to look at propaganda may be easier if you go in through the back door. Luckily, there's an old tale that's a perfect opener for this important conversation.

Hype Versus Substance: The Emperor's New Clothes

Hans Christian Andersen's tale about a clothes-hound emperor is an excellent starting point for discussing propaganda with your students. You will recall that this ruler was clothing-obsessed, commissioning a different suit for every hour of the day. He hires two tailors who promise to make him a remarkable new outfit that will be invisible to anyone who is either incompetent or stupid. When the emperor goes to preview his new togs, he sees nothing, for the tailors are swindlers, pantomiming the sewing process and pocketing the money. Afraid of looking deficient, the emperor pretends to be delighted and parades through the town in his invisible attire. His subjects cheer and clap because they've heard the weavers' tale and fear exposure. But, the bubble burst when an innocent child loudly exclaims that the Emperor is as naked as a jaybird.

Start by reading this story to your students. There are dozens of versions on the Internet as well as in your school library. Find the one that's most appropriate for your students' age and language development. After reading the story, ask:

- What words would you use to describe the tailors?
- What did they promise the emperor? What did they deliver?
- How did the tailors get away with it?
- Why did the emperor and his subjects say they saw the clothes?
- What do we call it when someone makes a person believe something that isn't true? (trick, lie, false advertising, deceive, fool, dupe, cheat, swindle)
- Can you think of any other examples of people doing that?
- How is this story similar to the way products or ideas are sold today?

Truth in Advertising

Give your students an opportunity to analyze the style and content of an advertisement, by providing a wide assortment of magazines (sports, food, news, gossip). Have them scan the advertisements and choose one that appeals to them. Ask them to pay close attention to the design elements (color, images, size, typeface, placement) and decide: *What mood does the design create?* Now have them focus on the text to determine the message the advertisers are using to sell the product. *What do the words say? What do they mean?*

Now teach your students the five propaganda techniques typically used in advertising:

1. *Bandwagon:* Advertisers try to persuade people to do something by letting them know others are doing it.
2. *Testimonial:* This technique uses the words of a famous person to make the product more appealing.
3. *Transfer:* Names or pictures of famous people are used, but not direct quotations.
4. *Repetition:* The product name is repeated at least four times.
5. *Emotions:* Words associated with the product or service make you feel strongly about someone or something.

Have them revisit their print advertisements to identify the main techniques used to sell these products so they can discover how advertising works. Ask them to consider the following points:

- Is the message about the product itself, the consumer, or the effect it will have on the consumer?
- Who is the target audience?
- What technique is the advertiser using to convince consumers to buy this product or service?
- Do you think it is an effective ad? Would you buy this product? Why?

Television is truly the prime arena in which advertisers capture the appetite and whining power of young consumers. So it's well worth your time to tape five to ten commercials from prime-time television—about five minutes of hard-core propaganda. Screen the television advertisements and ask your students to identify the techniques being used. Then have them group the ads according to technique. Ask:

- Which is the most common technique used? Why?
- Which is the most effective? Why?

Have students write their own commercials for a product, service, or idea using one or more propaganda techniques and present them to the class. Have the listeners analyze the presentations to identify the techniques in each and rate them for effectiveness.

Politics and Propaganda

Beyond advertising, there is an additional set of propaganda techniques used by the military, the media, in politics, and in many human interactions. This is the PhD level for propagandists, but the techniques are widely employed to influence the public, particularly during election season. If you happen to be teaching when the presidency is up for grabs, you'll have an unlimited supply of campaign commercials that can give your students some batting practice. Teach them the following propaganda techniques and then look for examples together. You'll have a field day.

- *Name Calling:* This technique consists of attaching a negative label to a person, cause, or thing. People engage in this type of behavior when they are trying to avoid supporting or stating their own opinion with facts. Rather than explain their beliefs, they tear their opponent down.
- *Glittering Generalities:* This technique uses important-sounding positive words that have little or no real meaning in that context. These words are used in general statements that cannot be proved or disproved. Words like *good, honest, fair, best, democracy, freedom, family values, rights* are examples of feel-good words.
- *False Analogy:* In this technique, two things that may or may not really be similar are portrayed as being similar. For example: *People are like dogs. They respond best to clear discipline.* When examining the comparison, you must ask yourself how similar the items are. In most false analogies, there is simply not enough evidence available to support the comparison.
- *Plain Folks:* This technique uses a folksy approach to convince us to support someone or something because they are just like us—plain folks. The

candidate or cause is identified with common people from everyday walks of life. The idea is to make the candidate/cause come off as grassroots and egalitarian.

- *Card Stacking:* This term comes from stacking a deck of cards in your favor. Card stacking is used to slant a message. Keywords or unfavorable statistics may be omitted in an ad or commercial, leading to a series of half-truths. Keep in mind that an advertiser, or political campaign, is under no obligation "to give the truth, the whole truth, and nothing but the truth."
- *Either/or Fallacy:* This technique is also called "black-and-white thinking" because only two choices are given. For example: *You're either with us or against us.* In this type of statement, there is no middle ground, no shades of gray. It is used to polarize issues, and negates all attempts to find a common ground.
- *Fear:* This approach presents a dreaded circumstance and then follows it up with the kind of behavior needed to avoid that horrible event. This technique is very popular among political parties and campaign organizers.

Ask students to think back to the story of the *Emperor's New Clothes.* What propaganda techniques were the tailors using? (Bandwagon and fear.)

Batting Practice

It's been said that the best propaganda omits rather than invents meaning so that when students are trying to detect propaganda, they'll need to look for what's *not* there, listen for what's *not* said, to read between the lines. To provide vital practice, log on to some Internet sites or get printed promotional material from organizations that promote a particular concern—Save the Whales, Save the Bay, Gun Control, National Rifle Association, Immigration Rights, Border Protection, Homeland Security, Clean Energy, Global Warming, The Democratic or Republican Parties, the Marines, Army or Navy, Energy Efficient Automobiles, Prison Reform, Drug Abuse Prevention, Anti-Smoking, or any other cause that is trying to influence people's actions or opinions by providing information or promulgating certain ideas.

Ask students to analyze the text, images, and design of the campaign to identify the techniques being used to sway people. Discuss the idea that propaganda may not be lying but it does use the truth selectively. Then teach them to ferret out the distortions by subjecting the claims, slogans, threats or promises to the following set of questions. Ask:

- According to whom? What is the source of this information or idea?
- What information is left out?

- Why did they do that?
- What do the producers have to gain by presenting this information?
- Who else does this benefit?
- Could someone be harmed by this information and the way it is presented?

Through critical thinking and ruthlessly applied questions students can pierce the veil created by propaganda techniques, and learn to think for themselves.

 ## Action

Using Knowledge About Point of View

Throughout this chapter we've focused on reading between the lines in social studies as a cautionary tale. But there are many positive activities that involve point of view and persuasion. This section suggests activities that allow students to share their cultural heritage, join in a cause, and use their writing skills to teach others about point of view.

Environmental Protection

If students develop an interest in an environmental cause, have them contact one of the activist organizations. Analyze the organization's website, message, and graphics for effectiveness. Encourage students to get involved on a local or global level, and share their passion with others. Start with the following websites:

- **Greenaction Youth Site for Health and Environmental Justice** (www .greenaction.org) This is a website for and by students to promote environmental justice through art, awareness, and action.
- **Green Arts Web** (www.greenarts.org) Extensive site explaining and linking to examples of eco-art.
- **The EnviroLink Network** (www.envirolink.org) This nonprofit organization is dedicated to providing the most comprehensive, up-to-date environmental resources available on the Internet. EnviroLink is a grassroots online community uniting millions of people around the world.

Creative Writing and Point of View

Using the point-of-view fairy tales as models, encourage students to choose another familiar story that can be told from various points of view. This could be another fairy tale, such as Jack and the Beanstalk told from the giant's point of view. Or you could find a section of your social studies text that has a distinct point of view—such as landing at Plymouth Rock—and tell it from other points of view. Students could use a narrative format, do a series of drawings like a comic book, or create a picture book. Be sure to arrange time for the authors to share their writing and hold a discussion on point of view to introduce the concept to other students. You may want to display the books in the school library with notes on point of view, bias, and propaganda.

Propaganda Posters

Students who are very interested in advertising or Internet sites that advocate for a cause, can teach other students about propaganda by making a set of posters showing blatant images, text, slogans, or promises lifted from print advertising or websites that illustrate explicit examples of propaganda. These can be like the old Wanted posters, with text to explain the "wanted" advertiser's or source's distortions or propaganda techniques. Display the posters for viewing by other students and arrange a time for your students to talk about their creations.

Artistic Statements: A Sculptor's Point of View

Many contemporary artists use their work as a vehicle to communicate their point of view about conditions in our society—how we treat children and each other, how we use and abuse the environment, and how we solve problems that lead to famine and war. Their goal is to move, persuade, touch the conscience, and stir the viewer to action through words, music, visual images, or drama. Encourage your students to research artists who are activists, starting with Maya Lin.

Maya Ying Lin designed the Vietnam Memorial when she was studying architecture at Yale. It was built to honor the memory of those who died in the Vietnam War. Over 58,000 names are inscribed in chronological order in the black granite memorial. The names show the war as a series of individual human sacrifices and give each name a special place in history.

Unlike other monuments that stand up high, this is shaped like an open book, and sunk into the park that surrounds it. To read the names visitors must stand below the horizon—six feet under—in the space of the dead. This memorial makes no grand statements about politics or American ideals. Its sole message is that the cost of war is human life. If you wish to discuss this sculpture as point of view, you can find numerous images on the Internet, including entire websites devoted to The Wall. After looking at the image of The Wall with your students, have a discussion focusing on the power of art as advertising or propaganda. Ask:

- What do you see?
- Why do you think it's important to remember certain individuals and events in history?
- What do you think Maya Ying Lin wanted to communicate about war?

- Do you think that art can change the way people think about the problems of war, human rights, and the environment?
- Do you think it can change the way people act?

For a more detailed look, log on to The Virtual Wall: The Vietnam Veterans' Memorial (www.virtualwall.org/) for remembrances, poems, photos, letters, and citations honoring those named on the Vietnam Veterans Memorial in Washington, DC.

The Learning Ledger

The Learning Ledger is a tool for regular, focused self-assessment. Learning Ledgers help students account for their day, like a memoir, diary, or journal with the expressed purpose of capturing concrete descriptions of their efforts to read between the lines, and understand culture, bias, and propaganda.

Basic Three Questions for the Learning Ledger
- What did I do?
- How did I do it?
- What did I learn?

Questions Related to Point of View
- What did I discover about the _____'s point of view toward _____?
- What do I think about their view?
- What's my point of view? Why?
- What did I learn about propaganda?
- What do I think about using propaganda?
- How would I recognize propaganda in my life?
- What would I do about it?
- What do I still wonder about?
- What else do I want to find out?
- What could I teach someone else about _____?

Additional Questions for the Learning Ledger
- What did I enjoy most about my work today?
- What do I want to try next time?
- What did I learn about how I am smart?
- Who helps me learn?
- What helps me learn?
- How do I help other kids learn?
- What did I learn about working as a group?

- How did I help the group?
- How did I get help from the group?

In Closing

Every four years, I gird my loins emotionally and cognitively, preparing for the assault of political commercials as the presidential season heats up. I've tried being calm or philosophical, but it always ends badly. There's the candidate (choose your party) starring in a multimillion dollar campaign to win my heart, and there I am, screaming at the television, "What does that mean?!"

My only consolation was to tape the commercials and replay them in class, with my finger on the pause button, so that my kids could examine each sentence and come to their own conclusions. By the end of the year, they had turbocharged crap detectors, and I felt confident about sending them out into the world. But reading between the lines isn't just about recognizing crap in the world beyond. It's about being more honest about the origins and validity of our own beliefs. That's the only way we can truly combat the subtle but crippling effects of bias and bigotry in our classrooms, in our society, and in ourselves.

8

Does This Still Happen?

Linking History to Current Events

The newspaper is history written in a hurry.
—Anonymous Newspaper Editor

What's the Big Idea About Current Events?

"We had just finished lessons on American history and slavery," said Barbara
Vogel. "I saw this article in the newspaper and wanted to share it with my students." That was the day a group of fifth graders in Colorado learned that the
human slave trade was alive and thriving in the twenty-first century. "I have been
teaching for twenty-five years and saw the shuttle blow up with my students
watching, and we've talked about the Oklahoma City bombing, but I've never
seen children touched like this. I saw boys and girls crying and they said, 'We
thought slavery was over,' and I said, 'So did I.'"

Vogel's students—many African Americans—were shocked to learn that
African women and children were once again being kidnapped, abused, and
traded as slaves—this time in Sudan. History and current events collided with
such velocity that their world was permanently altered. They would not rest until
they conceived an adequate response.

Without that current events article, slavery would have been just another
topic that Barbara Vogel's students checked off their list of abysmally low points
in history. Without their history lessons, the article would have been one more
depressing headline about depravity and human exploitation. But taken together,

they demonstrated a connection between past and present, and illustrated the persistence of certain human dilemmas. The students were enraged that such tragic history was repeating itself. But they knew they weren't powerless. Their history lessons taught them that centuries of slavery could be eradicated, if people embraced the notion of freedom for all and were willing to work. Their horror galvanized them to use the nineteenth-century American abolitionists as models for their contemporary effort to stop slavery in the Sudan. Their efforts became the S.T.O.P. Campaign, which stands for Slavery That Oppresses People. S.T.O.P. has raised more than fifty thousand dollars to help redeem enslaved Sudanese and return them to their villages. To date, more than a thousand former Sudanese slaves have regained their freedom due to the work of this student-organized movement.

Groundhog Day

Current events time in some classrooms is a bit like watching a low-budget version of the movie *Groundhog Day*—without the popcorn. The same types of events are reported over and over and over—fourteen soldiers died in battle, the stock market is up, air pollution control legislation failed, and Punxsutawney Phil did not see his shadow. The presentations have a mildly gee-look-what-just-happened tone, with the occasional twinge of déjà vu, but no context. So it can seem like these events are happening for the first time, again and again and again.

But here's another view. The daily headlines are actually announcing that we humans are still working on problems that have stumped us since we came out of the caves. Today's arresting headlines—food shortages, persecution, unemployment, law and order, crime and punishment—mirror events twenty, fifty, two hundred, or even two thousand years ago. On every continent, in every era, we keep revisiting a short list of challenges—sometimes getting better, sometimes losing ground. Current events are simply evidence of our latest efforts.

To a very large extent, inhabitants of the twenty-first century face the same fundamental problems as people who lived in the Roman Empire, Elizabethan England, The Royal Court of Benin, and ancient Mesopotamia. Similar situations keep recurring in politics, international relations, social standards, personal behavior, civil rights, nation building, religious and ethnic persecution, and humanitarian zeal. For example, observe the similarities in the plight of Socrates, Alexander Solzhenitsyn, and Nelson Mandela—three citizens who were imprisoned, exiled, or put to death because they were considered threats to the state.

Of course it's true that no two situations are ever exactly alike, but the parallels are surely there. As Mark Twain observed: "The past does not repeat itself, but it rhymes." So your challenge is to take the *new* out of *news*, and instead help your students approach current events as a study of how humans continuously grapple with the four basic questions: *How do we survive? How do we thrive? How do we evolve?* and *What makes us devolve?* If these seem a bit abstract, replay in your mind the news coverage of New Orleans in the days immediately following Hurricane Katrina, and you will see these fundamental challenges writ large. Let's scan a sampling of current global headlines to see how they fit into these categories.

Headlines Related to the Question: *How Do We Survive?*

"Govt Restrictions on Imported Fresh Produce Met with Mixed Feelings" (Botswana)
Severe shortages of produce, such as potatoes in shops and supermarkets as well as exorbitant prices, which are sometimes twice higher than those of the imported produce, are some of the problems that the hospitality industry has had to deal with since the introduction of the restrictions.

"Cities Struggling to Keep Up Infrastructure" (Canada)
The postwar building boom tapered off in the late 1970s, matching a slowdown in economic growth that squeezed government budgets. And the former spending feast was followed by decades of famine that starved funding to replace aging infrastructure.

"African Famine to Last Until End of Year" (Africa)
The famine affecting fourteen million people across southern Africa is likely to last at least another year, the United Nations food agency has warned. This should be a time of rainfall across most of the region but in country after country the rains have been patchy and interspersed with dry spells.

"Warm Species Invading Antarctica" (Antarctica)
Scientists are calling for action to prevent foreign species from taking hold in Antarctica and wrecking the continent's unique ecosystems.

Headlines Related to the Question: *How Do We Thrive?*

"The 300 Millionth Footprint on US Soil" (United States)
By one count, more than half of all the people who have ever lived in the United States are living today. And their ranks are expanding. On any given day, 11,000 babies are born and 3,000 immigrants arrive, outnumbering the people who die or emigrate.

"Can a UN Convention Tackle Desertification?" (Zimbabwe)
Many dry land dwellers are already preparing to adapt to the changing climate, improving their incomes and investing in their lands, for example through innovative water-sharing schemes, small-scale sustainable agriculture, and plans to reforest degraded land. But they could do with more support.

Headlines Related to the Question: *How Do We Evolve?*

"Costa Rican Idea to Help Poor Countries" (Costa Rica)
Costa Rican President Oscar Arias plans to draft a formal proposal early next year for his idea of rewarding poor countries that focus spending on social programs with international aid. The Nobel peace laureate told the media he was convening a group of academics and experts to help.

"Micro-Credit Pioneer Wins Peace Prize: Economist, Bank Brought New Opportunity to Poor" (Bangladesh)
Bangladeshi economist Muhammad Yunus and the Grameen Bank he created won the Nobel Peace Prize for leveraging small loans into major social change for impoverished families.

Headlines Related to the Question: *What Makes Us Devolve?*

"JVP Fears Dictatorship" (Sri Lanka)
The JVP yesterday warned that the introduction of an electoral system to establish a powerful Parliament besides the existing Executive Presidency would eventually lead the country to a dictatorship.

"N. Korea Reports 1st Nuclear Arms Test" (United Kingdom)
Less than a week after Pyongyang threatened to do so, North Korea said Sunday night that it had set off its first nuclear test, becoming the eighth country in history, and arguably the most unstable and most dangerous, to proclaim that it has joined the club of nuclear weapons states.

"An Arsenal of Oppressive Laws" (Egypt)
The Egyptian Organization for Human Rights' sixteenth annual report dismisses claims that violations in Egypt are on the decline; however, a security official insists otherwise.

So What?

Some adults shun current events, in particular the newspaper, saying, *If it's on the front page, it's already happened. I can't do anything about it anyway, so why bother?* But when you look at the primary purpose of social studies instruction, it's hard to imagine trying to pull it off without studying current events. Social studies is supposed to:

- Foster individual and cultural identity along with understanding of the forces that hold society together or pull it apart.
- Include observation of and participation in the school and community.
- Address critical issues and the world as it is.
- Prepare students to make decisions based on democratic principles.
- Lead to citizen participation in public affairs.

Let's step back in time to see how monitoring current events could help teachers and their students achieve those social studies goals. The year was 1965. The place—Alabama. Martin Luther King Jr. and his colleagues had been laboring against impossible odds to register black voters in Selma. Impossible because the state of Alabama enforced a complicated system of voter registration, including a test, to prevent African Americans from qualifying to cast ballots. State officials used not one test but one hundred variations, to make it difficult for people to prepare for the test. Generally each test had three parts: (1) Copy or write from dictation an excerpt from the U.S. Constitution; (2) Answer four questions based on the excerpt just copied; (3) Answer four general knowledge questions about state and national citizenship. This meant that applicants had to be able to read, write, spell, and be well-informed about the intricacies of state and federal laws, conditions white people didn't have to meet. Failure was a given.

Eventually, King and his supporters decided that the only way to break through the voting blockade was to organize nonviolent protest marches that would bring the civil rights violations to the nation's attention. One small march ended in the shooting death of protester, Jimmy Lee Jackson. Jackson's memorial march ended in violence and bloodshed, as marchers were attacked by law enforcement with tear gas, nightsticks and bullwhips, and beaten and trampled by horses until they dispersed. Dr. King filed a lawsuit in federal court requesting a permit for the march to proceed. The result was groundbreaking intervention by President Johnson, who deputized nineteen hundred state troopers to protect the peaceful demonstrators, and the march was completed.

Students and citizens following these events in the newspaper or on television were body-slammed by the forces that hold society together or pull it apart—class, race, and access to economic and political power. Headlines shrieked and wire photos graphically captured the effects of the civil rights conflict on our nation as a community. Readers cringed at the sight of the world as it is. The readings, discussions, and debates that transpired in current events lessons during the marches forced students to consider how we make decisions based on democratic principles, and how we enforce them in the face of organized, violent, illegal opposition. People all over the country, sickened by the injustice and brutality, made some very tough decisions. They *chose to act.* Galvanized by the courageous marchers, they poured into Alabama to support their cause. That's how Viola Liuzzo came to be in Selma on the night of March 25. The thirty-nine-year-old white woman left her home and five children in Detroit to lend her voice to the protest. She was shuttling marchers between Montgomery and Selma in her 1963 Oldsmobile when three Ku Klux Klan members fired directly into the driver's window of her car, killing her. Scores of other protesters were wounded, jailed, or killed. Throughout the movement, concerned citizens discovered that there was much that they could do about the injustice, if they decided to participate in this public affair.

What About Standards?

Poring over the newspaper is like gazing at a monitor tracking the vital signs of the planet. It may be the most efficient, interesting, and relevant way to address a plethora of social studies goals. With just a few minutes practice each day, your students can become experts at spotting current events that mirror the past and thinking about ways to improve the future. When you decide to incorporate current events in your social studies programs using the newspaper, the Internet, or other media sources, your students will develop and demonstrate skills that are fundamental to a rigorous standards-based approach to social studies. The following list suggests the range of learning challenges students face as they examine the link between past and present and consider possible responses to unfolding events.

Students will:

- Identify problems and dilemmas in the past and their counterparts in the present.
- Analyze the interests and values of the various people involved in current events.
- Identify causes of problems or dilemmas.
- Propose alternative choices for addressing problems in the present.
- Formulate a position or course of action on an issue.
- Identify possible solutions.
- Evaluate the consequences of various solutions.
- Conduct research on issues and interests.
- Gather, evaluate, and synthesize data from a variety of sources to develop media literacy skills.

 ## Awareness

Assessing Prior Knowledge About Current Events

The goal of the Awareness section is to find out what your students know about current events and the news media. How do people keep informed about the world around them, and how did they get the news in the past? These activities encourage your students to reveal what they already know, so they can feel smart before you start teaching. As you flush that information out into the open, you build an authentic foundation from which to launch the Exploration and Inquiry stages of the learning cycle.

You Are Here: What's Happening?

A simple way to describe current events is "what's going on now." As such, it can include events taking place across the street, in another state or on another continent, out in space or under the ocean. Topics can range from the discovery of an Egyptian tomb to the discovery of a cure for cancer. Your first task is prospecting to uncover what your students actually know about events in the world beyond your classroom—the issues, countries, and personalities on their radar screens.

So let's get started. Give students a piece of plain paper. Ask them to draw a picture or symbol in the center of the paper that represents them, then use words and sketches to show anything that's happening that day—local, national, and global events; issues related to people, animals, technology, science, or the environment. Students might draw melting glaciers to show the destruction of the polar ice cap, a space station, wars and antiwar demonstrations, a meeting at the United Nations, the Super Bowl, a horse race, miners, auto workers, fishermen, people voting or building a pipeline, or teaching school in a refugee camp.

When students have completed their drawings, have them pair up or meet in small groups to share their pictures. Then have the students reconvene and tell you "what's happening now." Make a list of all the events or issues they identified. Then ask: *How would we find out more about what's going on in the world right now?* Students list possible news sources (text messaging, Internet, radio, television, newspaper).

Waking Magoun's Brain: All the News That's Fit to Cry

Most of your students have watched the news on television. It may be their major portal for news about the outside world. Ask them how they think people living before radio, television, and the Internet got their news? Then share the following information about town criers and discuss that form of broadcasting.

Town Criers

Town criers or bellmen were the newscasters in times past. The tradition started in ancient Greece, when heralds announced the severing of diplomatic relationships, which preceded a proclamation of war. The first use of criers in the British Isles dated back to Norman times, when the cry "oyez, oyez, oyez" (old French for "hear ye") was used to draw the attention of the mostly illiterate public to matters of importance. Royal proclamations, local byelaws, market days, advertisements, even news of special sales were all proclaimed by a bellman or crier throughout the centuries. Town criers were protected by the ruling monarch, as they sometimes brought bad news, for example, tax increases. To injure or harm a Town Crier was seen as an act of treason against the ruling monarchy. This is how the phrase "don't shoot the messenger" came about. To this day, Town Criers in the British Commonwealth are protected under old English law—they're not to be hindered or heckled while performing their duties.

Ask your students:

- What do you think would be important skills for a town crier?
- Why do you think the crier needed the protection of the king?
- Why do you think we no longer have town criers?
- If we had a crier in our town today, what might he or she be announcing?
- What kind of news would a crier announce about our school?

Go to www.americantowncriers.com, the website of American Guild of Town Criers, where you can see pictures of town criers and hear them ringing their bells, calling the townspeople to order, and making historic announcements. Ask for volunteers to be the town crier for your room and make daily announcements.

Exploration

Discovering More About Current Events

Kids of all ages feel like adults when they're browsing through the newspaper. It's as grown-up as they can look until they're old enough to loaf around Starbucks and drink lattes. Even modest local newspapers have lots of topics in the various sections, from yard sales to crime reports, so students with a wide range of interests and reading abilities can dig in, especially if they work in pairs. And even if they're just reading the horoscopes or sports section at first, they're reading. That's a big step for some, particularly the voluntary illiterates who can read at Concorde speed, but treat books as if they're infectious. Newspapers lure them back into reading.

One of the most compelling aspects of using the newspaper in your classroom is that you can trade in your five-year-old textbooks for history that was written last night. This fresh, relevant instructional material is also incredibly cheap—or free. Most major newspapers support *Newspapers in Education*, a program that gives teachers free class sets once a week, and plenty of teaching suggestions. Most towns also have free local newspapers published at least once a week. They're generally small but super-relevant, covering events right in your backyard, such as Beach Clean-Up Day, which means your kids can be informed *and* involved. Scoop up an armful and you have at least a week's worth of timely, well-written reading material. Since the price is right, they can be cut apart, marked, clipped, pasted, posted, filed, and recycled in an almost endless cycle of learning activities.

The activities in this Exploration section are designed to let students roam through their world via newspaper headlines and photographs. They can browse, formulate questions, pursue hunches, make discoveries, and compare their impressions with other students. The goal is to build their comfort level with using the newspaper as a source of information about the big problems of our times, and to challenge them to recognize similarities between the past and present.

Getting to Know Your Newspaper by Browsing

When you drag a bundle of newspapers into your class, your kids may react as if you just broke out the snacks. Whatever you do, don't try to curb their enthusiasm. Let them dig with both hands. Pass out the papers, let each student choose a partner and give them time, fifteen minutes or so, to browse through the newspaper together, reading anything they want. At some point, pause and ask students to share the most interesting thing they've discovered so far. As kids talk about their horoscopes, used car prices, movie openings, a sale at the sporting goods store, you'll see the others flip through the paper to find what they missed. After the discussion give them more time for exploration, then focus on the idea of current events. Ask: *So what do we know about what's going on in the world today from looking at the newspaper?* List all of their ideas on a chart or the board. Then ask: *Do you think anything like this ever happened in the past?* List any connections they suggest.

Scavenger Hunt

Most newspaper fans take a buffet approach, rarely reading dutifully from front to back. Instead, they head for their favorite parts first—the horoscopes, ball scores, obits—leaving other sections unwrinkled, unread. But from a social studies point of view, there's valuable information in every section, so your students need to be omnivores. You can encourage them to sample each section by creating a scavenger hunt. Develop a list of items, such as the following, that will propel them through the pages, scanning to find:

- A number greater than one thousand
- The price of a pound of meat
- The high temperature in a major U.S. city
- The name of two countries other than the U.S.
- The name or photo of a person in the government
- An international dateline
- The name or photo of an animal
- A sports headline
- The price of a used car
- A game
- A letter

- A job you would like to have
- The score of a game
- The TV channel that broadcasts a news program at 6:00 P.M.

Ask your students to search through the newspaper to find the items on your scavenger list, then circle them and record the section and page number where they're located. When they're finished, ask what was the most interesting thing they discovered? What section was their favorite? Now that they're familiar with the contents, give them more time to browse and read.

Headlines: Focusing on the Big Ideas

Newspaper journalists have just a few column inches to capture readers' attention, but headline writers have the biggest challenge of all, because headlines sell papers. Their tightly compressed messages—just four to seven words—are like verbal fireworks. They explode in the brain, capturing our attention, even our awe. When they succeed, we dig for loose change.

Headlines are almost like code, so kids enjoy deciphering the meaning of a handful of words written in a stilted style—"President Declares Celebration," "Forgotten Brother Appears," "Drivers Protest Pay Cuts." The brevity represents a high thinking-to-reading ratio, so smart kids with reading difficulties can be champs in this activity.

Simply reading the headlines is a good way to monitor what's going on in the world and to track how the daily news relates to the continuous human effort to solve the four problems—how do we survive, thrive, evolve and devolve? Ask your students to bring in headlines or provide them with a generous pile of newspapers and let them cut out headlines and stick them on a bulletin board. When you have a fairly good collection, ask students to choose a headline and speculate with a partner about what the words mean.

Then ask students to group headlines that they think go together—by issue, location, effort, or people, and ask students to give their categories a title, such as *environmental protection, crime and law enforcement, disaster relief, safety, the economy, homelessness,* or *global warming.*

Photographs as Journalism

The newspaper is like a family photo album for the human race. There we are—at the launch of a space shuttle, the funeral of a former president, in warfare, in calamity, or in celebration. The pictures speak volumes about the challenges we face, our successes, and our plight. And the photos are the work of expert photojournalists, so they convey huge amounts of information in a single shot. Newspaper photos are invaluable tools for helping all kids understand current events, but especially second-language learners and students with strong visual and interpersonal intelligence. Here's a short list of activities using newspaper photographs to explore social studies.

1. Cut out photographs that focus on topics relevant to your studies and remove the captions. Give your students plenty of time to study the picture, and then ask: *What do you think this story is about? What clues do you see that can tell us more about who, what, where, when, why?*

2. Have students cut dozens of pictures from the newspaper and then classify them by subject or theme—science, environment, politics, education, inventions, entertainment, power struggles, the law, or cultures in conflict.

3. Make a photo bulletin board with the caption, "What's Happening in Our World?" Have students supply their own captions or brief explanations for the pictures.

4. Let students choose their favorite newspaper photo of the week or month and write a story about the event, using a point of view that's different from the original newspaper article.

Students with an interest in photography can visit The Best in Photojournalism (http://bop.nppa.org) to see award-winning photographs and related stories. There are some really stunning images to provoke more questions about current events.

Where in the World?

One of the amazing feats accomplished by a newspaper is connecting us with life on the other side of the planet. Reading the daily newspaper is like spinning the globe and eavesdropping on any of the seven continents, plus outer space. Ask students to look through the newspaper to find: five stories from cities in their home state, five stories from states other than their own, and five stories from countries other than the United States. They can record the names of these cities, states, and countries, then locate them in an atlas or on the Internet.

Mapping Events

Geography often plays a role in current events. The big newsmakers are natural disasters such as floods, fires, avalanches, tsunamis, and volcanic eruptions. But many other articles have an important geographic element, such as the report from the Arctic region finding that indigenous peoples and animals in the area are among the most chemically contaminated on earth, or coverage of logging in Brazil—ten thousand square acres of rain forest gone—and the significant local and global consequences of deforestation. So it's important that your students can tell the Amazon from the Arctic. They simply must know their way around the map, and the newspaper gives them vital practice, while linking current events and geography.

Arrange students in groups and have them choose one international story in the news. Ask them to find the location of the event on a map, then work through the following questions to explore the effect of geography on events.

- In what city did the story take place?
- In what country is that city?
- What's the capital of that country?
- On which continent is that country located?
- What lies to the north, south, east, and west of this country?
- How would you describe the geography and topography of the region in which this story occurred?
- Did the physical characteristics of the country contribute to the events in the story?
- Did the event or events have any effect on the physical characteristics or natural resources of the country?

Other News Sources

If you use the newspaper as your main source of current events, try to include a variety of other sources, including television, radio, the Internet, and magazines. You may want to select one news story and compare how it is handled by the different media. Four good sources are:

Scholastic News for Kids (http://teacher/scholastic.com/scholasticnews/news) will deliver the top stories of the day to your computer desktop to download for discussion or duplication five days a week.

New York Times Learning Network (www.nytimes.com/learning/) has news of the day and a special social studies section with articles and lesson plans.

TeachableMoment.org provides educators with timely teaching ideas to encourage critical thinking on issues of the day and foster a positive classroom environment. It is a project of Educators for Social Responsibility Metropolitan Area. Topical activities are available for elementary school, middle school, and high school levels.

500 Nations is a news network devoted to news of Native Americans. The website (www.500nations.com) is jam-packed history, anthropology, current events, even casino news—just about everything you can imagine relating to Native Americans. You will find information broken down by U.S. state and Canadian Provinces. Reading items from this website can stimulate an excellent conversation about what's news, who decides what's news, and how do we know what we're missing. Download several pages or articles and discuss them with your students. Locate the tribes on a map or atlas. Ask:

- What news does this website cover that we don't see in our newspaper? What do you think is the reason for the difference in content?
- What is the effect of this absence of news coverage about Native Americans in the mainstream media?

For your own global monitoring, log on to any of the following:

Amnesty International, www.amnesty.org Information about human rights issues and links to news reports of human rights violations around the world
Asia Today, www.asiasource.org/news
CNN: World News, www.cnn.com/WORLD Organized by region with some video and audio
European Newspapers, www.world-newspapers.com/europe.html Organized by country
Flying Inkpot News, www.inkpot.com/news Links to many national and international newspapers—searchable by category, keyword, or region
Latin American Newsletters, http://latinnews.com
NewsHub: World, http://newshub.com/ Headline news updated every fifteen minutes
New York Times Online: International, http://nytimes.com/pages/world
Middle East Online, www.middle-east-online.com

 Inquiry

Digging Deeper into Current Events

As a teacher, I valued the newspaper as a compressor—consolidating most of our academic targets in a single, highly accessible medium. At the same time, it was an expander—blowing out the classroom walls and transporting my students to distant places, far more complex and fascinating than our neighborhood. The goal of this Inquiry section is to encourage students to focus on a current events topic of their choice, probe deeply, devise and test theories of their own, and become an expert on one particular aspect of human activity in twenty-first-century life.

Now remember the real goal. You're studying current events to see how we humans are doing at solving the big problems. With that in mind, you don't want students to read the newspaper, listen to the news, or log on to the Internet and swallow current events whole, as if they are isolated incidents unrelated to anything past or present—requiring no scrutiny or explanation.

But how do you achieve that? Having a fifteen-pound bale of newspapers dropped on your classroom doorstep is just the first step. Even having students scour every section daily won't do the trick, and who has that kind of time? Instead, they need to make the leap from readers to inquisitors who observe, investigate, and wonder if there are bigger issues behind the headlines. Thinking is the way they find the connections between events in the present and the past. Thinking can expose the larger, unstated agendas that are driving issues that on the surface seem to be isolated, random, or benign. High-functioning inquisitors pursue the possibilities for change and improvement.

Here's how the process of inquisitive thinking might look. Picture this headline.

City Approves First 7 Story Building—Affordable Housing Promised

Now picture a steady stream of questions crawling beneath that headline, like the subscript on a news channel, prodding and poking the reader to think before swallowing. For example, without even reading the article about the seven-story building, an inquisitive thinker might ask:

- Why now? We have plenty of empty units in the city.
- Did they change the four-story ordinance, or just waive it for this project?
- Why? What did the city get in exchange? How will the city benefit?
- Who are the developers?
- Who voted to approve the building?
- What does *affordable* mean? To whom?
- What percentage of the units will be affordable?
- What does *promised* mean?
- How do we ensure that low-income citizens know about this opportunity?
- What is the process for applying? Who decides? Is it a public process?
- Do we know anyone who needs this information?
- How can we be sure they get it?

That's *inquisitive thinking.*

This will be easy for some students who already have an obsessive curiosity about events in their world. But you'll need to model this process to help most students learn to dissect newspaper articles for their content, implications, and connections to the past. Here is a process to help you get started.

Part 1: Just the Facts

In journalism, the Five Ws—also known as the Five Ws and one H—is a concept in news reporting, research, and police investigations that most people consider fundamental. It's a formula your students can use to dig the facts out of an article, before they drill for meaning, ferret out connections to the past, and create possible solutions. As you approach any article, remind students to begin looking for information that answers the following six questions:

- Who? (is the story about)
- What? (is the story about, what happened)
- Where? (did it take place)
- When? (did it happen)
- Why? (motives, consequences)
- How? (methods)

Part 2: What Does It Mean?

This is the level where students go beyond *what* to *so what?* The following questions promote analysis and synthesis, so that students realize that the purpose of reading the newspaper is not to prep for a current events quiz show, but to understand motives and implications.

- What were the people in this article concerned about?
- What was their problem?
- What do you think they were trying to accomplish, fix, change, invent, or avoid?
- Did culture play a role in their situation or actions?
- Would the situation have been different if they were living in a (desert, mountains, etc.)?
- What did they do?
- Why did they do it?
- What was the effect?
- Did it achieve their goals?
- What else happened as a result?
- What do you wonder about them?
- What would you have done?
- Do you have a different idea?

Part 3: Connections

This is the final leap, where students link contemporary events to human dilemmas in the past and assess the possibilities for making another try at a solution.

- What questions come to mind after reading this article?
- What is the problem attempting to be discussed, exposed, or solved?
- How long has this been a problem?
- Was this a problem in history? Where? When?
- How have people tried to solve the problem?

- What's worked?
- What is standing in the way of solutions? What would help?
- What factors influence finding a solution?
- How can we research this issue?
- Can we influence it?

A Picture Is Worth a Thousand Words

Since we know that many kids are visual learners, it's important to find ways to augment current events lessons with images, especially when you are trying to help kids understand the connection between location and events. Atlas-type maps offer a limited source of contextual information about topographic details or natural features, but there are two amazing sources on the Internet to help you add visual material to current events.

The first is Google Images. If you haven't used this yet, you're in for a treat. It's simple. Go to Google.com. Above the box for keywords you'll see the word *Images*. Click, then type in your keyword. Instead of text, you get dozens, even hundreds of images that you can print out or project.

A second source of images related to current events is on the website of the Library of Congress in the American Memory Project (http://memory.loc.gov/ammem/ gmdhtml/). In the section called *Places in the News*, there are hundreds of maps that illustrate the geography and history of cities in the news. The other section that's worth a look is *Cities and Towns*. This category runs the gamut from maps that depict individual buildings to panoramic views of large, urban areas. These maps record the evolution of cities through images of educational and religious facilities, parks, street patterns and widths, and transportation systems. The panoramic map section is mesmerizing.

Current Events Portfolio

Once your students get comfortable with scavenging for news and probing behind the headlines, they'll naturally start to gravitate toward certain topics, so devote some of your current events time to individual pursuits. Encourage each student to choose one topic about which they can become an expert. They can work on their own or in small groups of students who share the same interest.

Some Current Events Topics Students Can Investigate
- natural disasters: earthquakes, floods, storms, blizzards
- man-made disasters: building or mining collapses, fires, explosions
- transportation accidents: ships, trains, planes, highway collapses
- invasions, war, and peace
- crime and punishment
- inventions/cures

- accolades and prizes for special individuals
- drought, famine, involuntary migrations
- widespread diseases, epidemics
- elections and assassinations of leaders
- artists, musicians, actors
- cultural events and entertainment
- celebrations and rituals

Current Events Scrapbook Should Include

- information related to geography and location of their topic
- maps
- photographs
- downloads from the Internet
- newspaper or magazine articles
- video clips from television or the Internet
- written analysis and synthesis

After monitoring the current events of their choice, students should be able to discuss the following questions:

- Why is this event happening?
- Who are the people affected?
- How are they being affected?
- Are nature, animals, or the environment being affected? How?
- Who is trying to help?
- What solutions are being attempted?
- Is this happening anywhere else in the world now? Where?
- Has this happened before? When? Where? Link to history.
- What are your thoughts on the event?
- What do you think might happen in the future?

Culmination

Set aside time when students can present a symposium on their research, organized by topic, theme, continent, or people in the news. Invite knowledgeable, interested adults to create a dialogue with students.

 ## Action

Using Knowledge About Current Events

The purpose of social studies is to help students acquire the habits of good citizens, globally aware individuals, and productive adults. And habits come from action. In-the-world, in-the-moment, strategic, bold, creative action. Action lets students use their knowledge to address problems, work on solutions, create new knowledge that can be shared, and see the impact of their learning in the world. So what can your students do with their current events knowledge?

Activities Using Current Events

Helping Others Through Pro Bono Efforts

Throughout this book, you've seen examples of students organizing to help others. Barbara Vogel's kids created S.T.O.P., and kids in Salt Lake cleaned up toxic dumps. The opportunities are unlimited, because the need is unlimited. Challenge your students to put their shoulders into the effort to improve one situation they've monitored in the news. They can contact existing organizations to become members, set up local chapters of organizations such as S.T.O.P., or find their own cause and organize.

What Do You Think?

Students can extend their own learning about current events and spread the word by creating questionnaires to circulate among peers and adults. For example, if they are concerned about pollution in a local stream, a questionnaire will raise public awareness and expose areas where information is clearly needed, so students can shape a targeted publicity campaign. Students can design questionnaires to elicit input on: changes in local ordinances, attitudes toward recycling, education measures that will be on the ballot, zoning laws that curb efforts to support the homeless, or community use of public facilities such parks, beaches, and libraries.

Film at Eleven

Another way for students to bring their current events concerns to a broader audience is to get in front of a camera. With a simple video camera, they can film reports, like news broadcasts, complete with data, charts, interviews with experts, and testimonials from activists. Planning and creating the script or storyboard for these dramatic pieces can be a cooperative learning activity. It could be played at public meetings or put on the local town or city's website.

Back to the Future News

Students can use video cameras to tape news with a twist. They report on an event in the present, then flash back to a time or place where the same type of event was occurring. For example, after reporting on torrential rains in their town, students interview a peasant living in fourteenth-century Italy, who reports that it has rained continuously for six months. The fields are sodden, it's impossible to plant crops, and famine is just around the corner. Or students may report on the safe return of astro-nauts from space, then interview Lewis and Clark about their expeditions. Students can work with partners to gather information and write the script for their interview.

The Way We See the World

Writing their own weekly newspaper is another way for students to focus on cur-rent events that have a direct impact on their world while they practice their journalism skills. They can also include articles on sports, conduct restaurant reviews, give film suggestions, and write letters to the editor. Here's a formula to help students craft an effective article.

- *First Paragraph* In the first one or two sentences tell who, what, when, where, and why. Hook the reader by beginning with a clever or surprising statement. Try opening the article with a question or a provocative statement.
- *Second/Third/Fourth Paragraphs* Give the reader the details. Write in the third person (*he, she, it, they*). Be objective, but use quotes to include opin-ions from other people.
- *Last Paragraph* Wrap it up. Try ending with a quote or a catchy phrase.

Professional Curiosity

Invite a reporter from a newspaper or a television news station to come and ex-plain expectations and challenges of the profession. Student should prepare a se-ries of questions, such as:

- How did you become a journalist?
- What is the most important skill a journalist needs?
- What sources do you use?
- What do you like about your job?
- What do you dislike?
- What was the most interesting story you wrote?
- What's the hardest part about writing?
- What kind of stories would you like to cover?
- What should students study if they want to be journalists?

 ## The Learning Ledger

The Learning Ledger is a tool for regular, focused self-assessment. Learning Led-gers help students account for their day, like a memoir, diary, or journal with the expressed purpose of capturing concrete descriptions of their work with current events and its effects on them.

Basic Three Questions for the Learning Ledger
- What did I do?
- How did I do it?
- What did I learn?

Questions Related to Current Events
- What did I learn in current events?
- How did I find this information?
- What do I think about what's happening in _____ (country, city, event)?
- Why do I think this is happening?
- How is this like things that happened in the past?
- What might it take to change the circumstances, outcome, or events?
- What would be a better outcome?
- Who might be able to change the circumstances, outcome, or events for the better?
- What do I still wonder about?
- What else do I want to find out?
- What could I teach someone else about _____?

Additional Questions for the Learning Ledger
- What did I enjoy most about my work today?
- What do I want to try next time?
- What did I learn about how I am smart?
- What did I learn about myself?
- What's the best thing I did all month?
- Who do I enjoy working with?
- Who helps me learn?
- What helps me learn?
- How do I help other kids learn?
- What did I do with other students?
- How did I do it?
- What did I learn about working as a group?
- How did I help the group?
- How did I get help from the group?
- What did I do well?

In Closing

I have to admit—I love newspapers. I can squander a whole morning with a pot of coffee and a five-pound Sunday paper. I think of it as a highly indulgent form of learning, and *learning* is the key word here. If you get your kids hooked on the newspaper habit, you can rest assured that they'll be learners for life.

Consider the following. When your students leave school at the end of twelve or thirteen years, that will be the end of textbooks. For some, sadly, it will also be their last contact with novels and poetry and industrial-strength academic discourse. But newspapers are everywhere. It's nearly impossible to get a latte or a seat on the subway without caressing the soft, rustling pages that whisper news of the world, cultural reviews, political opinions, and consumer information. It's consistently good writing, delivered fresh daily to feed the brain. But more than that, the newspaper is a vital tool for maintaining a democratic society, and building an informed and compassionate planetary community. All that for pocket change.

9

Who Do We See About That?

Social Justice Projects Beyond the Classroom

I have moments of real terror when I think we might be losing this generation. We have got to bring these young people into the active life of the community and make them feel that they are necessary.

—Eleanor Roosevelt

Thematic Strands:
Power, Governance, and Authority
Civic Ideals and Practices

Learning Layers: Geography, environmental science, media literacy, history, sociology, economics, civil rights, the legal system, crime and punishment, Internet research, persuasive writing, public speaking, advocacy, community organizing, strategic thinking, consensus building, negotiation, compromise

What's the Big Idea About Social Justice?

Let's cut right to the chase. In an era of homogenized, shrink-wrapped, germ-free curriculum, social justice is the renegade. It's untidy, exhausting, discouraging, even dangerous work. None of that, however, stopped veteran teacher Bill Coate and his fifth-grade students from fighting to preserve and honor a forgotten community, poised on the brink of extinction.

Bill is a superb teacher with an unbridled passion for history and social justice. Each year his students haunt the newspaper archives, county morgue, tax assessor's office, and City Hall in their town of Madera, California, usually intent on resurrecting a long-forgotten resident of the town. But one fine afternoon, Bill and his kids stumbled upon seven headstones in a neglected field four miles outside of town, and their sleuthing morphed into a crusade to right a very old wrong. The only clues they could glean from the weed-choked plot were Chinese characters etched in stone. They scanned the area for informants and spied the Madera Irrigation District right across the road. "Let's go over and ask who owns this field," Coate suggested.

Bill readily admits that if he detects a hint of injustice, a whiff of something unfair, "That's like saying *sic 'em* to a dog," so the nervous, furtive, half-answers they got from the irrigation officials told him that something was amiss—and the hunt was on. With his band of amateur snoops, Bill grilled the tax assessor, who declared, "That's not a cemetery." Bill replied, "Well, somebody ought to tell the people who are buried there!" Despite repeated official denials, the students persisted, and their prying eventually uncovered the forgotten Chinese community of Madera, including the burial ground. The field held the remains of immigrants who arrived in California during the Gold Rush, built the railroad, and worked the ranches. Yet they lived, died, and were buried as outsiders.

Bill and his students were initially thrilled with their discovery. Then they hit a snag. The cemetery was on private land, the taxes hadn't been paid since the last descendants left town, so the plot was scheduled for a quiet sale to developers. With that transaction, the last traces of the Chinese immigrants would be wiped off the face of Madera. "My kids were hooked. They were determined to save the cemetery, so they decided to raise money to pay the back taxes. But we were foiled again—the county informed us that we wouldn't be allowed to pay the taxes."

Here's where Bill Coate, teacher, turns social justice crusader—and a brilliant one at that. With the cemetery doomed to destruction, his kids planned a *Ceremony of Remembrance* to honor the dead, and invited twelve honored guests, including Secretary of State March Fong Eu, the Chinese Consul General, and of course, the media. On the day of the ceremony, the guests were ushered to seats under a white canopy facing the graves. Bill's students presented their research, bringing the extinct Chinese community of Madera back to life, including the seven who rested at their feet. In closing, the students asked the twelve to act as an informal jury. "Should this sacred ground be designated an historic site? How would you vote as citizens of our community?" As the CNN cameras whirred, each cast a yes vote, including the representative from the Irrigation District.

The rest, as they say, is history. The Borden Chinese Cemetery earned protection as an historic site. The students published Forgotten Field, Forgotten People, the most definitive study of the Chinese experience in Madera County. The long-dead residents gained their place of honor in history, thanks to a teacher and his students who worked for justice and got it.

Improve Yourself, Improve Your Community

Most children experience or think about social justice issues. They know instinctively when something's unfair—whether they're puzzled by the way certain kids are bullied out of playground games, or deeply troubled wondering where homeless people sleep at night. Kids rarely accept injustice as the status quo. Instead, they look to the adults in their lives—parents, teachers, coaches, relatives—to help them decide what to do. But sometimes the response is less than inspiring—squirming, changing the subject, turning a blind eye. *Drop it* is the unspoken message.

Let's think about how children might respond to the discovery that the topic of social justice is off-limits. They could think:

- Injustice is a fact of life—no point in trying to change human nature.
- Injustice is unfortunate but getting involved is too discouraging.
- Perhaps the victims brought it on themselves. They deserve it.

Some kids might never get that far in their thinking, but could simply be left with a vague uneasiness that if they were ever in dire straights, no one would come to their rescue.

Younger students may not be able to define social justice, but they can list the attributes we value in human relationships—friendship, responsibility, equality, fairness, mutual support, collaboration, and caring. Adults reinforce those values when they encourage, rather than avoid, authentic conversations about our collective dilemmas—civil rights, environmental protection, economic justice, and violence. In the best-case scenarios, adults embrace the inevitable question, *What can we do about it?* and teach students to act. This was precisely the scenario at 99th Street School, where a group of students decided that social justice meant living without the fear of gun violence.

Early one warm afternoon, a band of second- and fifth-grade students crowded the curb, shouting and gesturing at the approach of an ice cream truck. It was a typical scene on 99th Street in Los Angeles, where several brightly painted trucks regularly trawl for hungry customers. But this afternoon was different. As the truck slowed to a crawl, anticipating a brisk round of open-air sales, the students raised a flutter of hand-lettered demands, *No more guns. Don't sell guns. Throw away guns.* The disappointed vendors sped away with a freezer full of Popsicles and their supply of toy guns untouched. These students had decided that their community didn't need another weapon—real or look-alike—so they campaigned for fellow students to boycott the gun-toting sweets distributors.

Across town, a group of eight-year-olds were discouraged by the profusion of broken furniture and large appliances dumped on the sidewalks ringing their school. The municipal trash trucks that plied the neighborhood twice a week didn't make a dent in the rubbish. So these students launched a telephone research campaign. With the zeal of telemarketers on commission, they contacted one government office after another until they discovered the name of the large haulers who could remove the unsightly debris—but only by special arrangement. The kids made the call, the sofas and refrigerators vanished, and in a moment of jubilant inspiration, they collected any beautiful junk left behind, and created a ten-foot-high commemorative sculpture for the entrance of their school.

With a little prompting, older students enlarge their sphere of concern, zeroing in on injustice related to socioeconomic status, exploitation, and the abuses of power. They won't use those words, but they'll definitely recognize the issues. They'll notice that certain ethnicities seem to be overrepresented on the homeless roles in their own town, and underrepresented in the local power structure. They'll wonder how hotel workers could risk their jobs to demonstrate for a living wage, only to be aggressively ignored at city council meetings. And now that classrooms have Internet access, it won't take long for your students to discover sweatshops, child labor, hazardous waste, discrimination, and the devastation of the natural environment on a global scale. All of which would be emotionally daunting for kids, if it were just an exercise in cataloguing calamities and human indifference. But social justice education encourages students to act. So when you embrace social justice as a pillar of learning in your classroom, you declare that we're all responsible for improving our world.

The Covenant

Whether your students are organizing a lunchtime feeding program for the poor, protesting racist comments at sporting events, or tackling slavery on another continent, the philosophical starting point is always the same. We, the people—humans, citizens—agree to live by certain guidelines we call a *covenant*, which defines how we will behave toward each other in a community, whether you define *community* as a prairie town or the planet. If individuals, or the town fathers or federal officials violate the covenant, then we attempt to restore social justice through concerted action.

But kids can't do this alone. They need adult mentors to help them translate their ideas into action. With your guidance, they can go from passively spectating their way through a text to focusing their energy on a solution that could save a childhood, an education, or a life. They master effective strategies, contact key people, and gather critical resources—because something real and terribly important is hanging in the balance.

What About Standards?

When you include social justice projects in your social studies program by teaching your students what activists do and think and know, they will develop and demonstrate skills that are fundamental to a rigorous standards-based approach to social studies. In fact, teachers who are bold enough to embrace an activist approach to teaching find themselves scrambling to *add* to the standard curriculum—impromptu lessons in trickle-down economics, writing a press release, making an effective speech in under three minutes, graphic design principles for posters, and the fundamentals of negotiation. Their students exceed expectations on dozens of standards, and experience the thrill of road testing their courage, persistence, ingenuity, intelligence, and diplomacy—not to mention the pride of contributing to the welfare of others.

The following list suggests the range of learning challenges students will face as they undertake the intellectually and morally challenging process of identifying contemporary issues that violate social justice norms, choosing an issue that they want to address, and developing the skills necessary to create a more just society.

Students will:

- Examine what it means to be a citizen of the United States.
- Identify the rights and responsibilities of people in the United States.
- Identify ways people can participate in their government.
- Discuss the importance of political leadership and public service.
- Conduct research on social justice issues by posing questions and generating ideas.
- Locate, access, organize, and apply information about an issue of public concern.
- Employ a wide range of strategies to select, develop, and promote social justice projects.
- Use spoken, written, and visual forms of communication effectively with a variety of audiences to promote their social justice efforts.
- Use knowledge of government, law, and politics to make decisions about and take action on local, national, and international issues to further the public good.
- See issues from others' points of view.
- Learn to recognize stereotyping and classifying or marginalizing people through generalizations.
- Understand your own beliefs, feelings, and abilities and how they affect relationships with others.
- Examine and develop their ethical and moral reasoning.

Clearly there are some pretty compelling academic reasons to include social justice in your curriculum. You may already be regretting some missed opportunities and turning over a new leaf. But it's only fair to warn you about the downside. For a start, social justice work is amorphous. There are very few right answers. For every earnest activist, there are dozens of well-educated and well-funded countervailing voices explaining why the situation can't or shouldn't change. So you and your students must grapple with the question: *Are there some behaviors or conditions that are simply unjust, no matter the opposition?*

And there's so much to be done, even in our own neighborhoods. Many projects turn out to be a tiny first link in a long, arduous chain of effort to achieve one change. Think of the thousands of discrete actions required over decades to achieve civil rights for minorities in this country. So your kids may never have the thrill of seeing a bill signed into law, or a shelter renovated, or even a municipal code modified to allow public feeding of the homeless. They may fix one part of a problem only to discover that they've uncovered a greater injustice or need. Social activists eat disappointment and frustration every day, but keep on trying.

And social activism is potentially dangerous. Herbert Kohl, a veteran educator, tells the story that one of his students warned him, "You know, Mr. Kohl, you could get arrested for stirring up justice." You have only to look at the history of the civil rights movement to know how right he was. Utah teacher and author Barbara Lewis got that message, too, when she received threatening letters because her students targeted the toxic waste polluters in their neighborhood.

Social justice projects don't just push the envelope—they're several leagues outside of the box. You may feel intense discomfort when your kids first seize upon a cause. You wonder, *What will people think if they see my kids parading up and down the sidewalk carrying signs?* Some schools or districts exert intense pressure to color inside the lines when it comes to curriculum. In addition, innovative teaching may earn looks of disdain, cynicism, or open hostility—so you could feel like a leper entering the faculty lounge. Just repeat in your head *No good deed goes unpunished,* and give those naysayers a dazzling smile. With luck, they'll conclude that you're mildly insane and give you a wide berth.

Awareness

Assessing Prior Knowledge About Social Action

The goal of the Awareness activities is to find out what your students know about social justice issues, and what experiences they've already had in trying to solve problems in the community. Giving students the opportunity to share their prior knowledge lets them feel smart from the outset, and you gather valuable details about their individual skills and interests. These activities can be done in pairs, small groups, or as a whole class. Working collaboratively models two notions that are fundamental in social activism—cooperation and collective effort. One person may have a great idea, courage, even an abundance of charismatic leadership, but change requires support and effort from like-minded people. Martin Luther King Jr. certainly galvanized the civil rights movement, but it gained its velocity and impact from the thousands of people who gave their time, money, speeches, or lives for the cause. It's never too soon for kids to learn to cooperate for a cause.

You Are Here: Social Action Autobiography

Most of us become social activists through inspiration. We meet or read about someone who puts everything on the line for a cause, and we're moved—or deeply disturbed—by the realization that we, too, possess the power to make a difference. It takes skill, perhaps some courage—certainly we'll have to give up some TV time—but we're capable. Some kids have already had that epiphany, even on a microscale, but may not see themselves as activists yet. That's your starting point.

The Social Action Autobiography helps all kids recognize the ways that they've acted for the good of others. Begin by helping them recall a time when they helped someone or something, and changed a situation for the better. For younger kids, the prompt might be something like: *Think of a time when you helped someone.* This could range from taking care of a neighbor's cat to playing with a child who had no friends. They can respond by writing or drawing a picture, or making an annotated drawing with images and words. Even kindergarteners can do this reflective activity, by drawing a picture or a series of pictures, and then dictating to a scribe, perhaps an older student, parent, instructional aide, or the teacher. If you can't arrange for scribes, ask students to talk about their pictures in small groups.

For older students, ask them to think about a problem that involved other people, the community, the environment or animals, and what they did to help. You can pose a series of questions like the following to help them remember details and analyze their actions:

- How did you find out about the problem?
- What did you think was a good solution?
- What did you need to do to make it happen?
- Did other people help you?
- How did you feel about the solution?
- What did you learn from the process?
- How did you feel about yourself?

As students share their experiences, they're building a template for how to pursue social action, and starting a list of potential projects.

Waking Magoun's Brain

Suppose your students don't have a clue about activism? Their idea of social justice is being first in the cafeteria line at any cost. It's not hopeless—they're probably just not paying attention. But rather than waiting around for them to discover social justice, you can jump-start the process by introducing them to some extraordinary kids—just like them—who are experts at this game. Get Phillip Hoose's book, *It's Our World, Too: Stories of Young People Who Are Making a Difference*

(1993). It celebrates fourteen heroic kids who saw problems in their world and changed them. Your students will be dazzled from the very first page. There's Justin Lebo, who rebuilt bikes from used bicycle parts and gave them to kids who were homeless, had AIDS, or were orphans. In all, he reconstructed nearly two hundred bikes, using donations and all his spare time. They will meet James Ale, whose friend was struck by a car while they were playing ball in a busy street. James wondered, *Why do we have to play in the street, while the kids in the rich part of town have parks?* He transformed his anger into a campaign, and eventually convinced city officials to build a park in his neighborhood.

After sampling or devouring this book, ask your students, *Why do you think these kids were successful? What did they know or learn how to do?* Have them list the personal traits and skills that helped these young activists succeed. Post the list prominently and refer to it often as you close in on your own projects.

I've used Hoose's book dozens of times, with adults and children, and the reaction is always the same—awe and discontent. Students recognize that these kids are doing something real and important. That's the awe factor. But they're filled with questions. *Could I do that? Would I? Are there problems like that in my community? How would I find them? Do I have the courage to act?* The status quo has been replaced with a new standard of behavior, and kids wonder if they can measure up. That's what causes the discontent, and that's a perfect platform for exploration.

Exploration

Discovering More About Social Justice

Ben Franklin—printer, writer, and revolutionary—was one of the earliest global citizens, and a true social activist. Guided by his motto, *Improve yourself, improve your community*, he organized the first lending library, the first volunteer fire department, and crossed the Atlantic countless times to work for peace. Now, thanks to the virtual revolution, we're all global citizens. Every day you and your students can flip on the television or fire up your computer, and there's the world in living, sometimes painful, color. The question is, will your students be planetary eavesdroppers—aware but unmoved—or will they embrace their vastly expanded citizenship through action? Using the Exploration activities in this section, students can commit to daily activism with the click of a mouse and shadow activists through literature and biographical research.

Click for a Cause

Once students have shared their own Social Action Autobiographies and met Phillip Hoose's heroes, they may be itching to get involved again. Click for a

Cause is a simple way to connect kids to global efforts, and give them the instant gratification of contributing, all via the Internet. Here's how it works. Social justice organizers enlist sponsors for their cause—hunger, landmine removal, the rainforest. When you click a button on their websites, the sponsor gives a specified donation to the cause—sometimes just a penny or two, but it adds up. You can log on once a day, every day. If your students recruit friends, relatives, and parents, together they can make a difference. Here are five sites that welcome you to click for a cause. Bookmark these sites and let your students take turns being the designated donor-for-the-day.

www.clearlandmines.com Each year 26,000 people are killed or mutilated by landmines. 8,000 are children. You can help support the foundation that is trying to eradicate landmines, by clicking on their site once per day.

www.thehungersite.com Each year approximately thirty-one million Americans are food insecure, meaning they were either hungry or unsure from where their next meal will come from. Twelve million are children. Once a day, you can click on the "Give Free Food" button and fund the purchase and distribution of a cup of staple food for a person in need.

www.therainforestsite.com According to The Nature Conservancy, eight million square miles of tropical rain forest once encircled the planet. More than half have been burned, bulldozed, and obliterated. Funds generated by your daily click are used primarily to purchase rain forest land for preservation.

www.theanimalrescuesite.com The Animal Rescue Site is an online activism site that gives Internet users the daily opportunity to help an abandoned or neglected animal awaiting adoption. Visitors to The Animal Rescue Site can click on the "Feed an Animal in Need" button and provide at least one bowl of food.

www.thechildhealthsite.com According to the United Nations, over ten million children die annually from preventable causes, and many millions more are severely injured. The goal of The Child Health Site is to save lives and preserve the health of at least one thousand children per day.

Exploring Social Justice Through Biographical Research

Another way for students to explore social activism is to meet people who are doing it. Start by asking them to name people—living or dead—who dedicated themselves to social justice causes. They'll probably mention people like: Harriet Tubman, Rosa Parks, Oskar Schindler, Ghandi, Mother Teresa, Cesar Chavez, and Martin Luther King Jr. In addition, there's an impressive group of lesser-known social activists who battled to help agricultural workers, displaced Native Americans, exploited factory workers, and victims of racial discrimination. Your students shouldn't miss Nellie Bly, a journalist who exposed inhumane conditions in mental institutions, sweatshops, and jails. Or Fannie Lou Hamer, a lifelong activist who worked to secure voting rights for African Americans.

While studying environmental justice with my students, I came across *Red Ribbons for Emma* (Preusch et al. 1981), the story of Emma Yazzie, an elderly Navajo sheepherder—and to this day I think of this solitary, fierce figure whenever I flip a light switch, or disconnect my telephone charger, or conserve electricity in even the smallest way. The book describes Emma's heroic efforts to halt the strip mining that destroyed vegetation and polluted the water needed to raise her sheep on the Navajo reservation. She single-handedly disrupted expansion at the Four Corners Power Station by pulling up their red-ribboned surveying stakes. One day we called the power station to ask about Emma, and the supervisor assured us that he could see her hogan from his window, and that she battled on, alone but determined.

Social Activists: A Sampler

Emma Yazzie is just one of the many activists who can act as role models for your students. Here are eleven more for your consideration.

- **Ida Wells-Barnett** was a full-time journalist in 1891 who defied mob violence and terror to expose the national disgrace of lynching.
- **Dr. Ralph Bunche** mediated the first Arab-Israeli war in 1950, and played a major role in the formation of the United Nations.
- **LaDonna Harris** founded Americans for Indian Opportunity, crusaded for the rights of children and women and for the elimination of poverty and discrimination.
- **Dolores Huerta,** co-founder of the United Farm Workers of America, directed the UFW's national grape boycott taking the plight of the farmworkers to the consumers.
- **Aung San Suu Kyi** is a Nobel Peace Laureate currently under house arrest for her commitment to human rights and democracy in Burma.
- **John Mercer Langston**, the first African American elected to public office in the United States, worked for the fair and equal treatment of African American soldiers in the Union Army and struggled for African American voting rights.
- **Russell Means**, an Oglala Lakota, brought worldwide attention to the injustices and privation faced by Native Indians past and present.
- **Lucretia Mott** was dedicated to achieving equality for all of America's disadvantaged and disenfranchised, including Indians, women, slaves, and free blacks.

- **Frances Perkins** witnessed the infamous Triangle Shirtwaist Factory fire, which claimed the lives of 164 female workers. She spent her life as an activist for industrial reform, tackling worker safety, child labor laws, and wage and hours regulations.
- **Mary Ann Shadd**, the first African Amercian woman to be editor of a newspaper in North America, worked for racial integration in the United States and equal education for people of color.
- **Dr. Daniel Williams** earned his medical degree in 1883 and fought so that African Amercian doctors would be allowed to operate at Chicago hospitals.

The activists listed in this section are exemplars—intelligent, dedicated, and courageous—with much to teach your students. You can also find photographs and biographies of sixty activists on the Picture History website, www.picturehistory .com. Introduce each figure briefly, then encourage students to research one person on the Internet or at the library. Through their research, students can vicariously experience life as a crusader, and identify the skills needed to promote change. Give them the following questions to guide their research.

- What makes this person special or interesting?
- What are the adjectives you would most use to describe the person?
- What examples from their life illustrate those qualities?
- What skills did this person use to work for justice?
- What events shaped or changed this person's life?
- Did he or she overcome obstacles? Take risks? Get lucky?
- What effect did he or she have on the world? On other people?
- Would the world be better or worse if this person hadn't lived? How and why?

Remember that reading activists' autobiographies, biographies, diaries, and journals during literature time provides models of social justice projects, describes the skills activists use, and reveals the obstacles they face. Students can puzzle through their own social justice dilemmas and improve literacy skills in one fell swoop.

Inquiry
Digging Deeper into Social Justice

There are five big topics that tend to dominate social justice agendas in elementary and middle school classrooms. They are:

Civil Rights Slavery, child labor, exploitation of workers, discrimination, voters rights, free elections, sweatshop labor, equity for disabled, gender equity
Economic Justice Poverty, homelessness, health care, famine, diseases, housing, welfare, Fair Trade products, unemployment

Planetary Issues Environment, pollution, depletion of resources, recycling, AIDS, destruction of the rain forest, global warming, endangered species
Nonviolence War, prison reform, landmines, the death penalty, Geneva conventions, military conscription, pacifism, prevention of cruelty to animals, juvenile justice systems

> The greatest sin of our time is not the few who have destroyed, but the vast majority who have sat idly by.
> —Dr. Martin Luther King Jr.

Cultural Identity and Preservation Destruction of indigenous environments, cultural heritage sites, historic preservation, genocide

This section provides a model for inquiry learning by examining one social justice issue—child labor—in the past and the present, using photography as the primary research medium.

Photography as Tool for Social Justice

One of the most direct and powerful ways to help your students think about social justice issues is to take them to the scene of the crime through photographs, because a picture is frequently worth at least a thousand words. You won't need to say much when you present your students with photos of a rodent-infested tenement, a six-year-old, twelve-hour-a-day carpet weaver or images of civil rights protesters mown down by high-powered water hoses. Most of the social justice movements of the past two centuries have been documented in photographs that are available on the Internet. You can literally Google the major events that have shaped the social landscape and let your students investigate with their eyes.

It's critical to note that most social justice photographers were not content with simply documenting history. These people used their cameras as tools to *shape* history. Think photograph as lever. Their images were intentionally created to inform the viewer, influence public opinion, and goad people and governments into action. In the right hands, cameras make history.

A Camera and a Cause: Using Photographs to Learn About Child Labor

One of the most photographically compelling issues of modern times is the problem of child labor, which was first captured on film by Lewis Hine (1874–1940). As a university student he studied sociology and became a teacher, but when he picked up a camera, he found his calling. Hine used photography to express his social concerns, beginning with the plight of Ellis Island immigrants. In 1908, he left teaching to work as an investigative photographer for the National Child Labor Committee on their campaign against the exploitation of American children. For four years, Hine criss-crossed America, photographing children as young as three years old working long hours, under dangerous conditions, in factories, mines, and fields. In 1909, he published the first of many photo essays depicting child laborers. Some of his images are among the most famous photographs ever taken. Attempts at child labor reform continued, aided by the widespread publicity from Hine's photographs. As a result, many states passed stricter laws banning the employment of underage children. In 1938, Congress passed the Fair Labor Standards Act, which protects children from exploitation in the workplace. The Act was declared constitutional in 1941 by the U.S. Supreme Court.

Despite advances in child labor protection, Cesar Chavez found that seventy years after Hine's photo essay, conditions were still dire for the children of migrant workers. In his 1984 speech to the Commonwealth Club he stated that, "Child labor is still common in many farm areas. As much as 30 percent of Northern California's garlic harvesters are under-aged children. Some 800,000 under-aged children work with their families harvesting crops across America. Babies born to migrant workers suffer 25 percent higher infant mortality rates than the rest of the population. Malnutrition among migrant workers' children is ten times higher than the national rate."

Almost one hundred years have passed since Lewis Hine published his groundbreaking work, but child labor hasn't gone away. It's largely migrated to other countries as the gap between the first and third worlds widens. The appetite for affordable clothing, sports equipment, and shoes has sent manufacturers to countries where child laborers are vital to their families' economic struggle to survive.

Begin your study of child labor with a visit to The History Place and then Hine's collection, *Child Labor in America, 1908–1912* (www.historyplace.com/ unitedstates/childlabor/). There you'll find sixty photographs by Lewis Hine including the original captions. Hine's images drew the nation's attention to the plight of its children.

A Walk Inside a Photograph

After looking at an array of Hine's photographs, select one for discussion. Ask your students to imagine that they could walk inside Hine's photograph. Have them concentrate on what they see, smell, hear, and feel. Ask:

- Where are you? Describe the setting.
- What do you see children doing?
- Does it feel hot or cold?
- Is it clean or dirty?
- Is it easy to see where you're going or dark?
- What is underfoot?
- What do you hear?
- What are the children saying?

- What are adults saying?
- What would you say to the children?
- What would you say to the adults?
- What emotions would you feel? Why?

Look again at a selection of Hine's photographs of child laborers. Use the following sequence of questions to help students understand the role of Hine's photographs in forcing this issue into the public gaze. Ask:

- What is unusual or surprising about these photographs?
- Can you tell how these children feel?
- How would you feel if you had to do this twelve hours per day?
- How does it make you feel to see this child?
- Why do you think Lewis Hine took such sad pictures?
- How do you think adults in America felt when they saw these pictures?
- How do you think the President and Senators felt when they saw them?
- What do you think they tried to do?
- Did the pictures work? Did Hine achieve his goal?

Now push their inquiry into the present. Have your students spend some time researching child labor in the twenty-first century. There are numerous websites that present photographs of children performing dangerous jobs, underpaid or exploited, testifying to the persistence of this problem. They also tell students how they can help—in effect, continuing Hine's work. Review the following sites then select several that are appropriate for your students.

www.boondocksnet.com/gallery/nclc/index.html *The Campaign to End Child Labor: Child Labor,* photographs by Lewis Hine

www.cis.yale.edu/amstud/inforev/riis/title.html *How the Other Half Lives,* Jacob Riis, 1890s photographs of child laborers in New York

http://www.hsph.harvard.edu/gallery/ *Stolen Dreams,* photographs by David Parker, MD. Images of child laborers in the United States, Mexico, Thailand, Nepal, Bangladesh, Turkey, Morocco, and Indonesia

http://www.digitaljournalist.org/issue0208/cc_intro.htm Afghan Child Labor, photographs by Chien-Min Chung

After researching, ask your students to compare and contrast the child labor situation as Hine portrayed it with the current conditions of child laborers. Pose questions like the following to prompt your discussion.

- How have things changed in America since Lewis Hine took those photographs?
- Why did they change?

- What are the laws about child labor like today?
- Do any children in the United States work? Under what conditions?
- How is child labor different in other countries? Why is it different?
- What kind of work do children do in other countries?
- What happens to children who run away from their jobs?
- How can we decide what work children should and shouldn't do?
- How can people from many countries protect all children from unfair work?
- Are there any rights of children that are still being ignored or unfulfilled in the United States? (hunger, education, poverty)
- What needs to be done?
- What might we as students do to help?

Other Cameras, Other Causes

Your students may be passionate about other social justice causes that have been documented through photography. The library, the Internet, and the daily newspaper are all sources for outstanding photographs created to inform the public and call for action. Students can research any of the following topics through photo archives:

- AIDS memorial quilt
- civil rights movement
- Holocaust and its survivors
- homeless in America
- Hurricane Katrina
- migrant workers
- Native American relocation to reservations
- peace demonstrations
- sweatshops
- Vietnam War

Sources of Photographs for Social Justice Discussions

Civil Rights Movement

- http://afroamhistory.about.com/library/blphotos_civilrights_index.htm
- Civil rights photography of Charles Moore—*Powerful Days*. Charles Moore was one of the unsung heroes of the Civil Rights movement. Without the publishing of his dramatic photographs in *Life* magazine, and the work of other photojournalists, the public perhaps would not have been galvanized into action against the atrocities of segregation. www.kodak.com/US/en/corp/features/moore/mooreIndex.shtml
- www.time.com/time/newsfiles/civilrights/

Poverty in the U.S.

Soup Kitchen Photos: http://hazel.forest.net/skjold/photo_pages/soup_kitchen.htm

Sweatshops

The Triangle Factory Fire in New York City: www.ilr.cornell.edu/trianglefire/narrative1.html

 Action

Using Knowledge About Social Justice

The best social action projects are like an earthquake. One minute you're comfortably ensconced in your classroom, earnestly working through your curriculum, and the next minute, the ground shifts. Even before the room stops rocking, you sense that you're in new territory—face to face with a genuine adventure. The best projects come organically from the work and conversations you have with your students every day. Sometimes a kid will burst through the door on red-alert and demand that his peers sit up and take notice.

> *We must be the change we want to see.*
> —Mahatma Gandhi

Dump Busters

This was exactly the case with the students of Salt Lake City's Jackson Elementary School, and their teacher Barbara Lewis. In the 1980s, a hazardous waste site was located just three blocks from the Jackson school grounds. Students often played in the abandoned industrial lot that served as a graveyard for more than fifty thousand barrels, many of which contained residue from toxic chemicals.

The students had seen sludge in the bottom of the barrels and thought that it might be poisonous so they talked to their teacher. She responded by sharing a map of toxic dump sites in Utah. From that moment, they made it their business to find out if toxic wastes were being released into their neighborhood.

The students researched ground water and its contamination through toxic chemicals. Armed with maps, photos, and the latest scientific information, they contacted government officials. At first the results were discouraging. Time and again the students were told that nothing could be done about the abandoned barrels, and that probably there was nothing dangerous about the location. But they didn't give up. Instead they conducted surveys in the neighborhood, collected data, and warned residents about the danger of the toxic dump. They got in touch with the Environmental Protection Agency (EPA) and the site's corporate owner. They wrote public service announcements, created flyers, published articles in local and national papers and magazines, spoke to civic and university groups, and appeared on radio and TV. The students circulated a petition, talked to other students, and wrote a flurry of letters to every level of government. They met with Salt Lake City Mayor Palmer DePaulis, who was impressed with the student's initiative and promised to join their effort to have the site cleaned up.

In response to the growing publicity generated by the students, the EPA came to Utah to study the barrel storage site. The tests revealed that soil at the site had been contaminated as deep as thirty feet below the surface by heavy metals, toxic chemicals, and pesticides. The site posed a distinct threat to the quality of the water supply used by almost four hundred thousand area residents. The barrel storage site was immediately placed on the national Priorities List for hazardous waste clean up. Within one year, the barrels had been removed from the location near Jackson Elementary School. For their efforts they won the 1989 President's Environmental Youth Award.

Save Henshey's

I had my own headlines-as-hand-grenade experience when I was studying local history with my third-, fourth-, and fifth-grade multiage class. We were obsessed with old buildings—as rare as Bald Eagles in a seaside town being devoured by ravenous developers—and we'd discovered a real beauty while on a field trip to the Historic Society. It was a turn-of-the-century department store with the name of its founding family carved in the cornice. Days later the newspaper announced it was slated for demolition. My students were outraged and disgusted and determined to save Henshey's by petitioning for Landmark status. The irony was that Henshey's would be sacrificed to create building space for none other than Toys 'R Us—a kid's best friend. But not my kids.

We talked at length about the David-and-Goliath aspect of the situation, and I was blunt with them about our chances—disappointment was more likely than success because they were squaring off against landowners, real estate developers, the Chamber of Commerce, a huge national corporation, and our own city fathers who had approved the deal. Goliath would have been a cupcake by comparison. Undeterred by the odds, they spent the next six months in hand-to-hand combat. They organized petitions, wrote letters, circulated flyers, and made posters. They wrote to the president of Toys 'R Us, explaining the value of the building and promising a boycott if the toy store came to town. They held meetings with city officials, the owners, preservation architects, and finally spoke before the Landmarks Commission. They battled to save Henshey's. Ultimately they won and lost. It was declared an historic landmark, but subsequently bulldozed, when the owners convinced the city that its decrepit condition made it a safety hazard.

It was heartbreaking to watch the wreckers gouge and tear at this elegant structure until it was rubble. But our campaign was not a pyrrhic victory by any means. For my students, it was a great learning experience about their power in the community. I had been trying to instill in my students an activist's mind-set— if life, your country, or your situation isn't what you want, then do something about it. With the Henshey's project, they discovered their muscles. As one of the youngest, fiercest voices, Kyle Miller summed it up this way: "When you get so hyped up that the government and older people who can really make a decision pay attention, it makes you feel strong." That's what I tried to instill in my students . . . the idea that they have power.

Taking Sides: How to Choose a Social Justice Project

Since you are the person who bears the ultimate responsibility for educating your students, you must evaluate every project for its potential to promote social justice *and* guarantee learning, by linking school skills to a real-world problem. All kinds of learners must be able to get involved, not just the honor rollers or zealots. Ask yourself: *Does the project need writers, designers, speakers, thinkers, coaches, artists, advocates, devil's advocates?* Here are a few more questions you need to answer before you settle on a social justice project:

- Is this an issue that is within your students' experience, or can be directly related to their lives?
- Is firsthand, direct investigation possible?
- Are there sufficient resources for students to do research and take action to achieve their goals?
- Is it related to your curriculum goals?
- Is it sensitive to the local culture and the cultures of your students?
- Does it represent a cause or an issue that adults feel is worth the time students will invest?
- Is it a project in which parents can participate, support, or learn from their children without feeling defensive (as in antismoking campaigns)?

Another consideration relates to learning. We know learning is most effective when students start with what they know and build on that. Social justice learning is no exception. Since children are the experts on how children live in their own community in the twenty-first century, your social justice efforts will be more compelling if your students focus on projects that directly affect other children. They can compare and contrast their lives with children living elsewhere, and take action if they feel some kids are being treated unfairly.

For example, Canadian students decided to help children in Africa and Afghanistan by raising money to remove landmines from schoolyards. Another way that kids help kids is through Amnesty International Kids (www .amnestyusa.org/aikids), a subset of a global organization to ensure human rights. Each month they post an Urgent Action on their website, usually a call to help save a child. For example, a recent request for action focused on Hmong children in the Laos jungle who are starving and wounded. Each Urgent Action is issued with instructions about how your kids can help, including tips for writing letters and who to contact.

If you are looking at questions about the rights of children, tell your kids about the UN Convention on the Rights of the Child, written in 1989. It is very explicit about the protections that all children should enjoy, and it is widely embraced by nations around the world. Students can research this document at www.unicef.org/crc or simply type in keywords *UN Convention on the Rights of the Child*.

Here are two resources you should investigate while you're prospecting for a project:

> The Rethinking Schools website is loaded with ideas about effective teaching for a better world. *Rethinking Globalization: Teaching for Justice in an Unjust World* is a four hundred page teaching resource (www.rethinkingschools.org/ publication/rg/index.shtml). Sections cover colonialism, global sweatshops, child labor, along with culture, consumption, and the environment. The book is available from Rethinking Schools.

> *Green Teacher* (www.greenteacher.com) is a magazine by and for educators to enhance environmental and global education across the curriculum at all grade levels. Each issue contains ideas for rethinking education in light of environmental and global problems, reports of what successful teachers, parents, and other youth educators are doing, cross-curricular activities for various grade levels, book reviews, and announcements of events.

Starting Points

Once your kids begin to close in on a problem with action in mind, they need to determine if the problem is common knowledge or their private discovery. *Do they have allies who can lend their expertise to the effort? Is there an organization already in place that could use their muscle?* The fastest way may be to Google the topic and review the citations. Then pose some questions that will help them focus their research and come up with a plan.

- What do we need to know if we want to help?
- What's already being done? Who's doing it?
- What still needs to be done?

- What skills or resources do we already have to lend to the effort?
- What skills/resources/information will we need to learn/acquire?
- What problems might we confront?
- How will we handle them?
- Who else may want to help us?

A Social Activist's Toolbox

Social justice is not a spectator sport. It requires students to abandon passive learning and take some level of action in their community or society to achieve a positive change. Teachers contemplating a social justice curriculum need to rigorously train their students in research techniques, critical thinking, and public relations skills.

Successful student activists use the following tools to get their message out and achieve their goals.

- Write petitions and collect signatures.
- Organize letter-writing campaigns.
- Create an education campaign with flyers, bulletin boards, and displays.
- Create and distribute surveys to gauge public interest and awareness.
- Give speeches to interested groups.
- Develop media awareness.
- Write press releases, Letters to the Editor, newsletters, magazine articles.
- Contact like-minded individuals.
- Lobby elected officials who support your cause.
- Demonstrate, protest, and boycott.
- Negotiate.

Prepping Students for Action: Politics 101

If your students decide to abandon their classroom for a more public learning venue, they'll be playing with the big boys. And no matter how patronizing adults are to kids when the cameras are on, I've yet to meet an entrepreneur who will sit idly by while a band of well-coached ten-year-olds derails his plans for yet another strip mall. So you will need to teach your kids to think politically about both the causes of problems and roadblocks to solutions. Because they're young and rather pure, they'll formulate solutions that are logical and doable, even affordable, but haven't been done. At first glance they may wonder why it's so easy for kids to find solutions, and so hard for adults. Before they start congratulating themselves for being brilliant, step in. It's time for Politics 101.

Thinking politically requires students to focus on *who* rather than *what*. Problems don't just exist like natural laws. Most of them are the result of human behavior. So your kids need to uncover the *who* behind the problem. For a start, challenge your kids by asking them to consider the following questions about their project:

- If so many people know about this problem, why do you think it still exists? (Understanding an individual or group's motivation can help kids get the leverage they need to create change.)
- Who might be benefiting from this situation as it currently exists? Who else?
- What values might be motivating them? What do they want or need?
- Have they already tried to block solutions? How? What happened?
- What kind of solutions would appeal to them?
- What kind of pressure or action might move them to change and cooperate with a solution?

Questions like these hone analytic thinking and encourage research. But be prepared for some disillusionment. As the veil is lifted, your students may conclude that many adults are good, and some are even heroic, but a disappointingly large number behave as if they live in a community of one—themselves. That doesn't mean kids have to give up. Remind them of all the other kid-warriors who have succeeded.

Meet the Press

I'm sure you've heard the question, *If a tree falls in the forest and no one's there to hear it, does it make a noise?* Well, that same question applies to social justice campaigns. Your students can be smart, organized, and energetic, but if the word about their cause never gets out, little will happen. Smart activists know the power of the press and they use it. A critical element in your project work is to identify local news outlets—press, television, and radio. Get the names, fax and phone numbers of the reporters who cover local happenings, education or human interest stories and get their attention. Your students have an advantage because the press likes to run occasional feel-good stories, and remarkable kids are always a popular subject. The difference this time is that your students may have gone where many adults fear to tread. That's a hook that could capture a reporter's attention, giving you a chance to inform the public and garner support for your cause.

Breaking through to the front page or prime time is very difficult. Stories are prioritized from minute to minute up to press time. *If it bleeds, it leads,* means that every time there's a high-speed car chase or a natural disaster, your story will be cut. Your kids need to be prepared for disappointment and just keep on trying. If you're having trouble attracting the press, try an oblique approach. Most Board of Education meetings and almost all city council meetings are televised, and members of the press routinely show up looking for a story. If your students speak during Public Comments about your project, they will get the word out to the broader community and perhaps attract a reporter or two in the process.

The most important thing about press coverage is credibility. You may only have one shot at an article in the newspaper or a thirty-second spot on television, so when the opportunity comes around, your kids need to be ready. Whether they're on camera or face-to-face with a reporter, they must be clear, accurate, articulate, and serious. Message discipline is essential. No freelancing. No mugging for the camera. So before you go public with your campaign, you need to rigorously train every student. Do mock interviews and critiques with your whole class—not just a few hand-picked speakers. You never know who will capture the limelight. All students need to be ready to think on their feet and speak for the cause.

If you do snag some press time, don't miss the opportunity to compare the coverage to the real event. Have your students analyze articles or television spots in which they appear to see if their message was distorted, diluted or came through loud and clear. *What was their goal? What was the reporter's goal? Did the reporter's view match what they said and did?* If there is a gap between their presentation and the reporter's version of things, guide your students to think about the implications for other things they read in the press or see on television. Once students begin to take a critical look at the media based on personal experience, they will be much more discerning media consumers.

The Learning Ledger

Quantifying student growth through social activism is a challenge. You're convinced that your students have learned more through one social justice project than they would in a year of text-driven lessons. But to prove that, you will need to do some task analysis that shows how authentic learning addresses the course of studies for your grade or subject. For example, take a look at the standards for language arts. Then think of all the talking, researching, speechwriting, demonstrating, lobbying, leafleting, and cajoling your students have done on behalf of their cause. You'll be amazed at how many standards have been mastered—not covered, but mastered. And here's a thought. What if your students save a life—human, animal, or arboreal—but don't finish their textbook? It's worth pondering because that's a potentially rich dilemma created by social justice education. Students engaged in social justice projects will have a lot to say in their Learning Ledgers. Some days they may be frustrated or discouraged, so it's good to have a place to vent. And over time, the ledger acts as a diary or journal with the expressed purpose of capturing concrete descriptions of their work and its effects on them.

Basic Three Questions for the Learning Ledger

* What did I do?
* How did I do it?
* What did I learn?

Questions Related to Social Justice Projects

* What did I do that I've never done before?
* How did I do it?
* What did I learn from this new experience? About myself?
* What did I do to solve a problem?
* How did I do it?
* What did I learn about helping people? Helping myself? Making changes?
* What do I still wonder about?
* What else do I want to find out?
* What could I teach someone else about _____?

Additional Questions for the Learning Ledger

* What did I enjoy most about my work today?
* What do I want to try next time?
* What did I learn about how I am smart?
* What did I learn about myself?
* What's the best thing I did all month?
* Who do I enjoy working with?
* Who helps me learn?
* What helps me learn?
* How do I help other students learn?
* What did I do with other students?
* How did I do it?
* What did I learn about working as a group?
* How did I help the group?
* How did I get help from the group?
* What did I do well?

In Closing

Skill development could be reason enough to steer your kids toward social action. But there's a second reason to pursue this brand of education, and quite frankly, this is the one that sent me to the barricades: citizen apathy. I was teaching my students about the ancient world, raving on about the Greeks, the invention democracy, and the wonder of citizens-as-decision-makers, when I got a reality check that was more like a body blow. Our local election failed to attract one in three of my neighbors. A scant 31 percent of the eligible voters managed to carve fifteen minutes from their day to mutilate chads. It appeared that for the fine citizens in my community, democracy was a spectator sport. At that moment I decided that my kids wouldn't just know their way around a democracy. By the time I got through with them, they'd be able to redraw the map if they decided it was the right thing to do.

As a classroom teacher, you hold the next generation of voters, politicians, and corporate heads in your hands. Teaching children about interdependence and responsibility through social action is a lesson that can stick. With your guidance, students discover their power to help people, animals, or the environment, through the political process. Active, inquisitive citizenship can begin when kids are very young. They should act out early and often, until championing worthy causes becomes a habit they can't break. It's your call, but believe me, you won't regret a minute you spend guiding your students to discover their roles as stewards of the environment and champions of human rights.

Postscript

As I mentioned in Chapter 1, while I was working on this book, I found myself thinking about all my "kids"—now college-graduated adults—and wondering what effect this approach to instruction and assessment had on them. I was touched and humbled by their responses. In closing, I want to share a letter with you. It's from Melody Huskey, a bright star in the firmament, if ever there was one. Melody writes:

> Dear Laurel,
>
> I learned community activism(I actually wrote about our fight to save Henshey's in my law school personal statement—I didn't get in but I don't think that was because the story wasn't good). It was a valuable lesson at 10 years old that I could stand up in front of the City Council and read a letter, and they would think about what I had said.
>
> I am a good researcher—we dove into our projects so deep that I now understand that a project on Michelangelo just is not complete until I know what he ate for breakfast and how he treated his back pains.
>
> I remember the little things, like illuminated manuscripts, that I owned the general store in our reenactment of Williamsburg (and I still have a metal shot from that general store when we visited), and that everyone's version of Utopia was different (and we were only 5th graders!).

I think that because you made learning so fun, and something
that wasn't just reading a textbook and answering questions,
I was still interested in learning when I moved on to high school
and college, where its imperative that you still WANT to learn
because it's not going to be fun and drawings anymore. I love
that I got to take my learning as far as I could imagine.

Melody

Dear reader, I can rest on that.

Resources

Professional Organizations and Centers

- Center for Civic Education: www.civiced.org
- National Center for History in the Schools: www.sscnet.ucla.edu/nchs
- National Council on Economic Education: www.ncee.net
- National Council for Geographic Education: www.ncge.org
- National Council for the Social Studies (NCSS): www.ncss.org
- Organization of American Historians: www.oah.org

Social Studies Professional Publications

- *Social Studies and the Young Learner*, a quarterly magazine published by NCSS, features a regular column on books appropriate for elementary social studies and suggestions for use
- *Theory and Research in Social Education*, a research journal of the National Council for the Social Studies
- *Teacher Magazine*, a leading information source for K–12 teachers
- "Notable Trade Books for Young People": www.socialstudies.org/resources/ notable/ A list compiled annually since 1972 by the Children's Book Council in cooperation with the National Council for the Social Studies (NCSS). Careful attention is paid to authenticity and historical accuracy.
- *An Annotated Bibliography of Historical Fiction for the Social Studies, Grades 5–12*, by Fran Silverblank (Kendall/Hunt for the National Council for the Social Studies)

Primary Source Documents and Other Instructional Resources

- African American Perspectives: Pamphlets from the Daniel A. P. Murray Collection, 1818–1907—American Memory: http://memory.loc.gov/ammem/ aap/aaphome.html
  Presents a review of African American history and culture as seen through the practice of pamphleteering. The site includes sermons on racial pride

and essays on segregation, voting rights, and violence against African Americans.

- American Memory at the Library of Congress: http://memory.loc.gov
- Digital History: www.digitalhistory.uh.edu
  Huge site with major section on children in history including their journals and diaries.
- EdSitement: http://edsitement.neh.gov/
- Education World History Sites Review: www.education-world.com/awards/past/topics/history.shtml
  Hundreds of history websites are rated for content, aesthetics, organization, and general usefulness to teachers.
- Historic American Sheet Music: http://scriptorium.lib.duke.edu/sheetmusic/
  This collection presents a broad perspective on American history and culture through a variety of music types including minstrel songs, protest songs, sentimental songs, patriotic and political songs, plantation songs, and spirituals.
- The Historical New York Times Project: www.nyt.ulib.org/
- Internet History Sourcebooks Project: www.fordham.edu/halsall
- Mapping Our City: http://mapcity.terc.edu
  In this project, students and teachers in three middle schools in Boston explored their urban environment for four years (1995–1998) and created maps and other documents based on their findings. This site includes the article, "Mapping Our City: Learning to Use Spatial Data in the Middle School Science Classroom" by Harold McWilliams and Paul Rooney.
- National Archives' Digital Classroom: http://www.archives.gov/education/
- Our Documents: www.ourdocuments.gov
- Virtual Jamestown: www.iath.virginia.edu/vcdh/jamestown
  Site contains an interactive segment, maps and images, court records, labor contracts for indentured servants, public records, letters, firsthand accounts, and virtual panoramas of Jamestown based on the paintings of John White.

Strategies for Teaching Social Studies

- César E. Chávez Foundation: www.chavezfoundation.org
  Resource guides are available through the website promoting topics such as peer mediation, homelessness, and economic justice. The Chávez service-learning resource guides are aimed at engaging K–12 youth in high-quality service-learning programs based on César's ten core values by providing a step-by-step project module while allowing for individual creativity.
- History Matters: http://historymatters.gmu.edu/browse/makesense/
  This website features a section for helping students and teachers make effec-

tive use of primary sources. Making Sense of Documents provides strategies for analyzing a wide variety of primary materials, such as maps, photographs, letters, songs, and more. For each type of material there are interactive exercises and a guide to traditional and online sources.

- Improving Writing Skills through Social Studies, ERIC Digest No. 40: www.ericdigests.org/pre-926/writing.htm

  This ERIC digest discusses (1) recent research on the linkage between writing and learning; (2) successful approaches to teaching writing; and (3) suggestions for including an effective writing component in the social studies curriculum.

- ReadingQuest: Making Sense in Social Studies: www.readingquest.org

  This website is designed for social studies teachers who want to engage their students more effectively with the content in their classes. The site clearly presents the underlying principles of content literacy and offers numerous strategies for the social studies classroom.

Museums and Other Education Organizations

- National Anthropological Archives: www.nmnh.si.edu/naa/about.htm
- National Gallery of Art, Education: www.nga.gov/education/index.shtm
- National Geographic EducationGuide: www.nationalgeographic.com/education
- Smithsonian Education: www.smithsonianeducation.org
- Smithsonian National Museum of American History: http://americanhistory.si.edu
- Smithsonian National Museum of the American Indian: www.nmai.si.edu
- Smithsonian National Portrait Gallery: www.npg.si.edu

Works Cited

Anderson, Richard C. 1985. *Becoming a Nation of Readers: The Report of the Commission on Reading.* Champaign, IL: National Academy of Education, National Institute of Education, and Center for the Study of Reading.

Beal, Merrill. 1963. *I Will Fight No More Forever: Chief Joseph and the Nez Perce War.* Seattle: University of Washington Press.

Bellairs, John. 1989. *Trolley to Yesterday.* New York: Dial.

Bernhard, Virginia. 1990. *The Durable Fire.* New York: Morrow.

Bonniwell, George. The Gold Rush Diary of George Bonniwell. www.emigrantroad .com/gold01.html.

Bryson, Bill. 1992. *Neither Here Nor There.* New York: Avon.

Burton, Virginia. 1943. *The Little House.* Boston: Houghton Mifflin.

Cerf, Christopher, and Victor Navasky. 1984. *The Experts Speak.* New York: Pantheon.

Chávez, César. 1984. Commonwealth Club Address. Authenticated text posted on web-site of the Commonwealth Club, www.commonwealthclub.org/archive/20thcentury/ 84-11chavez-speech.html.

Clemens, Samuel (Mark Twain). 1872. *Roughing It.* Hartford, CT: American Publishing Co.

Cresswell, Helen. 1990. *Time Out.* New York: Atheneum.

Collier, James, and Christopher Collier. 1974. *My Brother Sam Is Dead.* New York: Simon & Schuster.

Denenberg, Barry. 1996. *When Will This Cruel War Be Over? The Civil War Diary of Emma Simpson.* New York: Scholastic.

Dewey, John. 1897. "My Pedagogic Creed." *The School Journal* 54 (3): 77–80.

———. 1899. *The School and Society.* Chicago: University of Chicago Press.

———. 1910. *How We Think.* Boston: D. C. Heath.

———. 1997. In *California History–Social Science Curriculum Framework.* California Department of Education.

Duncan, Dorothy. 1981. *The Artifact: What Can It Tell Us About The Past?* Toronto: On-tario Historical Society.

Filipovic, Zlata. 1994. *Zlata's Diary.* New York: Viking.

Fischer, Max. 1997. *American History Simulations.* Westminister, CA: Teacher Created Materials.

Fleischman, Sid. 1986. *The Whipping Boy*. New York: Greenwillow.

Fox, Mem. 1993. "Men Who Weep, Boys Who Dance: The Gender Agenda Between the Lines in Children's Literature." *Language Arts* 70: 84–88.

Fradin, Judith Bloom. 2004. *The Power of One: Daisy Bates and the Little Rock Nine*. New York: Clarion Books.

Goodlad, John. 2004. *A Place Called School*. New York: McGraw-Hill.

Grandin, Temple. 1995. *Thinking in Pictures and Other Reports from My Life with Autism*. New York: Vintage.

Greer, Gery. 1988. *Max and Me and the Time Machine*. New York: HarperCollins.

Griffin, Peni. 1993. *The Switching Well*. New York: Margaret K. McElderry.

Grimes, Nikki. 2002. *Talkin' About Bessie*. London: Orchard.

Grogan, Ewart. 1900. *From the Cape to Cairo: The First Traverse of Africa from South to North*. London: Hurst & Blackett.

Gutman, Dan. 2001. *The Edison Mystery*. New York: Simon & Schuster.

———. 2002. *Qwerty Stevens, Stuck in Time with Benjamin Franklin*. New York: Simon & Schuster.

Hall, Ruby Bridges. 1999. *Through My Eyes*. New York: Scholastic.

Hamor, Ralph. 1957. "A True Discourse of the Present State of Virginia." Richmond: Virginia State Library.

Hoffer, Eric. 1951. *The True Believer: Thoughts on the Nature of Mass Movements*. San Bernardino, CA: Borgo Press.

Hoose, Phillip. 1993. *It's Our World, Too: Stories of Young People Who Are Making a Difference*. Boston: Little, Brown.

———. 2001. *We Were There, Too: Young People in U.S. History*. New York: Farrar, Straus & Giroux.

Hurmence, Belinda. 1982. *A Boy Called Girl*. New York: Clarion Books.

Junior League of Baton Rouge. 1959. *River Road Recipes*. Baton Rouge, LA: Junior League.

King, Martin Luther Jr. 1958. *Stride Toward Freedom*. New York: Harper & Row.

Larpenteur, Charles. 1933. *Forty Years a Fur Trader on the Upper Missouri: The Personal Narrative of Charles Larpenteur, 1833–1872*. Chicago: Lakeside Press.

Levstik, Linda S. 1996. "The Relationship Between Historical Response and Narrative in a Sixth Grade Classroom." *Theory and Research in Social Education* 14 (Winter): 1–19.

Lewis, Barbara A. 1991. *The Kid's Guide to Social Action: How to Solve Social Problems You Choose and Turn Creative Thinking into Positive Action*. Minneapolis: Free Spirit.

Lewis, William Mather. 1938. "Public Opinion on the Campus." *The Public Opinion Quarterly* 2 (1): 35–36.

Lunn, Janet. 1983. *The Root Cellar*. New York: Atheneum.

Lytle, Robert. 2000. *Three Rivers Crossing*. Spring Lake, MI: River Road.

Macaulay, David. 1976. *Underground*. New York: Houghton Mifflin.

———. 1979. *Motel of Mysteries*. New York: Houghton Mifflin.

McCusker, Paul. 1996. *Stranger in the Mist*. Colorado Springs: Chariot Victor.

Mill, John Stuart. 1869. *On Liberty*. London: Longman, Roberts and Green.

Murphy, Jim. 1998. *The Journal of James Edmond Pease: A Civil War Union Soldier*. New York: Scholastic.

Napoli, Donna Jo. 1993. *The Magic Circle*. New York: Dutton Juvenile.

National Geographic–Roper Public Affairs. 2006. "Geographic Literacy Study." Washington, DC: National Geographic Education Foundation.

Nelson, Lynn, and Trudy Nelson. 1999. "Learning History Through Children's Literature." *History and Literature Digest*. www.indiana.edu/~ssdc/hislitdig.htm.

New York Times. 1964. "Martin Luther King Wins the Nobel Prize for Peace." *New York Times*, 14 October. http://www.nytimes.com/learning/general/onthisday/20061014.html

Ogawa, Louise. 1942. www.smithsonianeducation.org/educators/lesson_plans/japanese_internment/letter_c.html

Peet, Bill. 1966. *Farewell to Shady Glade*. Boston: Houghton Mifflin.

———. 1974. *The Wump World*. Boston: Houghton Mifflin.

Pinkwater, Daniel. 1991. *Chicago Days/Hoboken Nights*. New York: Addison Wesley.

Postman, Neil. 1969. *Teaching as a Subversive Activity*. New York: Doubleday.

Preusch, Deb, Tom Barry, Beth Wood, and the New Mexico People and Energy Collective. 1981. *Red Ribbons for Emma*. Berkeley, CA: New Seed Press.

Ravitch, Diane. 2003. *The Language Police: How Pressure Groups Restrict What Students Learn*. New York: Alfred A. Knopf.

Robin, Diana. 1997. *Collected Letters of a Renaissance Feminist: Laura Cereta*. Part of the series *The Other Voice in Early Modern Europe*. Chicago: University of Chicago Press.

Rodgers, Mary. 1993. *Freaky Friday*. New York: HarperCollins.

Russell, Sharman. 1994. *The Humpbacked Fluteplayer*. New York: Knopf.

Scieszka, Jon. 1989. *The True Story of the Three Little Pigs!* New York: Viking Juvenile.

Scott, Deborah. 1988. *The Kid Who Got Zapped Through Time*. New York: HarperTrophy.

Service, Pamela. 1989. *Vision Quest*. New York: Atheneum.

Steinbeck, John. 1962. *Travels with Charley in Search of America*. New York: Viking.

Theroux, Paul. 2003. *Dark Star Safari: Overland from Cairo to Cape Town*. New York: Houghton Mifflin.

Twain, Mark. 1899. *Connecticut Yankee in King Arthur's Court*. New York: Charles L. Webster.

VanSledright, Bruce A. 1995. "How Do Multiple Text Resources Influence Learning to Read American History in Fifth Grade?" *Newsletter of the National Reading Research Center* (September): 4–5.

VanSledright, Bruce A., and Christine A. Kelly. 1996. "Reading American History: How Do Multiple Text Sources Influence Historical Learning in Fifth Grade?" *Reading Research Report* 68.

Weinberg, Karen. 1991. *Window in Time*. Shippensburg, PA: White Mane.

Woodruff, Elvira. 1991. *George Washington's Socks*. New York: Scholastic.

———. 1997. *The Orphan of Ellis Island*. New York: Scholastic.

Index